T0244222

LEARN
DUTCH

TARGET:
LANGUAGES

LEARN
DUTCH
Beginner level
A2

Ineke Paupert

Adapted for English speakers
by Elise Bradbury

THE TARGET: LANGUAGES SERIES

THE COMMON EUROPEAN FRAMEWORK OF REFERENCE FOR LANGUAGES

When, exactly, can someone say they 'speak' a foreign language? When can they claim to speak it 'correctly' and fluently? Language mastery is an issue that has long exercised educationalists and linguists. It might have remained a topic of academic debate, and language acquisition just another subject on the educational curriculum, were it not for the fact that today's learners need to demonstrate or prove the skills they have acquired, especially when working in a professional environment, applying for a job, or even moving to another country.

Various systems and scales have been developed to measure language proficiency, including the International English Language Testing System (IELTS), the ALTE Framework and, in the United States, the ACTFL Proficiency Guidelines and the ILR Scale.

In the European Union, which has more than 20 official languages (among the 120 or so spoken throughout Europe as a whole), the assessment issue has been a particularly critical question. This is why in 2001 the Council of Europe designed the Common European Framework of Reference for Languages (CEFRL). The main purpose of this initiative was to provide a method for learning, teaching and assessing that applies to all European languages so that they can be learned and practised more easily. Another of the original aims of the CEFRL, in addition to encouraging Europe's citizens to travel and to interact with each other, was to put some order into the multiple private assessment tests that were in use before then and were, in most cases, specific to just one language.

More than 20 years after the CEFRL was rolled out, it has proven hugely successful, not only in Europe but throughout the world. Now available in some 40 languages, the framework is widely used by educators, course designers, human resource managers and companies, who "find it advantageous to work with stable, accepted standards of measurement and format".[1]

---

[1] "Common European Framework of Reference for Languages: learning, teaching, assessment", Council of Europe, 2001

CEFRL LEVELS AND CATEGORIES

The Common European Framework comprises 3 broad categories and 6 common levels of competency:

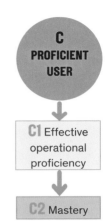

Each level of competency comprises detailed 'descriptors' of language proficiency and communication:
• spoken and written production
• reception (listening and reading comprehension)
• spoken and written interaction
• spoken and written mediation
• non-verbal signals.

For this Target: Languages course, we have restricted the communication activities to reception and basic production. Interaction, mediation and non-verbal communication will be learned at a later stage by meeting and interacting with native speakers, either in person or online.

A2 LEVELS AND SKILLS

At Level A2, the learner can:
• understand phrases and the highest frequency vocabulary
• read short texts and find information in simple materials
• understand short, simple personal letters
• communicate in simple, routine tasks
• describe in simple terms one's family and others, living conditions, educational background and job
• write short, simple notes and messages.

Most self-study methods refer to one of the CEFRL levels, generally B2, but few have been produced with those requirements specifically in mind. The Target: Languages collection has been designed using the descriptors and competencies outlined in the reference framework. The content of the dialogues has been enhanced with respect to the baseline specifications in order to meet the real needs of today's users. And, faithful to the Assimil philosophy, every effort has been made to make the learning experience enjoyable.

A word of advice to learners

By listening carefully to the dialogues, reading and understanding the grammatical explanations, and completing all the exercises, you will reach Level A2. There is no specific timeframe, so you can choose the pace that you feel comfortable with. But when you reach the end of the course, that's when the work really begins! You must immerse yourself in the language, taking every opportunity to talk with native speakers, watch movies, read books, articles and blogs – in short, to take every opportunity for using the knowledge you have acquired. That is the first most important step on the road to mastery, however it is officially measured!

* Comparative competency scales

CEFRL	ACTFL	ILR
A1	Novice Low Novice High	0 0+
A2	Intermediate Low Intermediate Mid	1
B1	Intermediate High	1+
B2	Advanced Advanced Plus	2 2+
C1	Superior	3 3+
C2	Distinguished	4 4+

Courtesy of The American University Center of Provence

LEARN DUTCH

TOPICS

LISTEN AND REPEAT!

The best way to learn how to pronounce a new language is to listen carefully and then try to imitate what you hear. Don't hesitate to exaggerate the accent as if you were acting, as this will help you pick up the distinctive sounds of the language. To help you, the Dutch texts in this course that are accompanied by audio are indicated with an audio symbol 🔊.

In this section, listen to each sound and then repeat it out loud. Play the sound as many times as you need to. In the lessons, do the same for the conversations and the recorded exercises: the secret is to practise, practise, practise!

PRONUNCIATION

While most of the consonants in Dutch are pronounced similarly to those in English, some of the vowel sounds are very different, so pay close attention to these.

One important distinction in the pronunciation of consonants is between voiced and voiceless consonants. Voiced consonants are produced with the vibration of the vocal cords: for example, put your hand to your throat and pronounce the letter **b**. Voiceless consonants are produced only with the mouth: for example, put your hand to your mouth and pronounce the letter **p**. More on this to follow!

◆ THE ALPHABET

Here are the letters of the alphabet and how they are pronounced in Dutch:
a [ah], **b** [bay], **c** [say], **d** [day], **e** [ay], **f** [eff], **g** [khay], **h** [hah], **i** [ee], **j** [yay], **k** [kah], **l** [ell], **m** [emm], **n** [enn], **o** [oh], **p** [bay], **q** [koo], **r** [air], **s** [ess], **t** [tay], **u** [oo], **v** [vay], **w** [vay], **x** [iks], **y** [aye], **z** [zett]

• Listen to each of these letters and repeat it out loud.
e [ay] / **g** [khay] / **h** [hah] / **i** [ee] / **j** [yay] / **v** [vay] / **w** [vay] / **x** [iks] / **y** [aye] / **z** [zett]

• Listen to these names and spell them out loud.
a. **Mark Jansen** : M A R K   J A N S E N
b. **Meneer Peters** : M E N E E R   P E T E R S
c. **David Smit** : D A V I D   S M I T
d. **Mevrouw Vriesman** : M E V R O U W   V R I E S M A N

◆ LETTERS AND LETTER COMBINATIONS

There are a few sounds in Dutch that are quite different from English.

G AND CH

The letter **g** and the letter combination **ch** are pronounced like the 'j' in Spanish or the 'kh' sound in the Scottish *loch* or the German *Bach*. It is a guttural sound made in the throat. Listen and repeat out loud.

gaan *to go*; **zacht** *soft*

J

The letter **j** is pronounced like the 'y' in *yes*.

ja *yes*; **je** *you*

N AT THE END OF AN UNSTRESSED SYLLABLE

While the **n** is usually pronounced in the same way as in English, note that at the end of an unstressed syllable, it is barely pronounced.

dans *dance*; **lopen** *to walk*

P, T AND K

Note that the letters **p**, **t** and **k** are pronounced without the puff of air that follows the English sound. Hold your hand in front of your mouth and say 'pan'. Did you notice the air that escapes just after the **p** sound? In Dutch, try to pronounce these letters without the puff of air. This makes the Dutch **p** sound similar to a 'b'.

S AND SCH

The letter **s** is pronounced as in English, although sometimes at the end of a word it can sound like 'sh'. The **sch** is an **s** followed rapidly by the Dutch sound **ch**.

les *lesson*; **straks** *soon*; **elektrisch** *electric*

V AND Z AT THE BEGINNING OF A WORD

In some regions, the **v** at the beginning of a word is pronounced more like an 'f'. In other regions, it is pronounced like a 'v'. The same is true for **z**, which is sometimes pronounced like an 's' and sometimes like a 'z' at the beginning of a word.

voor *for*; **zijn** *to be*

B AND D AT THE END OF A WORD

At the end of a word, **b** is pronounced like a 'p', and **d** like a 't'.

heb *have*; **hond** *dog*

R

The **r** is usually rolled, or can sound guttural or 'gargled'. At the end of a word, the **r** is pronounced in a similar way to the American 'r'.

over *over*; **meneer** *mister*

W

Before an 'r', the **w** is pronounced like a 'v'. Otherwise it is pronounced somewhere in between the English 'v' and 'w'. At the end of a word, it is pronounced 'oo'.

uw *your*; **eeuw** *century*

NG, NK, NJ, SJ, TJ

The letter combinations **ng** (as in the English 'ring') and **nk** are pronounced in a similar way as in English. But watch out for **nj** [nyuh], which is pronounced like the 'ny' in *canyon*. The combination **sj** is pronounced similarly to the English 'sh', and **tj** is pronounced similarly to the English 'ch'.

lang *long*; **bank** *bench*; **oranje** *orange*; **meisje** *girl*

THE ENDINGS -IG AND -LIJK

The 'j' is not pronounced in the ending **-lijk** [lik], and remember the guttural 'g' in the ending **-ig** [ikh].

heerlijk *delicious*; **gelukkig** *happy*

THE UNSTRESSED E

In some contexts, the **e** is a short, weak vowel pronounced something like the 'uh' sound at the beginning of *about*. This only occurs in unstressed syllables.

docente *teacher* (f.); **mevrouw** *madam*; **bedankt** *thanks*

THE FINAL E

In many English words, the final **e** is silent. However, in Dutch, the **e** at the end of a word is pronounced like the unstressed **e** [uh]. So, for example, the word **machine** has three syllables in Dutch: **ma** – **chi** – **ne**.

machine *machine*; **we** *we*; **aarde** *earth*

THE TREMA

When a trema (¨) is placed over a vowel, it indicates that it should be pronounced separately from the preceding letter. The **ë** in Dutch is pronounced [yuh].
Argentinië *Argentina*; **Italië** *Italy*; **ruïne** *ruin*; **coördinatie** *coordination*; **vacuüm** *vacuum*

SHORT AND LONG VOWELS

As in English, the length of a vowel (that is, the perceived length of the sound) can be short or long. It is important to distinguish short vowels from long vowels when listening and speaking, as the pronunciation can change the meaning of the word. Short vowels in Dutch are shorter than English vowels, so when pronouncing them keep them clipped. Some long vowels are pronounced in a more stretched way than in English – this is the case if they are followed by an 'r', for example. In some cases, a long pronunciation is indicated by doubling the vowel.

For instance, compare the word **man** *man* and **maan** *moon*: the first has a short vowel [mahn], while the second is stretched out [maahn] as in *arm*, but even longer. The short **e** is similar to the sound in 'met', while the long **ee** sounds more like 'may'.

• Listen to these pairs of words and then repeat them out loud. In each line, the vowel in the first word is short, and in the second it is long. Pronounce the first more tersely than in English, and the second more stretched out than in English.
a. **man** *man* / **maan** *moon*
b. **mes** *knife* / **mees** *titmouse*
c. **lip** *lip* / **liep** *walked*
d. **zon** *sun* / **zoon** *son*
e. **mus** *sparrow* / **muur** *wall*

EU AND OE

There is no equivalent in English to the **eu** in Dutch. To approximate it, pronounce the English vowel sound in *hurt*, but with the lips pursed.
neus *nose*; **leuk** *nice, funny*

The **oe** is very similar to the English 'oo' in *fool*, but is shorter and made further back in the mouth.
boek *book*; **moe** *tired*

THE DIPHTHONGS *EI/IJ, UI, OU/AU, OI, AAI, OOI, EEUW, IEUW*

A diphthong is a vowel combination in which one vowel sound glides into another.

The **ei/ij** sound is somewhere between the 'i' in *right* and the 'a' sound in *rate*.
dijk *dyke*; **wei** *meadow*

The **ui** sound can be approximated by pronouncing the diphthong in *mouse* with the lips tightly pursed and the tongue against the bottom teeth.
ui *onion*; **lui** *lazy*

The **ou/au** sounds similar to 'ow'.
kou *cold*; **blauw** *blue*

oi is pronounced like 'oy'.
hoi *hi*

aai is a blend of 'ah' and 'ee', something like in the word *sigh*.
saai *boring*; **aaien** *to stroke*

ooi is a blend of 'oh' and 'ee', something like in the word *boy*.
mooi *beautiful*; **dooien** *to thaw*

eeuw is a blend of 'ay' and 'oo' (the latter verging towards an 'oh').
leeuw *lion*; **eeuw** *century*

ieuw is a blend of 'ee' and 'oo' (the latter verging towards an 'oh').
nieuw *new*; **kieuw** *gill*

WORD STRESS

Word stress refers to which syllable in a word is more emphasized than the others. In Dutch, as in English, the stress generally falls on the first syllable of a word (e.g. WIND-mill or TU-lip). There are a few exceptions, for example, words with a foreign origin, such as **Française** *Frenchwoman* [frahn-SAY-suh], or if the first syllable contains an unstressed **e**. In the latter case, the word stress is on the following syllable. The same is true for a word starting with a prefix, such as **ver-**. Occasionally, the stress is on the last syllable. Keep this in mind when you listen to the audio and try to remember where a word is stressed.

• Listen to and repeat these words with the right stress (the underlined syllable):

a. **wonen** *to live*
b. **komen** *to come*
c. **nummer** *number*
d. **prima** *great*

e. **meneer** *mister*
f. **bedankt** *thanks*
g. **bedoelen** *to mean*
h. **vertellen** *to tell*

i. **Française*** *Frenchwoman*
j. **moment** *instant*
k. **retour** *round-trip ticket*
l. **boerderij** *farm*

* The word **Française** is pronounced as it is in French, but with an 'uh' at the end.

In compound words (words made up of two or three words – which is common in Dutch), the stress usually falls on the first word.

• Listen to and repeat the following compound words with the right stress (the underlined word):

a. **kaasmaker** *cheesemaker*
b. **Tulpenstraat** *Tulip Street*
c. **rekenmachine** *calculator*

d. **huisdier** *domestic animal*
e. **buurvrouw** *neighbour* (f.)
f. **achternaam** *surname*

ACCENTUATION AND SENTENCE STRESS

In addition to stressing a particular syllable in a word, certain words in a sentence can be stressed, which gives a language its rhythm.

The words that carry the essential meaning tend to stand out more than the other words in a sentence. Typically, that means the emphasis is placed more on words that convey key information, such as nouns, verbs and adverbs, and less on words such as articles, prepositions, etc.

• Listen to the following sentences from the conversation in the first lesson and then repeat them one by one out loud:

a. **Hoe heten jullie?** *What's your name?*
b. **Wonen jullie in de Tulpenstraat?** *Do you live in Tulips Street?*
c. **Goed, jullie staan op de lijst.** *Good, you are on the list.*
d. **Prima, bedankt en tot straks.** *Great, thanks, and see you later.*
e. **En waar woont u?** *And where do you live?*

I.
FIRST
CONTACT

II.
EVERYDAY
LIFE

III.
IN THE
CITY

IV.
FREE
TIME

I

FIRST

CONTACT

1.
FIRST ENCOUNTER

EERSTE KENNISMAKING

AIMS	TOPICS

- SAYING HELLO
- INTRODUCING YOURSELF
- ASKING SOMEONE THEIR NAME AND WHERE THEY LIVE
- SAYING GOODBYE

- INFORMAL AND FORMAL ADDRESS
- INFINITIVES AND THE PRESENT TENSE

HELLO

(Informal)

<u>Mark</u>: Hello.

<u>Hostess</u>: Hello *(Day).** **What are your names** *(How are-called you* [pl.]*)*?

<u>Mark</u>: **My name is** *(I am-called)* **Mark Jansen.**

<u>Bernie</u>: **And I'm Bernie.**

<u>Hostess</u>: **Have you come** *(Come you)* **for the cheese-tasting?**

<u>Mark</u>: **Yes.**

<u>Hostess</u>: **Do you live on** *(Live you in the)* **Tulips Street?**

<u>Mark</u>: **Yes, we live at** *(on)* **number 6.**

<u>Hostess</u>: **Good, you are** *(stand)* **on the list.**

<u>Mark</u>: **Great, thanks, and see you later** *(until soon).*

<u>Hostess</u>: **See you later.**

(Formal)

<u>Hostess</u>: **Good afternoon** *(Good-day).* **What's your name?**

<u>Mr Peters</u>: **Jasper Peters.**

<u>Hostess</u>: **Have you also come for the cheese-tasting?**

<u>Mr Peters</u>: **Yes.**

<u>Hostess</u>: **And where do you live?**

<u>Mr Peters</u>: **On** *(the)* **Birches Lane.**

<u>Hostess</u>: **In Amsterdam?**

<u>Mr Peters</u>: **No, in Zaandam.**

<u>Hostess</u>: **Oh, pardon me!**

---

* The words in parentheses and italics are literal translations of the Dutch to help you pick up the vocabulary and syntax.

Mark: Hallo.

Hostess: Dag. Hoe heten jullie?

Mark: Ik heet Mark Jansen.

Bernie: En ik heet Bernie.

Hostess: Komen jullie voor de kaasproeverij?

Mark: Ja.

Hostess: Wonen jullie in de Tulpenstraat?

Mark: Ja, we wonen op nummer 6 (zes).

Hostess: Goed, jullie staan op de lijst.

Mark: Prima, bedankt en tot straks.

Hostess: Tot later.

Hostess: Goedendag. Hoe heet u?

Meneer Peters: Jasper Peters.

Hostess: Komt u ook voor de kaasproeverij?

Meneer Peters: Ja.

Hostess: En waar woont u?

Meneer Peters: In de Berkenlaan.

Hostess: In Amsterdam?

Meneer Peters: Nee, in Zaandam.

Hostess: O sorry!

UNDERSTANDING THE DIALOGUE
SOME USEFUL STARTING POINTS

→ **Hallo** *Hello* is a very common greeting. It is more informal than **Goedendag**, literally 'Good day', of which **Dag** is the short form.

→ **Hoe heten jullie?** *What are your names?* ('How are-called you?'). Note that **jullie** is the informal plural *you*, used to address more than one person. The verb **heten** means *to be called, to be named.* The formal *you* is **u**, which has a different verb conjugation. There is also an informal singular *you* (**jij**), but we'll get to that later! See the section below for more about informal and formal address.

→ **kaasproeverij** *cheese-tasting* is a compound word formed from two words: **kaas** and **proeverij**. We see the same thing with **Tulpenstraat** *Tulips Street* and **Berkenlaan** *Birches Lane.*

→ The article **de** *the* is used before a street name: **in de Tulpenstraat** *in Tulips Street* (note the singular nouns **de tulp** *tulip* and **de berk** *birch*).

→ The preposition **op** means *on* (to give an address in Dutch, you use *on* rather than *at*: **op nummer 6** *at number 6*; **op de lijst** *on the list*).

→ **staan** *to be (standing)* is the verb used for things that are written or printed.

→ **bedankt** *thanks* and **sorry** are very commonly used and are fairly informal.

→ The preposition **tot** *until* is used in expressions such as **tot straks** *see you soon*, **tot later** *see you later.*

INFORMAL AND FORMAL ADDRESS

Unlike modern English, Dutch has two registers for addressing others: informal and formal. The informal second-person pronouns **jij** (singular) and **jullie** (plural) are generally used when speaking to family, friends and colleagues. Today, they are also often used between people that don't know each other, especially people of the same age, and even by companies addressing their clients. The second-person formal pronoun **u** (which is both singular and plural) is mainly used in conversations with superiors (although you will also hear the informal in these contexts), older people or in official settings.

Generally speaking, if the person you are speaking to introduces themselves with their first name, you can use the informal. But in situations in which it is important to show respect or to create a certain distance, opt for the formal address (**u**).

24

◆ GRAMMAR
FORMAL ADDRESS

As the formal **u** *you* can be used to address one person or a group of people, there is only one verb conjugation to remember for any formal situation. For example:
Hoe heet u? *What's your name?* or *What are your names?*
Komt u ook voor de kaasproeverij? *Have you* (on your own / you both / you all) *also come for the cheese-tasting?*

▲ CONJUGATION
INFINITIVES AND THE PRESENT TENSE

Dutch infinitives (the unconjugated form of a verb) almost always end in **-en**:
heten *to be called*; **komen** *to come*; **wonen** *to live*, etc.

The second-person plural (informal) is identical to the infinitive:
jullie heten *you are called*; **jullie komen** *you come*; **jullie wonen** *you live*.

In the formal present tense, the **-en** of the infinitive is replaced with **-t** (i.e. the verb stem + **-t**, unless the stem already ends in **-t**):*
u heet *you are called*; **u komt** *you come*; **u woont** *you live*.

* The vowel in the verb stem is doubled when some verbs are conjugated. For more on spelling rules, see lessons 3, 4, 8 and 10.

⬡ EXERCISES

The exercises accompanied by audio are indicated with a speaker icon. 🔊 In these cases, first listen to the recording, then answer the exercise questions. You may need to select 'Pause' if there are several steps. The exercise answers can be found at the end of the book.

1. LINK EACH QUESTION TO THE CORRECT RESPONSE.

a. Hoe heet u? •   • 1. We wonen in de Tulpenstraat.

b. Hoe heten jullie? •   • 2. Meneer Peters.

c. Waar wonen jullie? •   • 3. In Zaandam.

d. Waar woont u? •   • 4. Ik heet Mark. Ik heet Bernie.

2. CHOOSE THE CORRECT PREPOSITION FOR EACH SENTENCE.

a. Ik woon in/op de Berkenlaan.

b. We wonen in/op nummer 6.

c. Op/Tot later!

d. U staat om/op de lijst.

3. COMPLETE EACH SENTENCE WITH THE CORRECT FORM OF THE VERB.

a. Jullie (wonen) .... in Amsterdam.

b. (Heten) .... jullie Mark en Bernie?

c. (Komen) .... u voor de kaasproeverij?

d. En waar (wonen) .... u?

4. (I) READ THESE VERBS AS YOU LISTEN TO THE AUDIO: *HEET, HETEN, KOMT, STAAN, WOONT, WONEN.*
(II) COMPLETE EACH SENTENCE WITH THE CORRECT VERB FROM THE LIST ABOVE AND THEN READ THE SENTENCE OUT LOUD.
(III) LISTEN TO THE AUDIO AND CORRECT YOUR ANSWERS IF YOU NEED TO.

03

Example: Hoe .... jullie? → Hoe heten jullie?

a. Waar .... jullie?

b. .... u voor de proeverij?

c. De kaasmaker (*cheesemaker*) .... meneer Peters.

d. .... jullie op de lijst?

e. .... u in Amsterdam?

VOCABULARY

Note: These are the words from the lesson, listed in order of their appearance. The nouns appear with the definite article *the*: this is because in Dutch, *the* can be either **de** or **het**, depending on the type of noun it is used with.

We'll explain this in the next lesson, but for now just remember that when you come across a new word, it's best to try to learn the noun and the article together.

Hallo! / Dag! *Hello!* (informal)
de hostess *hostess*
Hoe? *How?*
heten *to be called, to be named*
jullie *you* (informal plural)
ik *I*
en *and*
komen *to come*
voor *for*
de kaasproeverij *cheese-tasting*
Ja. *Yes.*
Nee. *No.*
wonen *to live*
in *in*
de straat *street*
de tulp *tulip* (**tulpen** *tulips*)
we *we*
op *on*
het nummer *number*

goed *good*
staan *to be (standing* or *upright)*
de lijst *list*
Prima! *Great!*
Bedankt. *Thanks.*
tot *until*
straks *soon*
later *later*
Goedendag. *Good afternoon. Hello.* (formal)
u *you* (formal singular & plural)
de meneer *mister*
ook *also*
Waar? *Where?*
de laan *lane*
de berk *birch* (**berken** *birches*)
O! *Oh!*
Sorry. *Excuse me. Sorry.*
de kaasmaker / de kaasmaakster *cheesemaker* (m./f.)

2.
TALKING ABOUT YOURSELF

OVER JEZELF VERTELLEN

AIMS

- SPELLING A NAME
- ASKING SOMEONE ABOUT THEMSELVES

TOPICS

- SINGULAR DEFINITE AND INDEFINITE ARTICLES (THE, A/AN)
- UNSTRESSED SUBJECT PRONOUNS
- THE PRESENT TENSE OF THE VERBS TO BE AND TO HAVE

THE NEW STUDENT

Teacher: Ah, here is the new student! Good morning. What is your name?

Student: Hi. I am David Smit.

Teacher: How do you spell that *(How spell you that)*?

Student: D-A-V-I-D.

Teacher: I mean your surname, not your first name!

Student: Like a blacksmith,* but with a 't'.

Teacher: Hey, don't be sassy *(Say, you are surely the funniest at home)*!

Student: My surname is spelled *(spell you)* S-M-I-T. And what is your name?

Teacher: I ask *(pose)* the questions here! Can you tell us anything about yourself *(Can you anything about yourself tell)*?

Student: I come from the village of Giethoorn. We have a house on the dyke. I have a brother and a sister: they are already grown up *(big)*. My brother is called Thijs and he has a cat. My sister is called Maud and she has a dog. Do you have a pet *(Have you a house-animal)*?

Teacher: Stop! You also certainly have *(have certainly also)* a calculator. We're going to begin.

---

* See the vocabulary list, p. 35

Docente: Ah, hier is de nieuwe leerling! Goedemorgen. Wat is je naam?

Leerling: Hoi. Ik ben David Smit.

Docente: Hoe spel je dat?

Leerling: D-A-V-I-D.

Docente: Ik bedoel je achternaam, niet je voornaam!

Leerling: Zoals een smid maar met een « t ».

Docente: Zeg, je bent zeker de leukste thuis!

Leerling: Mijn achternaam spel je S-M-I-T. En wat is uw naam?

Docente: Ik stel hier de vragen! Kun je iets over jezelf vertellen?

Leerling: Ik kom uit het dorp Giethoorn. We hebben een huis op de dijk. Ik heb een broer en een zus: ze zijn al groot. Mijn broer heet Thijs en hij heeft een kat. Mijn zus heet Maud en ze heeft een hond. Heeft u een huisdier?

Docente: Stop! Je hebt natuurlijk ook een rekenmachine. We gaan beginnen.

■ UNDERSTANDING THE DIALOGUE

→ **Heeft u een huisdier?** *Do you have a pet?* In English, questions often start with *Do/Does …?* In Dutch, to form a question you just swap the order of the verb and subject: **Heeft u …?** *Have you …?*

→ **Goedemorgen** *Good morning* is more formal than **Hoi** *Hi.*

→ **Wat is je naam?** *What is your name?* is synonymous with **Hoe heet je?**

→ The subject pronoun **je** *you* (informal sing.) has the more neutral sense of *one* in **Hoe spel je dat?** *How do you (does one) spell that?*

→ The nouns **achternaam** *surname* and **voornaam** *first name* contain the prepositions **achter** *after, behind* and **voor** *before, in front of.*

→ In the expression **Je bent zeker de leukste thuis!** *Don't get smart with me!* ('You are certainly the funniest in the house!'), we see the superlative **de leukste** *the funniest.* We'll come back to this.

→ **vragen stellen** *to ask questions* ('questions to-put'): the most frequent way to make a noun plural in Dutch is to add **-en** to the singular noun. More on this later, but for now be careful not to confuse plural nouns with infinitives!

→ In a question that doesn't start with a question word (e.g. *How? What? Where?* etc.), the conjugated auxiliary verb is at the beginning of the question, and the main verb (an infinitive) is at the end: **Kun je iets over jezelf vertellen?** *Can you tell us something about yourself?* ('Can you something about yourself tell?').

→ Note the preposition after this verb: **komen uit** *come from*: **Ik kom uit het dorp Giethoorn.** *I come from the village of Giethoorn.*

A FINAL 'D' IS PRONOUNCED 'T'!

If you don't want to be immediately signalled out as a foreigner, don't forget to pronounce the **-d** at the end of a word as a 't'! There are several examples in the dialogue – did you notice when you listened to the audio? You hear this in **Maud**, **David**, **hond**, as well as **Smit** and **smid**, which sound the same!

◆ GRAMMAR
SINGULAR DEFINITE AND INDEFINITE ARTICLES

As we've mentioned, there are two definite articles (*the*) in Dutch: **de** and **het**. Common nouns, also known as nouns of common gender, are preceded by **de**: **de leerling** *the student*, **de naam** *the name*. There are also neuter nouns, which are preceded by **het**: **het dorp** *the village*. Neuter nouns are less common. When you're learning a new word, get into the habit of learning it with its definite article. The good news is that there is only one singular indefinite article in Dutch: **een** *a/an*: **een broer** *a brother*, **een zus** *a sister*.

UNSTRESSED SUBJECT PRONOUNS

Some subject pronouns have an unstressed form. This means they are not stressed when speaking. This unstressed form is the one commonly used in speech unless special emphasis is required. The stressed forms of the subject pronouns are given in lesson 6, p. 65.

	Singular		Plural	
1st person	**ik**	*I*	**we**	*we*
2nd person	**je**	*you* (informal)	**jullie**	*you* (informal)
	u	*you* (formal)	**u**	*you* (formal)
3rd person	**hij**	*he*	**ze**	*they*
	ze	*she*		

▲ CONJUGATION
THE PRESENT TENSE OF *TO BE* AND *TO HAVE*

	zijn	*to be*	**hebben**	*to have*
ik	**ben**	*I am*	**heb**	*I have*
je (informal)	**bent**	*you are*	**hebt**	*you have*
u (formal)	**bent**	*you are*	**heeft/hebt**	*you have*
hij / ze	**is**	*he/she/it is*	**heeft**	*he/she/it has*
we	**zijn**	*we are*	**hebben**	*we have*
jullie (informal)	**zijn**	*you are*	**hebben**	*you have*
ze	**zijn**	*they are*	**hebben**	*they have*

● EXERCISES

1. REPLACE THE INDEFINITE ARTICLE WITH THE CORRECT DEFINITE ARTICLE.

a. een hond: ....   c. een leerling: ....

b. een huis: ....   d. een dorp: ....

2. COMPLETE EACH SENTENCE WITH THE CORRECT SUBJECT PRONOUN (THE ENGLISH EQUIVALENT IS GIVEN IN PARENTHESES).

a. .... (*I*) kom uit Utrecht.

b. .... (*they*) hebben een hond en een kat.

c. .... (*she*) heeft een broer.

d. Heeft .... (*you*, form.) een huisdier?

e. .... (*we*) zijn hier.

f. .... (*you*, inf. sing.) hebt een zus.

g. Waar wonen .... (*you*, inf. pl.)?

3. CHOOSE THE CORRECT FORM OF THE VERB.

a. Jullie heeft/hebben.   c. Hij is/zijn.

b. U bent/zijn.   d. Je hebt/hebben.

4. (I) SPELL THE FOLLOWING NAMES OUT LOUD: DAVID, BERNIE, MAUD, SMID, GIETHOORN. THEN LISTEN TO THE AUDIO TO CHECK IF YOU WERE RIGHT.
(II) LISTEN TO THE FOLLOWING SENTENCES AND THEN FILL IN THE MISSING WORD AND READ THEM OUT LOUD.
(III) LISTEN TO THE AUDIO AGAIN TO CHECK YOUR ANSWERS.

04

a. Mijn .... is David.

b. Ik .... Maud.

c. We komen .... Giethoorn.

d. Is uw .... Smid?

e. .... Bernie een huisdier?

● VOCABULARY

de *the* (with common nouns)
het *the* (with neuter nouns)
een *a / an*
nieuw *new*
de leerling / de leerlinge
  student, learner (m./f.)
de docent / de docente
  teacher (m./f.)
hier *here*
is *is* (see **zijn**, p. 33)
Goedemorgen. *Good morning.*
Wat? *What?*
mijn *my*
je *your* (informal)
uw *your* (formal)
de naam *name*
Hoi! *Hi!*
ben *am* (see **zijn** p. 33)
spellen *to spell*
je *you* (informal), *one*
dat *that*
bedoelen *to mean*
de achternaam *surname, family
  name, last name*
de voornaam *first name*
niet *not*
zoals *like, as*
de smid *blacksmith*
maar *but*
met *with*
zeggen *to say, to tell*
zeker *certainly, of course*
de leukste *the funniest*

thuis *at home*
stellen *to put, to pose*
de vraag *question*
  (**vragen** *questions*)
kunnen *to be able to (can)*
iets *something, anything*
over *over, about*
jezelf *yourself* (informal)
vertellen *to tell*
uit (komen uit) *from (come from)*
het dorp *village*
hebben *to have*
het huis *house*
de dijk *dyke*
de broer *brother*
de zus *sister*
al *already*
groot *big, tall*
ze *she, they*
hij *he*
de kat *cat*
de hond *dog*
het huisdier *pet*
stoppen *to stop*
natuurlijk *certainly*
de rekenmachine *calculator*
gaan *to go*
beginnen *to begin*

3.
DESCRIBING SOMEONE
IEMAND BESCHRIJVEN

AIMS	TOPICS
• INTRODUCING SOMEONE • DESCRIBING SOMEONE OR SOMETHING	• LONG VOWELS • CAPITALIZATION • ADJECTIVES • THE DEMONSTRATIVE PRONOUNS *DIT* THIS AND *DAT* THAT • THE PRESENT TENSE OF REGULAR VERBS

NICE TO MEET YOU!

Annette: I want to introduce you to my neighbour later *(I want you later just introduce to the neighbour-woman)*.

She comes from France. She is very nice.

She is French and her husband is Dutch.

They work in *(for the)* television: he is a presenter, and she works there as a translator.

They have three boys and one girl.

The boys speak Dutch and French.

The girl also speaks *(speaks also)* Spanish, because the childminder comes from Argentina.

They live in that big house with the *(those)* red shutters.

Do you see it *(See you)*? That house with the *(those)* plants on the windowsill.

Ah, here she is *(there is she)*!

Hey, Margot, may I introduce you *(may I you for-a-moment introduce)*?

Margot, this is Ben.

Ben, this is my French neighbour Margot. And that is the Argentinian childminder.

Ben: Nice to meet you! Hm, how do you say that in Spanish *(how say you that in the Spanish)*?

Annette: Ik wil je straks even voorstellen aan de buurvrouw.

Ze komt uit Frankrijk. Ze is erg lief.

Ze is Française en haar man is Nederlander.

Ze werken voor de televisie: hij is presentator en zij werkt er als vertaalster.

Ze hebben drie jongens en een meisje.

De jongens spreken Nederlands en Frans.

Het meisje spreekt ook Spaans, want de oppas komt uit Argentinië.

Ze wonen in dat grote huis met die rode luiken.

Zie je? Dat huis met die planten op de vensterbank.

Ah, daar is ze!

Hé Margot, mag ik je even voorstellen?

Margot, dit is Ben.

Ben, dit is mijn Franse buurvrouw Margot. En dat is de Argentijnse oppas.

Ben: Aangenaam! Eh, hoe zeg je dat in het Spaans?

■ UNDERSTANDING THE DIALOGUE

→ **Ik wil je even voorstellen.** *I want to introduce you.* **Mag ik je even voorstellen?** *May I introduce you?* The adverb **even** *just, awhile, momentarily* is not always translated, but is used frequently with the meaning 'just for a moment'.

→ **Hij is presentator en zij werkt er als vertaalster.** *He is a presenter and she works as a translator.* The pronoun **zij** *she* is the stressed equivalent of **ze** – it is used to put emphasis on the pronoun, here in the sense of 'as for her, she …'. Also note that no indefinite article is used before a job: **is presentator** *is a presenter.*

→ **Hoe zeg je dat in het Spaans?** *How do you say that in Spanish?* A definite article is used before a language, unless it follows the verb **spreken** *to speak.* **De jongens spreken Nederlands en Frans.** *The boys speak Dutch and French.*

CULTURAL NOTE

In the Netherlands, few houses have shutters, although some homes in rural areas do. But **de vensterbank** *windowsill* (**het venster** *window*), in this case, the inner ledge of the window, is frequently used to put plants, flowers and all sorts of decorative objects. Since there are no shutters and rarely curtains, passersby can look in to see what's on display. The Dutch don't seem to worry too much about others seeing their living space or the 'social control' that this might imply.

✳ SPELLING
LONG VOWELS

The long vowels can be spelled with a single or a double letter. In a syllable ending in a consonant, the <u>vowel is doubled</u>. In a syllable ending in a vowel, <u>a single vowel</u> is used. This means the spelling of a word can change if the ending changes:
groot → **grote** *big*; **rood** → **rode** *red* (see the section on 'Adjectives', next page)
spreken *to speak* → **ik spreek** *I speak*; **heten** *to be called* → **ik heet** *I am called*

CAPITALIZATION

As in English, countries, nationalities and languages are capitalized:
Ze komt uit Spanje. *She comes from Spain.* **Ze is Française.** *She is French.*
Ze spreken Italiaans. *They speak Italian.* **Mijn Britse buurvrouw** *My British neighbour.*

◆ GRAMMAR
ADJECTIVES

• An adjective can be placed after the verb **zijn** *to be*, just as in English:
Ze is erg lief. *She is very nice.* **Ze zijn aardig.** *They are kind.*
• Or an adjective can be placed before a noun to qualify (describe) it. In this case, an **-e** is added to the end:
het grote huis *the big house*; **de rode luiken** *the red shutters*; **de leuke buurvrouw** *the amusing neighbour*; **de kleine vensterbank** *the small windowsill.*

THE DEMONSTRATIVE PRONOUNS *DIT* THIS AND *DAT* THAT

The demonstrative pronouns **dit** *this* and **dat** *that* are used in a similar way to those in English in introductions or to point something out:
Dit is Ben. *This is Ben.* **En dat is de Argentijse oppas.** *And that is the Argentinian childminder.*
Dit is mijn zus Annette en dat is mijn broer Rob. *This is my sister Annette, and that is my brother Rob.*
Dit is een raam en dat is een luik. *This is a window, and that is a shutter.*

▲ CONJUGATION
THE PRESENT TENSE OF REGULAR VERBS

To form the first-person singular, just take off the **-en** (or **-n**) ending of the infinitive. For the second- and third-person singular, add a **-t** to the verb stem. The plural persons are all the same as the infinitive. (Don't forget about the long-vowel double or single vowel spelling rule.)

werken *to work*
ik werk *I work*
je werkt *you work* (informal)
u werkt *you work* (formal)
hij / ze werkt *he/she works*
we werken *we work*
jullie werken *you work* (inf. pl.)
ze werken *they work*

spreken *to speak*
ik spreek *I speak*
je spreekt *you speak* (informal)
u spreekt *you speak* (formal)
hij / ze spreekt *he/she speaks*
we spreken *we speak*
jullie spreken *you speak* (inf. pl.)
ze spreken *they speak*

● EXERCISES

1. COMPLETE EACH SENTENCE WITH THE CORRECT FORM OF THE VERB.

a. Ik .... (werken) voor de televisie.

b. .... (spreken) u Spaans en Frans?

c. De tulp is .... (rood).

d. Hij .... (wonen) in dat .... (groot) huis.

e. Ze *(plural)* .... (werken) in Zaandam.

2. MAKE THESE INTRODUCTIONS FOLLOWING THE EXAMPLE.

Example:
Margot/Mark: Mag ik je even voorstellen?
                    Dit is Margot en dat is Mark.
                    Aangenaam.

a. de buurvrouw / de oppas: ....

b. Maud/Thijs: ....

c. de nieuwe leerling / de nieuwe docente: ....

3. CHOOSE THE CORRECT FORM OF THE ADJECTIVE.

a. De Argentijns/Argentijnse buurvrouw   c. De meisjes zijn groot/grote.

b. Het huis is rood/rode.   d. De nieuw/nieuwe oppas

4. LISTEN TO THE SENTENCES AND FILL THEM IN, THEN LISTEN TO THE AUDIO AGAIN TO CHECK YOUR ANSWERS.

a. Ze komt uit ....

b. Hij spreekt .... en ....

c. Mijn .... oppas is niet lief.

d. Hij is .... en zij is ....

VOCABULARY

aangenaam *pleasant, pleasurable*
Aangenaam! *Nice to meet you!*
  Pleased to meet you!
willen *to want*
even *just, awhile, for a moment*
voorstellen *to introduce*
aan *to*
de buurman / de buurvrouw
  neighbour (m./f.)
Frankrijk (het) *France*
erg *very*
lief *nice*
haar *her*
de man *husband*
de Fransman / de Française
  Frenchman / Frenchwoman
de Nederlander / de Nederlandse
  Dutchman / Dutchwoman
de televisie *television*
de presentator / de presentatrice
  presenter (m./f.)
zij *she* (stressed pronoun, for
  emphasis)
er *there*
als *as*
de vertaler / de vertaalster
  translator (m./f.)
drie *three*
de jongen *boy*
het meisje *girl*
spreken *to speak*
het Nederlands *Dutch* (language)
het Frans *French* (language)

het Spaans *Spanish* (language)
het Italiaans *Italian* (language)
het Engels *English* (language)
want *because*
de oppas *childminder* (m./f.)
Argentinië (het) *Argentina* (country)
dat *that*
die *that, those*
rood *red*
het luik *shutter*
zien *to see*
de plant *plant*
de vensterbank *windowsill*
daar *there*
mogen *to have permission to (may)*
dit *this*
dat *that*
Frans *French* (adj.)
Argentijns *Argentinian* (adj.)
Brits *British* (adj.)
aardig *nice, kind, friendly*
klein *small*

4.
CHEERS!

PROOST!

<table>
<tr><td>

AIMS

- **SUGGESTING USING INFORMAL ADDRESS**
- **ASKING SOMEONE TO GO FOR A DRINK**

</td><td>

TOPICS

- **WORDS THAT INFLUENCE TONE**
- **TALKING ABOUT COUNTRIES, NATIONALITIES AND LANGUAGES**
- **DOUBLED CONSONANTS**
- **THE PRESENT TENSE OF REGULAR VERBS**

</td></tr>
</table>

CHEERS!

Ben: So you are the Argentinian childminder.

Julia: We can use the informal *(Say just ordinary '**jij**')*, it's fine!

Ben: Shall we go for a drink somewhere *(Shall we somewhere something go drink)*?

Julia: Yes, good idea. I know a nice café near here *(here nearby)*.

Ben: Great!

***

Ben: What do you want to drink?

Julia: I'll have *(I take)* a beer. And you?

Ben: For me, a glass of white wine. Have you been living in Holland a long time *(Live you already long in Holland)*?

Julia: We've been *(We are)* here since last year. And you?

Ben: We've been living here for ten years already *(We live here already ten years)*. We come from Portugal.

Julia: Ben? Is that a Portuguese name?

Ben: Actually, my name is Benjamin, but my friends call me Ben.

Julia: That's funny: my English teacher's name is Bernard, but we call him Ben too *(say also Ben)*. He comes from England and his wife comes from Italy. We speak two languages at home, but they speak three languages: English, Italian and Dutch.

Ben: Well, cheers! To polyglots!

Ben: Dus u bent de Argentijnse oppas.

Julia: Zeg maar gewoon 'jij', hoor!

Ben: Zullen we ergens wat gaan drinken?

Julia: Ja, goed idee. Ik ken een leuk café hier vlakbij.

Ben: Prima!

***

Ben: Wat wil je drinken?

Julia: Ik neem een biertje. En jij?

Ben: Voor mij een glas witte wijn. Woon je al lang in Nederland?

Julia: We zijn hier sinds vorig jaar. En jullie?

Ben: Wij wonen hier al tien jaar. We komen uit Portugal.

Julia: Ben? Is dat een Portugese naam?

Ben: Eigenlijk heet ik Benjamin, maar mijn vrienden noemen me Ben.

Julia: Dat is grappig: mijn docent Engels heet Bernard, maar we zeggen ook Ben. Hij komt uit Engeland en zijn vrouw komt uit Italië. Wij spreken thuis twee talen, maar zij spreken drie talen: Engels, Italiaans en Nederlands.

Ben: Nou, proost! Op de meertaligen!

■ UNDERSTANDING THE DIALOGUE

→ **Zeg maar gewoon 'jij', hoor!** *We can use the informal, it's fine!* This is the way someone may invite you to use the informal. See the section below to find out more about a few words in Dutch that are frequently used to influence tone.

→ **Zullen we ergens wat gaan drinken?** *Shall we go for a drink somewhere?* The auxiliary verb **zullen** *will, shall* is used with another verb to indicate the future. Here it is used as a proposition to do something.

→ **Ik neem een biertje.** *I'll have a beer.* In Dutch, you 'take' a beer: **nemen** *to take.* Note that we would use the future tense in this context, but in Dutch the present is used. **Biertje** ('small beer') is the diminutive of **het bier** *beer.* It can also be used in the plural: **twee biertjes** *two beers*, etc.

→ **Wij wonen hier al tien jaar.** *We've been living here for ten years already.* Here the present tense is used in Dutch, but the present perfect is required in English. The adverb **al** *already* is how the speaker indicates elapsed time.

→ **Eigenlijk heet ik Benjamin.** *Actually, my name is Benjamin.* In a simple sentence, the conjugated verb is always in the second position (that is, the second word in the sentence). As this sentence starts with a word that is not the subject, the order is: complement + verb + subject.

WORDS THAT INFLUENCE TONE

In Dutch, there are a variety of words that are used to nuance the tone in speech: for example, to soften a request so it doesn't sound like an order. These adverbs and interjections are very common and often can't be directly translated. Some examples in the dialogue are:

• **maar** *please*, *so*, *just* to add politeness to a request
• **hoor** *you know*, *listen*, *it's OK*, *you see* to emphasize something that's been said, often in a way that reassures the listener
• **nou** *Well!*, *So!*, *Really!* to express reactions varying from surprise to doubt to indignation. The context and the intonation will help you interpret the meaning.

TALKING ABOUT COUNTRIES, NATIONALITIES AND LANGUAGES

We've already seen a few of these, and there are a few more in this lesson's vocabulary list. Some names of countries end in **-rijk**, which means *kingdom*, or in **-land** *country.* Sometimes, as in English, the term for male inhabitants of a country ends in **-man**. Most of the time, the term for female inhabitants of a country ends in **-se**.

☀ SPELLING
DOUBLED CONSONANTS

To retain the pronunciation of the short vowel, the consonant is doubled when there are two syllables. If there is just one syllable, there is only one consonant:

wit + e → **wit**te *white*

ken + en → **ke**nn**en** *to know*

zeg + en → **ze**gg**en** *to say*

▲ CONJUGATION
THE PRESENT TENSE OF REGULAR VERBS

The frequently used verbs **kennen** *to know* and **zeggen** *to say* are regular in the present tense. (Don't forget the double consonant spelling rule.)

kennen: **ik ken; je / u kent; hij / ze kent; we / jullie / ze kennen**

zeggen: **ik zeg; je / u zegt; hij / ze zegt; we / jullie / ze zeggen**

⬤ EXERCISES

1. TRANSLATE THESE SENTENCES INTO ENGLISH.

a. Zij is Italiaanse en hij is Nederlander.

→ ....

b. Ze komen uit Portugal.

→ ....

c. Hij spreekt Nederlands, Frans en Spaans.

→ ....

d. We zeggen 'Frankrijk', maar 'Nederland'.

→ ....

e. Een Fransman spreekt Frans.

→ ....

2. LINK THE BEGINNING OF EACH SENTENCE WITH THE END.

a. Zullen we •   • 1. Italiaans en Portugees?

b. Ze wonen •   • 2. wat gaan drinken?

c. Spreekt zij •   • 3. hier al tien jaar.

d. Ik neem •   • 4. een glas witte wijn.

3. CIRCLE THE CORRECT SPELLING.

a. Ze zegen/zeggen Ben.   c. Hij neemt een glas wite/witte wijn.

b. Wij kenen/kennen een leuk café.   d. Dat is grapig/grappig.

06

4. LISTEN TO THE AUDIO AND COMPLETE THESE SENTENCES, AND THEN TRANSLATE THEM INTO ENGLISH.

a. ...., eigenlijk heet ik Bernard.

→ ....

b. Zeg .... gewoon Ben!

→ ....

c. Dat is een Nederlandse naam ....!

→ ....

50

VOCABULARY

Proost! *Cheers!*
dus *so*
maar *but, just*
gewoon *usual, ordinary*
jij *you* (informal sing., stressed)
Hoor! *You know! It's fine!* etc.
zullen *will, shall* (future auxiliary)
ergens *somewhere*
wat *something*
drinken *to drink*
goed *good*
het idee *idea*
leuk *nice, fun, pleasant*
het café *café*
vlakbij *nearby*
Wat? *What?*
nemen *to take*
het biertje *beer* (diminutive of **het bier**)
mij *me*
het glas *glass*
wit *white*
de wijn *wine*
lang *long*
Nederland (het) *the Netherlands*
sinds *since*
vorig *last*
het jaar *year*
wij *we*
tien *ten*
Portugal (het) *Portugal*
Portugees *Portuguese* (adj.)
eigenlijk *actually*

de vriend / de vriendin *friend* (m./f.)
noemen *to be named*
me *me*
grappig *funny, amusing*
de docent / de docente *teacher* (m./f.)
Engels *English* (adj.)
Engeland (het) *England*
het Engels *English* (language)
zijn *his*
de vrouw *woman, wife*
de man *man, husband*
twee *two*
de taal *language*
Italië (het) *Italy*
het Italiaans *Italian* (language)
Nou! *Well! Really!* etc.
de meertalige *polyglot, someone who is multilingual*
het rijk *kingdom*
het land *country*

5.
AT THE MARKET

OP DE MARKT

AIMS	TOPICS

AIMS

- ASKING THE PRICE OF SOMETHING
- ORDERING SOMETHING
- SPECIFYING FRUITS/ VEGETABLES AND WEIGHTS/ QUANTITIES
- UNDERSTANDING AND USING EXPRESSIONS FOR BUYING SOMETHING
- TALKING ABOUT COLOURS
- SAYING THANK YOU AND GOODBYE

TOPICS

- MAKING NOUNS PLURAL
- PLURAL DEFINITE AND INDEFINITE ARTICLES

AT THE MARKET

Greengrocer: Apples, pears and bananas!

Customer: Do you also have red currants?

Greengrocer: Yes indeed, 100 grams *(1 ounce)* of currants?

Customer: How much *(costly)* are they?

Greengrocer: 7 euros per kilo.

Customer: Give me *(Do please)* 200 grams *(2 ounces)*. And how much are *(cost)* the pears?

Greengrocer: They cost 4 euros per pound.

Customer: That's *(How)* expensive! No, thank you.

Greengrocer: And for madam, an orange cauliflower?

Customer: You have orange cauliflower?

Greengrocer: Yes, we have various colours of cauliflower: white, orange, green, yellow and even purple!

Customer: Goodness, purple cauliflowers! How much are they?

Greengrocer: 1 euro a piece.

Customer: A yellow and a purple then, please.

Fishmonger: What would you like? *(Say you it just!)*

Customer: A fresh herring.

Fishmonger: With onions *(little-onions)*?

Customer: Yes, gladly.

Fishmonger: A fresh fish for you, sir *(for mister)*. So that's *(That is then)* 2 euros.

Customer: Here you are.

Fishmonger: Thank you very much and see you *(until see)*!

<u>Groenteman</u>: Appels, peren en bananen!

<u>Klant</u>: Heb je ook rode bessen?

<u>Groenteman</u>: Jazeker, een ons bessen?

<u>Klant</u>: Hoe duur zijn ze?

<u>Groenteman</u>: Zeven euro per kilo.

<u>Klant</u>: Doe maar twee ons. En hoeveel kosten de peren?

<u>Groenteman</u>: Ze kosten vier euro per pond.

<u>Klant</u>: Wat duur! Nee, dank je.

<u>Groenteman</u>: En voor mevrouw een oranje bloemkool?

<u>Klant</u>: Heeft u oranje bloemkool?

<u>Groenteman</u>: Ja, wij hebben allerlei kleuren bloemkool: wit, oranje, groen, geel en zelfs paars!

<u>Klant</u>: Tjonge, paarse bloemkolen! Wat kosten ze?

<u>Groenteman</u>: Een euro per stuk.

<u>Klant</u>: Een gele en een paarse dan graag.

<u>Visboer</u>: Zegt u het maar!

<u>Klant</u>: Een verse haring.

<u>Visboer</u>: Met uitjes?

<u>Klant</u>: Ja, graag.

<u>Visboer</u>: Een vers visje voor meneer. Dat is dan twee euro.

<u>Klant</u>: Alstublieft.

<u>Visboer</u>: Dank u wel en tot ziens!

▣ UNDERSTANDING THE DIALOGUE

→ **groenteman** *greengrocer* is a compound noun made up of **groente** *vegetable* and **man**, and **visboer** *fishmonger* is made up of **vis** *fish* and **boer** *farmer*. A greengrocer can also be called a **groenteboer**.

→ There are several ways to ask how much something costs:
Hoe duur zijn ze? *How much are they?* ('How expensive are they?')
Hoeveel kosten de peren? *How much do the pears cost?*
Wat kosten ze? *How much do they cost?*

→ **een ons bessen** *100 grams of currants*. Note that the preposition 'of' is not used in this context in Dutch. The word **ons** translates to *ounce*, but it is not the equivalent weight measurement as the ounce in Britain or the United States. See the section below for more on weights.

→ **Doe maar twee ons.** *Give me 200 grams then.* We saw in the last lesson that **maar** is used to soften a request. The verb here is **doen** *to do*.

→ **Wat duur!** *That's expensive!* The word **wat** can mean *what, how* or *very*. In this type of expression, the verb is generally left out.

→ **dank je (wel)** *thank you (very much)* is synonymous with **bedankt**. The formal equivalent would be **dank u (wel)**.

→ **Zegt u het maar!** ('Just say it!') is the equivalent of *What would you like? What can I get you?* and is often heard in cafés and shops. It is also used in contexts in which two or more people might be speaking, in a similar way to *Go ahead!*

→ **(...) allerlei kleuren bloemkool** *(...) various colours of cauliflower.* The useful term **allerlei** means *all sorts, all kinds, all types, a variety of*.

→ **graag** *gladly, with pleasure* is often used in the sense of *please*.

→ **uitje** is the diminutive of **ui** *onion* and **visje** is the diminutive of **vis** *fish*. In Dutch, the diminutive is used frequently and does not always imply a small size. One of the many ways they are used is to specify something as a countable portion.

→ **Alstublieft!** *Here you are!* Informally you would say **Alsjeblieft!**

TALKING ABOUT WEIGHTS

When ordering by weight, the Dutch still frequently use **het pond** *pound* (half a kilo), as well as **het ons** *ounce*, which refers to 100 grams. You can also use metric weights: **100 (honderd) gram** or **500 (vijfhonderd) gram** or **een halve kilo** *a half kilo*. Note that the unit stays singular regardless of the number: **twee euro** *two euros*.

◆ GRAMMAR
MAKING NOUNS PLURAL

The most frequent way to make a noun plural in Dutch is to add an **-en**:
bes → **bessen**; **peer** → **peren**; **banaan** → **bananen**; **bloemkool** → **bloemkolen**.

Note the doubling of the consonant or the change to a single vowel when a plural ending is added. Certain nouns form the plural by adding an **-s**. In general, nouns with more than one syllable that end in an unstressed **-el** add **-s** in the plural:
appel → **appels** (the plural **appelen** is also possible, but it is less common).

PLURAL DEFINITE AND INDEFINITE ARTICLES

• The definite article *the* for all plural nouns is **de**. This is the case whether the noun is common or neuter: **de peer** → **de peren** *pears*; **het land** → **de landen** *countries*.
• The plural indefinite article (*some*) doesn't exist in Dutch, you just use the plural noun on its own: **een peer** → **peren**; **een land** → **landen**.

⬡ EXERCISES

1. ASK THE PRICE USING THE GIVEN WORDS.

a. bananen/duur →

   H .... ?

b. haring/kost →

   H .... ?

c. bessen/kosten →

   W.. ?

2. NOW ANSWER THE QUESTIONS USING THE GIVEN WORDS.

a. bananen / twee euro / kilo → De ....

b. duur / een euro / stuk → De ....

c. ons / kost / zeven euro → Een ....

3. MAKE THESE NOUNS PLURAL.

a. de bes → ....

b. de kleur → ....

c. een banaan → ....

d. een visboer → ....

e. de appel → ....

4. LISTEN TO EACH PHRASE, THEN SELECT THE RIGHT MEANING FROM EACH PAIR.

07

a. ❑ What would you like?   ❑ You said it!

b. ❑ That's expensive!   ❑ That's cheap!

c. ❑ Thank you very much. (informal)   ❑ Thank you very much. (formal)

d. ❑ Yes, please!   ❑ No, thank you.

VOCABULARY

de markt *market*
de groenteman/groentevrouw or
de groenteboer/groenteboerin
  greengrocer, vegetable seller
  (m./f.)
de groente *vegetable*
de appel *apple*
de peer *pear*
de banaan *banana*
de rode bes *red currant*
de klant *customer* (m./f.)
jazeker *yes indeed, sure, definitely*
het ons *ounce* (100 grams)
Hoe duur? *How much is it?*
zeven *seven*
de euro *euro*
per *per*
de kilo *kilo*
doen *to do*
Hoeveel? *How much?*
kosten *to cost*
vier *four*
het pond *pound* (half a kilo)
Wat ...! *How ... !*
duur *expensive, costly*
Dank je (wel). *Thank you (very
  much).* (informal)
Dank u wel. *Thank you very much.*
  (formal)
de mevrouw *madam*
de bloemkool *cauliflower*
allerlei *all kinds, all sorts, various*
de kleur *colour*

oranje *orange* (colour)
groen *green*
geel *yellow*
paars *purple*
zelfs *even*
Tjonge! *My goodness!*
het stuk *piece*
dan *then*
graag *gladly, with pleasure, please*
de visboer / de visboerin
  fishmonger (m./f.)
de boer / de boerin *farmer* (m./f.)
Zegt u het maar! *What would you
  like? What can I get for you?*
vers *fresh*
de haring *herring*
het uitje *little onion* (the diminutive
  of **de ui** *onion*)
Alstublieft! *Here you are!* (formal)
Alsjeblieft! *Here you are!* (informal)
Tot ziens! *See you!*
de gram *gram*
honderd *hundred*
vijfhonderd *five hundred*
half *half*

6.
FAMILY

DE FAMILIE

AIMS	TOPICS
• **TALKING ABOUT YOUR FAMILY** • **ASKING AND GIVING YOUR AGE**	• **STRESSED SUBJECT PRONOUNS** • **SPELLING CHANGE WHEN THE SUBJECT AND VERB ARE INVERTED** • **NUMBERS FROM 1 TO 19** • **MORE ON ADJECTIVES**

THE FAMILY ALBUM

Granny: How nice that you're all here *(fine that you there all are)*! Paul, do you have the photo album? Look, on that photo it's *(stands)* me with Grandad. And do you know who that is? No? That is Aunt Marijke and Uncle Joop.

Paul: And is that *(see I there)* our cousin Erik?

Granny: Yes, that's right. And that is your cousin Anja.

Paul: Don't they have *(Have they not)* a daughter who's *(of)* eight?

Granny: She is already nine *(year)*. She *(It)* is a happy girl!

Paul: And who is that?

Granny: That is Tom, the son of Ingrid and Ivo. He is thirteen.

Paul: And is this photo of your father and mother?

Granny: No, those are my grandparents.

Paul: They look so serious *(How look they gravely)*!

Granny: Look, on this photo are *(stand)* my four children and fourteen grandchildren. Lovely photos, eh?

Paul: Well, you have an adorable family!

Oma: Wat fijn dat jullie er allemaal zijn! Paul, heb jij het fotoalbum? Kijk, op die foto sta ik met opa. En weet je wie dat zijn? Nee? Dat zijn tante Marijke en oom Joop.

Paul: En zie ik daar onze neef Erik?

Oma: Ja, dat klopt. En dat is je nicht, Anja.

Paul: Hebben zij niet een dochter van acht?

Oma: Ze is al negen jaar. Het is een vrolijk meisje!

Paul: En wie is dat?

Oma: Dat is Tom, de zoon van Ingrid en Ivo. Hij is dertien.

Paul: En is die foto van je vader en moeder?

Oma: Nee, dat zijn mijn grootouders.

Paul: Wat kijken ze ernstig!

Oma: Kijk, op die foto staan mijn vier kinderen en veertien kleinkinderen. Mooie foto's hè!

Paul: Nou, je hebt een schattige familie!

■ UNDERSTANDING THE DIALOGUE

→ **Wat fijn dat jullie er allemaal zijn!** *How nice that you're all here!* The adjective **fijn** is here used in the sense of *agreeable, delightful,* and the pronoun **allemaal** means *everyone.* The adverb **er** is the unstressed form of **daar** *there.*

→ Note the useful expression **Dat klopt.** *That's right.*

→ **Hebben zij niet een dochter van acht?** *Don't they have a daughter who's eight?* Note the way the negative verb in this question is formed: **Hebben zij niet...?** ('Have they not ...?').

→ **Ze is al negen jaar.** ('She is already nine year.') As we saw in the last lesson, when used with a number, the unit is always in the singular.

→ **Het is een vrolijk meisje!** *She's a happy girl!* Although **het meisje** *girl* is technically a diminutive, there is no non-diminutive form of this word. The word **het** here is not the definite article, but a pronoun used for the third-person *it* or an impersonal subject. In English, the more specific pronoun *she* would be used.

→ **Wat kijken ze ernstig!** ('How look they gravely!') In Dutch, an adverb has the same form as the corresponding adjective: **ernstig** *serious* or *seriously.*

→ **Kijk, op die foto staan mijn vier kinderen...** *Look, on this photo are my four children ....* Don't forget that **staan** *to stand* is used rather than *to be* for things that are upright or are printed. Also note the irregular plural of **het kind** *child.*

→ **Mooie foto's hè!** *Lovely photos, eh?* If a noun ends in **-a**, **-o** or **-u**, the plural ending is always preceded by an apostrophe: **foto's.** Unlike in English, this does not indicate possession, it is simply the plural form.

→ **schattig** has a variety of affectionate meanings: *cute, adorable, lovely, sweet, darling, precious.*

TALKING ABOUT YOUR FAMILY

• As in English, the adjective **groot** *great* is used for grandparents: **grootvader** *grandfather* (or **opa** *grandad*) and **grootmoeder** *grandmother* (**oma** *granny*). But for *grandchildren*, Dutch uses **klein** *small*: **kleinkinderen.**

• The term **neef** can refer to a *cousin* (m.) or *nephew*, while **nicht** can refer to a *cousin* (f.) or *niece*. The context will usually make it clear which is meant.

• Note that nouns referring to people are almost all common nouns, except for the neuter nouns **het meisje** *girl* and **het kind** *child.*

◆ GRAMMAR
STRESSED SUBJECT PRONOUNS

We've seen the unstressed subject pronouns, which are more commonly used. The stressed forms are used when you want to put emphasis on the pronoun, so in speech these pronouns are accentuated. Several of the stressed pronouns end in **-ij**. (But note that **hij** *he* is used for both the stressed and unstressed forms.)

		Singular		Plural
1st person	**ik**	*I*	**wij**	*we*
2nd person	**jij**	*you* (informal)	**jullie**	*you* (informal)
	u	*you* (formal)	**u**	*you* (formal)
3rd person	**hij**	*he*	**zij**	*they*
	zij	*she*		

SPELLING CHANGE WHEN THE SUBJECT AND VERB ARE INVERTED

In a question, or when another word apart from the subject starts a sentence, the verb comes before the subject. In this case, in the second person informal (**je / jij**), the final **-t** of the conjugated verb is dropped, unless the verb stem ends in **-t**:

je / jij hebt → **heb je / jij** *you have*	**je / jij heet** → **heet je / jij** *you are called*
je / jij ziet → **zie je / jij** *you see*	**je / jij weet** → **weet je / jij** *you know*

NUMBERS FROM 1 TO 19

08

Many of the numbers up to 19 in Dutch resemble those in English, especially when you hear them pronounced. But note the following changes between the units and the teens: 3 = **drie**, but 13 = **dertien** and 4 = **vier**, but 14 = **veertien**.

1	een	6	zes	11	elf	16	zestien
2	twee	7	zeven	12	twaalf	17	zeventien
3	drie	8	acht	13	dertien	18	achttien
4	vier	9	negen	14	veertien	19	negentien
5	vijf	10	tien	15	vijftien		

MORE ON ADJECTIVES

Before a singular neuter noun (**het** nouns) used with the indefinite article (**een** *a/an*), an adjective does not add the **-e** at the end: *een schattig* **meisje** *a cute girl / een vers* **visje** *a fresh fish*. But if a neuter noun is used with a definite article (**het** *the*) or is plural (thus taking the article **de** *the*), the **-e** is required:

het vrolijke meisje *the happy girl* / **(de) vrolijke meisjes** *the happy girls*
het verse visje *the fresh fish* / **(de) verse visjes** *the fresh fish(es)*

● EXERCISES

1. WRITE OUT THESE NUMBERS IN WORDS.

a. 4 → ....   d. 18 → ....

b. 14 → ....   e. 3 → ....

c. 8 → ....   f. 13 → ....

2. TRANSLATE THESE SENTENCES INTO ENGLISH.

a. Zij hebben een dochter van zestien en een zoon van elf.

→ ....

b. Op die foto staan mijn opa en oma.

→ ....

c. Wat een schattig kind!

→ ....

d. Heb jij al kleinkinderen? Ja, ik ben al grootmoeder.

→ ....

3. CHOOSE THE CORRECT FORM OF THE ADJECTIVE.

a. een groot/grote huis   c. een leuk/leuke café

b. het groot/grote huis   d. het leuk/leuke café

● VOCABULARY

het familiealbum *family album*
de familie *family*
de oma *granny*
de opa *grandad*
fijn *fine, agreeable, enjoyable*
er *there* (unstressed form of **daar**)
dat *that*
allemaal *all, everyone*
het fotoalbum *photo album*
de foto *photo*
kijken *to look*
weten *to know*
Wie? *Who?*
de tante *aunt*
de oom *uncle*
onze *our*
de neef *cousin* (m.), *nephew*
de nicht *cousin* (f.), *niece*
kloppen *to be right*
Dat klopt! *That's right!*
de dochter *daughter*
de zoon *son*
van *of*
acht *eight*
negen *nine*
dertien *thirteen*
veertien *fourteen*
het jaar *year*
vrolijk *happy, merry, cheerful, jolly*
het meisje *girl*
de vader *father*
de moeder *mother*
de grootouder *grandparent*

ernstig *serious, severe, grave* (also
 seriously, severely, gravely)
het kind *child*
het kleinkind *grandchild*
mooi *beautiful, lovely*
schattig *cute, adorable, sweet*
Hè! *Eh?* (i.e. *Isn't it?*)

4. LISTEN TO EACH SENTENCE. IF THE SENTENCE BELOW MATCHES THE AUDIO, SELECT *WAAR* (TRUE), AND IF IT DOESN'T MATCH, SELECT *NIET WAAR* (FALSE).

	WAAR	NIET WAAR
a. Hij kijkt ernstig, maar zij kijkt vrolijk.		
b. Onze neef Tom is negentien en onze nicht is vijftien.		
c. Op die foto staan mijn twaalf kleinkinderen.		
d. Heb jij al een dochter van zeventien?		
e. Heeft zij een broer en een zus?		

7.
ON THE PHONE
AAN DE TELEFOON

AIMS	TOPICS

- TALKING ON THE PHONE
- USING THE DIMINUTIVE
- ASKING QUESTIONS

- HOW TO FORM A QUESTION
- QUESTION WORDS
- NUMBERS FROM 20 TO 102

ON THE PHONE

Ring, ring

Margot: Hello? *(With Margot.)*

Ben: Hi, it's Ben. Is Julia there *(at home)*?

Margot: No, she's not here *(is there not)*.

Ben: Do you know where she is?

Margot: No, no *(not-any)* idea!

Ben: Uh, and when will she be *(is she)* back?

Margot: I don't know that either *(That know I also not)*.

Ben: And what is she doing *(does she)* later?

Margot: Why do you want to know that *(want you that to-know)*?

Ben: I want to ask her over *(her to-invite)*.

Margot: Oh, okay! You can reach her on her mobile, the number is *(on number)* 09 45 98 36 72.

Ben: And I also want to send her a bouquet of flowers *(I want to-her also a bouquet flowers to-send)*. What is the address?

Margot: Naardenstraat 59, Maastricht. The postcode is 1933 WH.

Ben: Thanks and bye.

Ring, ring…

Vriesman: Vriesman here.

Ben: Sorry, who am I speaking to *(with whom speak I)*?

Vriesman: Ms Vriesman.

Ben: Oh, I have the wrong number *(then am I wrongly connected)*. Excuse me *(Take me not as malicious)*.

Ring, ring…

Julia: This is the voicemail *(answering-machine)* of Julia. I'm not at home at the moment, but leave *(record)* a message after the tone.

Tring, tring …

Margot: Met Margot.

Ben: Ja hallo met Ben. Is Julia thuis?

Margot: Nee, ze is er niet.

Ben: Weet je waar ze is?

Margot: Nee, geen idee!

Ben: Eh, en wanneer is ze terug?

Margot: Dat weet ik ook niet.

Ben: En wat doet ze straks?

Margot: Waarom wil je dat weten?

Ben: Ik wil haar uitnodigen.

Margot: O, oké! Je kunt haar bereiken op haar mobieltje, op nummer 09 45 98 36 72.

Ben: En ik wil haar ook een bosje bloemen sturen. Wat is het adres?

Margot: Naardenstraat 59, Maastricht. De postcode is 1933 WH.

Ben: Bedankt en tot ziens.

Tring, tring …

Vriesman: Met Vriesman.

Ben: Pardon, met wie spreek ik?

Vriesman: Met mevrouw Vriesman.

Ben: O, dan ben ik verkeerd verbonden. Neemt u me niet kwalijk.

Tring, tring …

Julia: Dit is het antwoordapparaat van Julia. Ik ben momenteel niet thuis, maar spreek een boodschap in na de piep.

■ UNDERSTANDING THE DIALOGUE

→ **Ja hallo met Ben.** *Yes, hello, it's Ben.* There are certain fixed expressions used when talking on the phone. One of these is the use of **met** *with* + name rather than *it's* + name as we would say in English.

→ **Geen idee.** *No idea.* The negative word **geen** translates as *no* or *none*. It's used in situations where the meaning is *not one*, *not any*.

→ **En wat doet ze straks?** *And what is she doing* ('does she') *later?* **Eh, en wanneer is ze terug?** *Uh, and when will she be* ('is she') *back?* While in English the present or future continuous would be used in the first question and the future tense in the second, in both contexts, the present tense is used in Dutch. Simple!

→ **Waarom wil je dat weten?** ('Why want you that to-know?') Don't forget the rule that the conjugated verb must be in the second position in a sentence (or clause), and the main verb (in the infinitive) at the end.

→ As we've mentioned, the diminutive is very frequently used in Dutch. It can refer to a small size (**mobieltje** *mobile phone*) or express affinity, affection or intimacy (**een bos(je) bloemen** *a bouquet of flowers*), among other nuances.

→ **dan ben ik verkeerd verbonden** ('then am I wrongly connected'). Note the Dutch way of saying you have the wrong number, as well as the word order (conjugated verb in second position, main verb in the infinitive at the end).

→ **Neemt u me niet kwalijk.** *Excuse me. Pardon me.* ('Take me not as malicious.') Another useful expression, here with the formal **u**.

→ **(…)** spreek **een boodschap** in **na de piep** ('record a message after the tone'). The verb here is **inspreken** *to record, to speak into*, which is a separable-prefix verb: when it conjugates, the prefix splits off and moves to another position in the sentence. We'll come back to this.

ANSWERING THE PHONE AND UNDERSTANDING POSTCODES

In the Netherlands, when someone answers the phone, rather than saying 'Hello?' they give their name (first or last), preceded by **met** *with*. In terms of postcodes, these have four digits, followed by a space and then two letters. The numbers correspond to a town or a district in a city. The letters specify the street or the part of a street. It is rare for two towns to have the same digits. Note that the number of the house or building comes after the street name in an address.

◆ GRAMMAR
FORMING QUESTIONS

As we've seen, to form a question, you simply swap the subject and verb – in Dutch there is no equivalent to *Do/does ...?*. If the question starts with a question word (*What? When? Where? Why? How?*), the question word comes first, followed by the conjugated verb, and then the subject pronoun:

Wanneer is ze terug? *When will she be back?*
Wat doet ze straks? *What is she doing later?*
Waarom wil je dat weten? *Why do you want to know that?*

QUESTION WORDS

Here are a few question words we've seen so far:
Waar? *Where?* **Wat?** *What?* **Wanneer?** *When?* **Waarom?** *Why?*

NUMBERS FROM 20 TO 102

09

Here things get a bit trickier, as in numbers such as 21, the unit comes before the ten, with **en** *and* inserted between them: 21 **een**en**twintig** ('one-and-twenty'). Also note how certain numbers change form: 3 = **drie**, but 30 = **dertig**; 4 = **vier**, but 40 = **veertig**; 18 = **achttien**, but 80 = **tachtig**.

20	twintig	30	dertig
21	eenentwintig	40	veertig
22	tweeëntwintig	50	vijftig
23	drieëntwintig	60	zestig
24	vierentwintig	70	zeventig
25	vijfentwintig	80	tachtig
26	zesentwintig	90	negentig
27	zevenentwintig	100	honderd
28	achtentwintig	101	honderdeen
29	negenentwintig	102	honderdtwee

73

● EXERCISES

1. WRITE OUT THE NUMBERS IN WORDS.

a. 88 →..   d. 28 →..

b. 49 →..   e. 99 →..

c. 36 →..   f. 101 →..

2. COMPLETE THE QUESTIONS WITH THE CORRECT QUESTION WORD.

a. .... werkt de buurvrouw? (*Where*)

b. .... wonen jullie in een huis op de dijk? (*Why*)

c. .... begint de kaasproeverij? (*When*)

d. .... is je naam? (*What*)

e. .... doe je straks? (*What*)

3. TRANSLATE THE SENTENCES BELOW INTO ENGLISH.

a. Goedemorgen, met meneer Hans. Is je vader thuis?

→ ....

b. Neemt u me niet kwalijk. Ik ben verkeerd verbonden.

→ ....

c. Je kunt haar bereiken op haar mobiel.

→ ....

d. Hallo, met wie spreek ik?

→ ....

e. Dit is het antwoordapparaat van Ivo. Spreek een boodschap in na de piep.

→ ....

4. LISTEN TO THE AUDIO AND COMPLETE EACH SENTENCE/QUESTION.

a. Hebben zij niet een .... van .... en een .... van ....? Ja, dat klopt.

b. .... doet ze ....? ....

c. Wat .... drinken? Ik .... een glas............................. En jij?

d. Zullen we .... gaan? Ja, ... idee!

e. Sorry, hij is ....

74

VOCABULARY

de telefoon *telephone*
er *there* (unstressed form of **daar**)
Geen idee! *No idea!*
Wanneer? *When?*
terug *back*
Waarom? *Why?*
haar *her*
uitnodigen *to invite*
Oké. *Okay.*
bereiken *to reach*
de mobiel *mobile/cell phone*
de bos *bouquet*
de bloem *flower*
sturen *to send*
het adres *address*
de postcode *postcode*
Pardon. *Pardon me.*
Met wie spreek ik? *Who am I
  speaking to?*
verkeerd verbonden *to have the
  wrong number*
Neemt u me niet kwalijk!
  Excuse me! (formal)
het antwoordapparaat
  answering machine, voicemail
momenteel *at the moment*
inspreken *to record, to speak into*
de boodschap *message*
na *after*
de piep *beep, tone*

II

EVERYDAY

LIFE

8.
A NEW
ID CARD

EEN NIEUWE IDENTITEITSKAART

AIMS	TOPICS
• MAKING AN APPOINTMENT • ASKING AND GIVING YOUR AGE • ANSWERING QUESTIONS ABOUT YOURSELF	• EXPRESSIONS: *NODIG HEBBEN* TO NEED AND *EEN AFSPRAAK MAKEN* TO MAKE AN APPOINTMENT • *OM TE* IN ORDER TO • FORMING THE NEGATIVE • FINAL CONSONANTS *-V* AND *-Z* • THE PRESENT TENSE OF VERBS SUCH AS *GEVEN* TO GIVE AND *REIZEN* TO TRAVEL

A NEW ID CARD

Lisa: I need a new ID *(I have a new identity-card need-of)*.

City official: You have to make an appointment first. I have a spot *(place)* on 6 October.

Lisa: I can't on Monday. Tuesday, 7 November, is that possible?

City official: Yes, I can do that *(that can)*. I'll note *(I note)* the date and give you this form in advance *(give you already this form)*.

Lisa: Do my children need a card as well?

City official: How old are they?

Lisa: They are 15 and 17.

City official: They need their own card in order to be able to travel abroad *(They have their own card need-of in-order towards the outside-country to be-able-to travel)*.

Lisa: Give me three forms then, please.

7 November

Lisa: I've come *(I come)* to pick up our cards.

City official: What is your name?

Lisa: Lisa Vos.

City official: One moment, I'll switch *(I switch)* the computer on … You are *(stand)* not in the file. I do see *(see well)* an Elisabeth Vos …

Lisa: How stupid of me! That's me *(That am I)*!

<u>Lisa</u>: Ik heb een nieuwe identiteitskaart nodig.

<u>Gemeenteambtenaar</u>: U moet eerst een afspraak maken. Ik heb plaats op 6 oktober.

<u>Lisa</u>: Ik kan niet op maandag. Dinsdag 7 november, is dat mogelijk?

<u>Gemeenteambtenaar</u>: Ja, dat kan. Ik noteer de datum en geef u vast het formulier.

<u>Lisa</u>: Hebben mijn kinderen ook een kaart nodig?

<u>Gemeenteambtenaar</u>: Hoe oud zijn ze?

<u>Lisa</u>: Ze zijn 15 en 17.

<u>Gemeenteambtenaar</u>: Ze hebben hun eigen kaart nodig om naar het buitenland te kunnen reizen.

<u>Lisa</u>: Geeft u mij dan maar drie formulieren.

7 november

<u>Lisa</u>: Ik kom onze kaarten ophalen.

<u>Gemeenteambtenaar</u>: Wat is uw naam?

<u>Lisa</u>: Lisa Vos.

<u>Gemeenteambtenaar</u>: Een momentje, ik doe de computer aan … U staat niet in het bestand. Ik zie wel een Elisabeth Vos …

<u>Lisa</u>: Wat dom van me! Dat ben ik!

UNDERSTANDING THE DIALOGUE

→ **Ik heb een nieuwe identiteitskaart nodig.** *I need a new ID card.* In this sentence we see the very useful expression **nodig hebben** *to need* ('need-of to-have'). Note that what is needed goes in between the verb and **nodig**, which moves to the end of the sentence.

→ **U moet eerst een afspraak maken.** *You have to make an appointment first.* When a modal auxiliary verb such as **moeten** *to have to, must* is used with another verb, it is conjugated and appears in the second position in the sentence, while the main verb (infinitive) moves to the end.

→ The preposition **op** *on* is used to give a date or a day: **op 6 oktober** *on 6 October*; **op maandag** *on Monday*. Note that in Dutch, the days of the week and the months are not capitalized.

→ As in English, the days of the week all end in **-dag** *day*: **maandag** *Monday*, **dinsdag** *Tuesday*, **woensdag** *Wednesday*, **donderdag** *Thursday*, **vrijdag** *Friday*, **zaterdag** *Saturday*, **zondag** *Sunday*.

→ **Hoe oud?** *How old?* Just as in English, in Dutch an age is given with the verb **zijn**, *to be*: **Hoe oud zijn ze?** *How old are they?* **Ze zijn 15 en 17.** *They are 15 and 17.*

→ **Ze hebben hun eigen kaart nodig om naar het buitenland te kunnen reizen.** ('They have their own card need-of in-order towards the outside-country to be-able-to travel.') This sentence is a bit trickier! It contains a structure we haven't seen yet: **om** + **te** + infinitive, *in order to* + verb. The **om** introduces the purpose, which is followed by **te** + infinitive at the end of the sentence. Here, the purpose is to be able to go to another country. The preposition **naar** *towards* is used to indicate going in the direction of something.

→ **Geeft u mij dan maar drie formulieren.** ('Give you me then just three forms.') Softening modal words can be used together, but they have to be in a certain order: as here with **dan maar** *then, please*.

→ In the phrase **ik doe de computer aan** *I'll switch the computer on*, we have the separable-prefix verb **aandoen** *to switch on, to start up*.

NICKNAMES

It's very common for people to be called by a shortened form or a variant of their given name: for example, **Elisabeth** might become **Bettie**, **Elisa**, **Ella**, **Els**, **Elles**, **Elsbeth**, **Ilse**, **Lies**, **Liesbeth**, **Lizzy** or **Lisa**. So the official first name that appears on a birth certificate or an ID is often rarely used in everyday life.

◆ GRAMMAR
FORMING THE NEGATIVE

There are two ways to form the negative in Dutch: with **niet** or **geen** *no, not*. We'll explain **geen** in lesson 13, but let's start with **niet**, which can be placed:

• just before an adjective or adverb to make it negative:
Hij is niet lief. *He is not nice.* **Ze is niet erg groot.** *She is not very tall.*

• generally, before a complement (a word or phrase that describes the subject or object of a sentence) when this is introduced by a preposition:
Ik kan niet op maandag. *I can't on Monday.*
U staat niet in het bestand. *You are not in the file.*

• after a complement relating to the subject – if possible, the **niet** should come at the end of the sentence – to make the whole sentence negative:
Ze is er niet. *She is not here.* **Dat weet ik ook niet.** *I don't know that either.*

To show a contrast with a previous statement that includes **niet**, the adverb **wel** *well* is often used, in a similar way to emphasizing a verb with *do* in English:
U staat niet in het bestand. Ik zie wel een Elisabeth Vos.
You are not in the file. I <u>do</u> see ('I see well') an Elisabeth Vos.

✳ SPELLING
THE FINAL CONSONANTS -*V* AND -*Z*

A Dutch word cannot end in **-v** or **-z**. To avoid this, a final **-v** is replaced by **-f**, and a final **-z** is replaced by **-s**. We'll see an example of this in the next section with the verbs **geven** *to give* and **reizen** *to travel*, but this rule does not only affect verbs.

▲ CONJUGATION
THE PRESENT TENSE OF VERBS SUCH AS *GEVEN* TO GIVE AND *REIZEN* TO TRAVEL

Remember the rule for forming the present tense. To conjugate the first-person singular, the **-en** ending of the infinitive is dropped, which for the verb **geven** *to give* would theoretically result in:

    geven → gev

However, the vowel needs to be doubled because the syllable ends in a consonant:

gev → **geev**

Plus, because of the rule that a word cannot end in a **-v**, the final consonant has to change to an **-f**:

geev → **geef** *I give*

In **reizen** *to travel*, the vowel (in this case a diphthong) doesn't have to be doubled, but the final **-z** becomes an **-s**. Note that this spelling change occurs even if the letter is followed by **-t** in the second and third person.

	geven	*to give*	**reizen**	*to travel*
ik	**geef**	*I give*	**reis**	*I travel*
je / u	**geeft**	*you give*	**reist**	*you travel*
hij / ze	**geeft**	*he/she gives*	**reist**	*he/she travels*
we	**geven**	*we give*	**reizen**	*we travel*
jullie	**geven**	*you give* (pl.)	**reizen**	*you travel* (pl.)
ze	**geven**	*they give*	**reizen**	*they travel*

● EXERCISES

1. LINK THE NICKNAME TO THE OFFICIAL NAME IT IS SHORT FOR.

a. Willie (girl's name) ●　　　　　　● 1. Beatrix

b. Julia　　　　　　●　　　　　● 2. Alexander

c. Bea　　　　　　●　　　　　● 3. Wilhelmina

d. Xander　　　　　●　　　　　● 4. Juliana

2. CHOOSE THE CORRECT PREPOSITION AND THEN MAKE THE SENTENCE NEGATIVE.

a. U staat in/op de lijst.

→ ....

b. Ik zie je naam in/op het bestand.

→ ....

c. We kunnen in/op donderdag.

→ ....

d. Ze reizen in/op 3 maart naar/op het buitenland.

→ ....

● VOCABULARY

de identiteitskaart *identity card*
nodig hebben *to need*
de gemeenteambtenaar /
de gemeenteambtenares
city official (m./f.) (**de gemeente**
local authority & **de ambtenaar /**
de ambtenares *civil servant* m./f.)
moeten *to have to, must*
eerst *first*
de afspraak *appointment*
een afspraak maken *to make an*
appointment
de plaats *place, space, availability*
plaats hebben *to have a place, to*
have availability
oktober (de) *October*
november (de) *November*
mogelijk *possible*
Dat kan. *It's possible. I can do that.*
noteren *to note*
de datum *date*
geven *to give*
vast *already, in advance, meanwhile*
het formulier *form*
de kaart *card*
Hoe oud? *How old?*
oud *old*
hun *their*
eigen *own*
om ... te *in order to*
naar *towards, to*
het buitenland *foreign country*
reizen *to travel*

ophalen *to pick up*
het moment *instant, moment*
aandoen *to switch on, to start up*
het bestand *file*
de computer *computer*
wel *well*
dom *stupid, silly*
me *me*
maken *to make*
maandag (de) *Monday*
dinsdag (de) *Tuesday*
woensdag (de) *Wednesday*
donderdag (de) *Thursday*
vrijdag (de) *Friday*
zaterdag (de) *Saturday*
zondag (de) *Sunday*
geen *none, not any*
lezen *to read*
de krant *newspaper*
vaak *often, frequently*

3. COMPLETE THE SENTENCES WITH THE CORRECT FORM OF THE VERB.

a. Ik (geven) .... u een nieuwe identiteitskaart.

b. Hij (lezen) (*to read*) .... de krant (*newspaper*).

c. Ze (*She*) (reizen) .... niet vaak (*often*).

d. (geven) .... u mij dan maar drie tulpen.

4. (I) READ THESE PHRASES OR WORDS: *EEN AFSPRAAK MAKEN, DAN MAAR, HEEFT NODIG, HOE OUD, KOMEN, OPHALEN.*
(II) LISTEN TO THE AUDIO.
(III) COMPLETE THE SENTENCES WITH THE CORRECT WORDS AND THEN READ THE SENTENCES OUT LOUD.
(IV) LISTEN TO THE AUDIO TO CHECK YOUR ANSWERS.

10

a. .... zijn je kinderen?

b. Jullie moeten eerst ....

c. We .... onze kaarten ....

d. Doe .... twee ons bessen!

e. Hij .... een nieuwe rekenmachine ....

9.
DAILY ACTIVITIES

DAGELIJKSE BEZIGHEDEN

AIMS	TOPICS

- ASKING AND GIVING THE TIME
- TALKING ABOUT SPECIFIC TIMES DURING THE DAY
- SAYING WHAT YOU WANT TO DO WITH *ZIN HEBBEN OM TE* TO FEEL LIKE

- THE TIME
- THE PRESENT TENSE OF VERBS SUCH AS *GAAN* TO GO AND *DOEN* TO DO

WHAT TIME IS IT?

Emma: What time *(How late)* is it?

Bram: It's 2:00 *(two hour)*.

Emma: In the afternoon or the morning *(in the night)*?

Bram: In the afternoon, of course! I'm going to get a little croquette *(I go a little-croquette out the wall to-pull)*.

Emma: I'm staying in bed. Are you going by *(with the)* tram?

Bram: No, I'm going by *(on the)* bike, and I'll take *(and with)* the ferry over the [river] IJ.

Emma: So far? What time will you be back *(How late are you back)*?

Bram: At around 5:00. It's already 10 after *(It is now already ten over)* two now. Aren't you getting up *(Get you not up)*?

Emma: In a *(little)* quarter of an hour. I **am** hungry, and I fancy fries with mayo *(I have well hunger and desire in a little-fries with mayo)*.

Bram: You know what? You get up, put your tracksuit on and *(you)* come along with me.

Emma: I feel like staying in bed *(I have desire in bed to stay)*.

Bram: Slacker! Are you staying in bed until 6:30 *(half seven)* tonight?

Emma: Hoe laat is het?

Bram: Het is twee uur.

Emma: 's Middags of 's nachts?

Bram: 's Middags natuurlijk! Ik ga een kroketje uit de muur trekken.

Emma: Ik blijf in bed. Ga je met de tram?

Bram: Nee, ik ga op de fiets en met de pont over het IJ.

Emma: Zo ver? Hoe laat ben je terug?

Bram: Om ongeveer vijf uur. Het is nu al tien over twee. Sta je niet op?

Emma: Over een kwartiertje. Ik heb wel honger en zin in een patatje met mayo.

Bram: Weet je wat? Je staat op, doet je joggingpak aan en je gaat mee.

Emma: Ik heb zin om in bed te blijven.

Bram: Luiwammes! Blijf je in bed tot half zeven vanavond?

■ UNDERSTANDING THE DIALOGUE

→ In Dutch, *What time ...?* is **Hoe laat ...?** ('How late ...?'): **Hoe laat is het?** *What time is it?* The response is formed with **Het is ...** *It is...* Note that **het** here is the impersonal pronoun *it*, which can be used to refer to something abstract.

→ Note that in conversation **uur** *hour* is only used on the exact hour, so after a time its meaning is in fact *o'clock*. And remember that after a number, the unit is singular: **Het is twee uur.** *It's 2 o'clock.*

→ **'s Middags of 's nachts?** *In the afternoon or in the night?* Usually, in conversation people use the 12-hour clock, if necessary specifying the time of the day with the expressions **'s nachts** *in the night*; **'s ochtends / 's morgens** *in the morning*; **'s middags** *in the afternoon*; **'s avonds** *in the evening*:

> **Het is twee uur 's middags.** *It's 2:00 in the afternoon.*
> **Het is twee uur 's nachts.** *It's 2:00 in the morning.*

→ The odd-looking form **'s middags** (pronounced [smiddakhs]) originates from **des middags** (and likewise for the other times of day), which is a fossilized genitive form. Note that if **'s** begins a sentence, it isn't capitalized: the following word is.

→ In timetables for flights, trains, buses, etc., when it's essential to know the exact time of day, the 24-hour clock is used, with **uur** in between the hour and minutes:

> **Het is eenentwintig uur zestien.** *It's 21:16.*
> **Het is negen uur achttien.** *It's 9:18.*

→ The prepositions used for different forms of getting around vary depending on the type of transport: **met de tram** *by tram* ('with the tram'); **op de fiets** *by bike* ('on the bike'); **met de pont** *on the ferry* ('with the ferry').

→ The preposition **om** *at* is used with times: **om vijf uur** *at 5:00.*

→ **Sta je niet op?** *Aren't you getting up?* contains the separable-prefix verb **opstaan** *to get up.* There are a few other separable-prefix verbs in the dialogue, for example, **aandoen** *to put on* and **meegaan** *to come along with, to join*: **Je staat op, doet je joggingpak aan en je gaat mee.** *You get up, put your tracksuit on and come with me.* We'll come back to this in lesson 16.

→ **Over een kwartiertje** *in a quarter of an hour.* This is the diminutive of **het kwartier** *quarter hour,* not to be confused with **het kwart** *quarter.*

→ **Ik heb wel honger en zin in een patatje met mayo.** Note that in Dutch you aren't hungry, you 'have hunger': **hebben honger.** The construction for *to feel like/fancy something* is **zin hebben in** + noun, and *to feel like doing something* is **zin hebben om** + **te** + infinitive: **Ik heb zin om in bed te blijven.** *I feel like staying in bed.* The **te** + infinitive is at the end of the sentence.

CULTURAL NOTE

Een kroketje uit de muur trekken *go get a croquette* ('a little-croquette out the wall pull'). A **kroket** *croquette* is a little breaded and fried ball of meat, potato or fish, and they are very popular in Holland. They are sold at snack bar counters or from vending machines on the wall next to fast-food restaurants, hence the expression.

Over het IJ *over the IJ*. The **IJ** is a river that separates the northern part of **Amsterdam** from the centre. It was previously part of the bay of **Zuiderzee**, which is now a freshwater lake, the **IJsselmeer**. Several ferries cross the **IJ** from its northern and southern banks and are mainly used by pedestrians and cyclists. The **IJ-tunnel** is reserved for cars.

GIVING THE TIME

There are some important differences in the way the time is given in Dutch. First off, the minutes are always given before the hour.

For the first 15 minutes after the hour, use **over** *after, over, more than*:

Het is vijf (minuten*) over twee. *It's five after two.*
Het is tien over twee. *It's ten after two.*
Het is kwart over twee. *It's a quarter after two.*

* The use of **minuten** is optional.

For the next 15 minutes (16 to 29), count the minutes <u>until</u> the half hour and use the preposition **voor** *before*. Another big difference: the half hour is given in reference to the coming hour, <u>not</u> the current hour:

Het is tien (minuten) voor half drie. *It's 2:20.*
('It is ten (minutes) before half three.')

Het is vijf voor half drie. *It's 2:25.*
Het is half drie. *It's half two* ('three').

For the next 15 minutes (31 to 44), count the minutes <u>after</u> the half hour, and use the preposition **over** *after*:

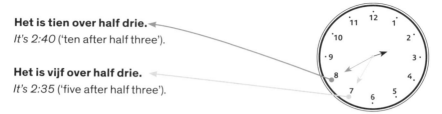

Het is tien over half drie.
It's 2:40 ('ten after half three').

Het is vijf over half drie.
It's 2:35 ('five after half three').

And for the final 15 minutes (45 to 59), count the minutes <u>until</u> the coming hour, and use the preposition **voor** *before*:

Het is vijf voor drie.
It's five to three.
Het is tien voor drie.
It's ten to three.
Het is kwart voor drie.
It's a quarter to three.

▲ CONJUGATION
THE PRESENT TENSE OF VERBS SUCH AS *GAAN* TO GO AND *DOEN* TO DO

• Verbs such as **gaan** *to go* and **doen** *to do* have a regular conjugation, with the exception that only the final **-n** is dropped before adding the conjugation ending (in other verbs **-en** is dropped).
• Remember that in the second-person singular (**je** *you*), if the verb and subject are swapped, the final **-t** is dropped, except if the verb stem ends in a **-t**.
• And don't forget to double the vowel **a** if the syllable ends in a consonant.

ik ga *I go*; **je /u gaat** *you go*, but **ga je** *go you*; **hij / ze gaat** *he/she/it goes*;
we gaan *we go*; **jullie gaan** *you go* (pl.); **ze gaan** *they go*

ik doe *I do*; **je / u doet** *you do*, but **doe je** *do you*; **hij / ze doet** *he/she/it does*;
we doen *we do*; **jullie doen** *you do* (pl.); **ze doen** *they do*

● VOCABULARY

Hoe laat is het? *What time is it?*
Hoe? *How?*
laat *late*
het *it* (neutral, impersonal pronoun)
het uur *hour, o'clock*
of *or*
natuurlijk *of course*
de kroket *croquette*
trekken uit *to pull out*
de muur *wall*
blijven *to stay*
in bed *in bed*
het bed *bed*
de tram *tramway*
de fiets *bicycle*
op de fiets *by bike*
de pont *ferry*
over *after, over, more than*
zo *so* (to such an extent)
ver *far*
om *at* (+ time)
ongeveer *about, approximately*
nu *now*
opstaan *to get up*
over *in*
de honger *hunger*
honger hebben *to be hungry*
de zin *desire*
zin hebben in (+ noun) *to feel like/*
  fancy something
zin hebben om + te (+ verb) *to feel*
  like/fancy doing something
de patat *fries*

de mayonaise *mayonnaise*
aandoen *to put on*
het joggingpak *tracksuit, sweatsuit*
meegaan *to come along with, to join*
de luiwammes *slacker* (m./f.)
tot *until*
's ochtends / 's morgens
  in the morning
de ochtend *morning*
de morgen *morning*
's middags *in the afternoon*
de middag *afternoon*
's avonds *in the evening*
de avond *evening*
vanavond *this evening*
vannacht *tonight*
's nachts *in the night*
de nacht *night*
de tunnel *tunnel*
het kwartier *quarter of an hour*
het kwart *quarter*
de minuut *minute*
voor *before*

◆ EXERCISES

1. GIVE THE TIMES IN NUMBERS AND CONVERSATIONALLY, SPECIFYING THE TIME OF DAY (SEE LESSON 6, P. 65, AND LESSON 7, P. 73, IF YOU NEED HELP WITH THE NUMBERS).

a. 9:45 → Het is ....

b. 17:05 → ....

c. 3:15 → ....

d. 20:35 → ....

2. COMPLETE THE SENTENCES WITH THE CORRECT PREPOSITION AND TRANSLATE THEM.

a. Het is tien .... half negen. (2 possibilities)

→ ....

b. Zij heeft zin ....een glas witte wijn en hij .... een patatje .... mayonaise.

→ ....

c. We hebben zin .... het buitenland te gaan.

→ ....

d. De pont komt .... een kwartier.

→ ....

e. Ga je een kroketje .... de muur trekken?

→ ....

f. Hoe laat ben je terug? .... negen uur.

→ ....

g. Ze blijven .... bed .... tien uur.

→ ....

3. COMPLETE EACH SENTENCE WITH THE CORRECT FORM OF THE VERB.

a. Ik .... (doen) mijn joggingpak aan en ik .... (gaan) mee.

b. .... (staan) Jasper niet op de lijst?

c. .... (gaan) u op de fiets of met de tram?

d. .... (blijven) je in bed tot twaalf uur of .... (staan) je nu op?

4. LISTEN TO THE AUDIO AND THEN COMPLETE THE SENTENCES. READ THEM OUT LOUD, AND THEN LISTEN TO THE AUDIO AGAIN TO CHECK YOUR ANSWERS.

a. Het is .... 's middags.

b. Heb je ....?

c. Ze nemen .... over ....

d. Hij .... een .... uit de ....

e. Doe je ....

94

10.
AN EMAIL
FROM EVA

EEN E-MAIL VAN EVA

AIMS	TOPICS

- **WRITING AN EMAIL**
- **GREETING AND SIGNING OFF IN WRITTEN COMMUNICATION**
- **ASKING FOR AND GIVING NEWS**

- **STRESSED OBJECT PRONOUNS**
- **NO DOUBLED CONSONANTS AT THE END OF A WORD**
- **THE PRESENT TENSE OF VERBS SUCH AS *STOPPEN* TO STOP AND *BEGINNEN* TO BEGIN**

AN EMAIL FROM EVA

Dear Tessa,

A quick note *(short message)* from me before the holidays begin.

I'm busy *(I have it busy)*, but all is well with me.

(With) My brothers are *(is it)* also great. I don't see them as much anymore *(so often more)* as they are both beginning their studies soon *(because they begin soon both with their studies)*.

(With) My sister is *(it)* fine. She stopped *(with)* her studies and is going to start her *(an)* own business. It's risky *(It is a risk)*, but she wants to give it a try *(chance)*!

But how is it going with you? And with your husband: how is he *(how is it with him)*? And the children? How are they *(How goes it with them)*?

I hope that your mother is doing better now *(that it meanwhile better with your mother goes)*. Give her my best! *(Do her the regards from me!)*

Well, hope to hear from you soon *(let just fast something from you to-hear)*! And you know, you're (pl.) always welcome at ours *(us)*.

Love,

Eva

Lieve Tessa,

Een kort berichtje van me, voordat de vakantie begint.

Ik heb het druk, maar alles is goed met mij.

Met mijn broers is het ook prima. Ik zie ze niet zo vaak meer, want ze beginnen binnenkort allebei met hun studie.

Met mijn zus is het oké. Zij stopt met haar studie en gaat een eigen bedrijf starten. Het is een risico, maar ze wil het een kans geven!

Maar hoe gaat het met jou? En met je man: hoe is het met hem? En de kinderen? Hoe gaat het met hen?

Ik hoop dat het inmiddels beter met je moeder gaat. Doe haar de groeten van me!

Nou, laat maar snel iets van je horen! En je weet, jullie zijn altijd welkom bij ons.

Liefs,

Eva

■ UNDERSTANDING THE DIALOGUE

→ **Lieve (…)** *Dear* (…) is the form of the adjective **lief** *sweet, nice, dear, lovable* when used before a noun. Remember that a word can't end in **-v**, so when the adjective is used after a verb the final **-v** is replaced by an **-f**.

→ **Een kort berichtje van me** *A quick note* ('short message') *from me.* Note that **me** *me* is the unstressed object pronoun in the first person. We'll come back to this in lesson 15.

→ **de vakantie** *vacation, break, holidays*: note that this is singular in Dutch, so it is used with a singular verb.

→ **Ik heb het druk.** *I'm busy.* ('I have it busy.') The word **druk** can mean *busy, occupied* or *stress, pressure*. This expression is formed with the verb **hebben** and the impersonal pronoun **het** *it*.

→ **Alles is goed met mij.** *Everything is fine with me.* You can also say **alles gaat goed met mij/me** or **het gaat goed met mij/me** ('all/it goes well with me'). The object pronoun **mij** *me* is the stressed form of **me** *me.* See the section on stressed object pronouns on the next page.

→ **Ik zie ze niet zo vaak meer.** *I don't see them as much* ('so often') *anymore.* Note the way to form the negation **niet … meer** *not … anymore.*

→ **Ze beginnen met hun studie.** *They are starting their studies.* **Zij stopt met haar studie.** *She is stopping her studies.* The preposition **met** *with* is used after **beginnen** and **stoppen** to introduce what is starting or stopping.

→ **dat het (…) beter met je moeder gaat** *that your mother is better (…)*: the preposition **met** *with* is also used in the various ways to say how someone is.

STARTING AND SIGNING OFF A LETTER/EMAIL

With close friends or family, you can start a letter or email with **Lieve** *Dear*, which expresses affection. At the end of the letter, you can sign off with **Liefs**, which has the same meaning and is equivalent to *Love, Affectionately*.

For a greeting that is less intimate but still warm, use **Beste** *Dear*. In this case, you can sign off with **Met vriendelijke groeten** *Kind regards* ('With friendly greetings') or **Hartelijke groeten** *Warmly, Cordially*.

A formal letter/email would start with **Geachte heer** *Dear sir* ('Esteemed sir') / **Geachte mevrouw** *Dear madam*. (Or if speaking out loud: **Dames en heren** *Ladies and gentlemen*.) At the end of a formal written communication, use **Hoogachtend** *Sincerely, Yours faithfully* ('Highly esteeming').

◆ GRAMMAR
STRESSED OBJECT PRONOUNS

An object pronoun indicates who or what receives the action of the verb. It sometimes follows a preposition. Like the subject pronouns, there are two forms in Dutch: stressed and unstressed. Here are the stressed forms, which can be used for both direct and indirect object pronouns (except *them*) and with or without a preposition.

mij *me*; **jou** *you*; **u** *you* (formal); **hem** *him, it* (common noun); **haar** *her*; **het** *it* (neuter, impersonal); **ons** *us*; **jullie** *you* (pl.); **hen** (direct object) / **hun** (indirect object) *them*.

• **hem** can refer to a male (*him*) or to a common noun (*it*):
Ik zie Hans. *I see Hans.* → **Ik zie hem.** *I see him.*
Hoe gaat het met hem? *How is he?* ('How goes it with him?')
Ik zie de krant. *I see the newspaper.* → **Ik zie hem.** *I see it.*

• **haar** refers to a female (*her*):
Ik zie Eva. *I see Eva.* → **Ik zie haar.** *I see her.*
Hoe gaat het met haar? *How is she doing?* ('How goes it with her?')

• **het** can refer to something impersonal or abstract or to a neuter noun:
Ik wil het een kans geven. *I want to give it a chance.*
Ik heb het druk. *I'm busy.* ('I have it occupied.')
Ik zie het formulier. *I see the form.* → **Ik zie het.** *I see it.*

• **hen / hun** (*them*)
→ **hen** can refer to a direct object or an indirect object after a preposition:
Ik zie hen niet. *I don't see them.* (direct object)
Hoe gaat het met hen? *How are they?* ('How goes it with them?') (indirect object)

→ **hun** refers to an indirect object if there is no preposition:
Ik geef hun de krant. *I give them the newspaper.* (indirect object)

However, it is common for Dutch people to get this wrong, and you'll often hear **hun** instead of **hen**. To avoid making this mistake, conversationally you can replace **hen/hun** with the unstressed pronoun **ze** *they*: **Ik zie ze niet zo vaak meer.** *I don't see them as much anymore.*

✷ SPELLING
NO DOUBLE CONSONANT AT THE END OF A WORD

A Dutch word can't end in a double consonant. So for verbs such as **stoppen** *to stop* and **beginnen** *to begin*, the extra consonant is dropped from the stem before adding the conjugation ending, except in the plural forms, which are identical to the infinitive.

▲ CONJUGATION
THE PRESENT TENSE OF VERBS SUCH AS *STOPPEN* TO STOP AND *BEGINNEN* TO BEGIN

In verbs with a double consonant, when the **-en** (or **-n**) of the infinitive is removed to leave the verb stem, in the singular persons the extra consonant is also removed:
stoppen *to stop* → **stop** *I stop,* etc. and **beginnen** *to begin* → **begin** *I begin,* etc.
ik stop; je / u stopt (but **stop je**)**; hij / ze stopt; we / jullie / ze stoppen**
ik begin; je / u begint (but **begin je**)**; hij / ze begint; we / jullie / ze beginnen**

⬢ EXERCISES

1. COMPLETE THE SENTENCES WITH THE CORRECT FORM OF THE VERB.

a. .... (stoppen) je met je studie?

b. De vakantie .... (beginnen) vanavond.

c. .... (zeggen) u het maar!

d. Hoe .... (spellen) je dat?

e. Ik .... (willen) je straks even aan hem .... (voorstellen).

2. LINK THE TWO ELEMENTS THAT GO TOGETHER.

a. Lieve Bram   •   •   1. Hartelijke groeten

b. Beste Ingrid   •   •   2. Liefs

c. Geachte mevrouw   •   •   3. en heren

d. Dames   •   •   4. Hoogachtend

● VOCABULARY

de e-mail email
kort short, brief
het bericht message, note
voordat before
de vakantie vacation, break, holidays
druk busy, occupied
het druk hebben to be busy
alles all, everything
ze them (conversationally)
niet ... meer not... anymore
binnenkort soon
allebei both
de studie study
oké okay, alright, fine
het bedrijf business, company
starten to start
het it (neuter, impersonal)
het risico risk
de kans chance, opportunity, possibility
Hoe gaat/is het met ...?
  How's it going with ... ?
  How are ... ?
hopen to hope
inmiddels in the meantime, meanwhile, by now
beter better
de groet greeting, salutation
de groeten doen to give one's regards, to give one's best
Nou ... Well ...
laten to let, to allow

snel fast, quickly
je you
horen to hear
iets laten horen to give news ('something to let hear')
altijd always
welkom welcome
bij at
Lieve Dear
Liefs Love, Affectionately
Beste Dear
Geachte heer Dear sir
Dames en heren Ladies and gentlemen
Met vriendelijke groeten
  Kind regards, Best wishes
Hartelijke groeten Warmly, Cordially
Hoogachtend Sincerely, Yours faithfully
mij me
jou you (informal object pronoun)
u you (formal object pronoun)
hem him, it (common noun)
haar her
het it (abstract, impersonal, neuter noun)
ons us
jullie you (plural object pronoun)
hen them (direct object, or indirect object with preposition)
hun them (indirect object, no preposition)

3. TRANSLATE EACH SENTENCE AND THEN LISTEN TO THE AUDIO TO CHECK YOUR ANSWERS.

a. Give her my regards!

→ ....

b. She is starting her own business.

→ ....

c. How are you *(formal)*?

→ ....

d. They hope that your father is doing better.

→ ....

4. LISTEN TO THE AUDIO OF THESE SENTENCES AND UNDERLINE THE WORDS/SYLLABLES THAT ARE STRESSED. THEN LISTEN TO THE AUDIO AGAIN TO CHECK YOUR ANSWERS.

a. Hoe gaat het met haar?

b. Hij heeft het druk maar alles is prima met hem.

c. We zien hen niet zo vaak meer.

d. Jullie zijn altijd welkom bij ons.

11.
LOOKING FOR AN APARTMENT

OP ZOEK NAAR EEN FLAT

AIMS	TOPICS
• **ASKING AND GIVING AN OPINION ON A FLAT/HOUSE**	• **VOCABULARY RELATED TO ACCOMMODATION**
• **DESCRIBING A FLAT/HOUSE**	• **THE DEMONSTRATIVE ADJECTIVES *DEZE*, *DIT* THIS; *DIE*, *DAT* THAT**
• **ASKING ABOUT THE RENT**	
• **EXPRESSING AND EXPLAINING A CHOICE**	• **MORE ABOUT FORMING THE PLURAL**
• **SAYING YOU WANT TO MOVE**	• **THE COMPARATIVE (MORE .../-ER)**

LOOKING FOR AN APARTMENT

Estate agent: What do you think of this flat? There is a spacious living room with an open kitchen and a bathroom, and there are two bedrooms.

Isa: This apartment is indeed bigger, but the *(that)* other property *(dwelling)* has more closets.

Estate agent: Well, but the advantage of this apartment is the extra storage on the ground floor.

Isa: Hm, the other one *(that other)* has a south-facing balcony *(balcony on the south)*! But I find the view here prettier. What is the rent? And when can I move in *(can I there-in)*?

Estate agent: This flat is a bit more expensive *(somewhat dearer)* of course, and it will be *(comes)* free in December.

Isa: Only then *(Then only)*! That's too late! I want to move at the end of this month *(I want end this month to-move-house)*!

<u>Makelaar</u>: Wat vindt u van deze flat? Er is een ruime woonkamer met een open keuken en een badkamer en er zijn twee slaapkamers.

<u>Isa</u>: Deze flat is inderdaad groter, maar die andere woning heeft meer kasten.

<u>Makelaar</u>: Tja, maar het voordeel van dit appartement is de extra berging op de begane grond.

<u>Isa</u>: Eh, dat andere heeft een balkon op het zuiden! Maar ik vind het uitzicht hier mooier. Wat is de huurprijs? En wanneer kan ik erin?

<u>Makelaar</u>: Deze flat is wel wat duurder natuurlijk, en hij komt vrij in december.

<u>Isa</u>: Dan pas! Dat is te laat! Ik wil eind deze maand verhuizen!

■ UNDERSTANDING THE DIALOGUE

→ **Wat vindt u van deze flat?** *What do you think of this flat?* The verb **vinden** means *to find*, and **vinden van** is used in the sense of *to think of* when asking or giving an opinion about something.

→ **Er is een ruime woonkamer en er zijn twee slaapkamers.** *There is a spacious living room, and there are two bedrooms.* Note the construction **er is** *there is /* **er zijn** *there are,* in which **er** *there* is an impersonal pronoun. The verb agrees with the following noun, as in English: **er is een woonkamer** *there is a living room,* but **er zijn twee slaapkamers** *there are two bedrooms.*

→ **open keuken** *open kitchen.* For the most part, adjectives ending in **-en** don't take the final **-e** when used before a noun.

→ **de begane grond** *the ground floor.* The noun **de grond** means *foundation, bottom* as well as *soil, ground.*

→ **de huurprijs** *rental price* is a compound word made up of **de huur** *rent* and **de prijs** *price.* Note also the verb **huren** *to rent.*

→ **En wanneer kan ik erin?** *And when can I move in?* The word **erin** is made up of the adverb **er** *there* combined with the preposition **in** *in.* In this question, there is no main verb, just the conjugated auxiliary verb **kan** with the term of movement **erin** ('can I in there?'). We'll come back to adverb + preposition combinations in lesson 19.

→ The conjugated verb in the phrase **komt vrij in december** *is available* ('comes free') *in December* is from the infinitive **vrijkomen** *to become free,* which is a separable-prefix verb. More on this soon.

→ **Dan pas!** *Only then!* In this exclamation, **pas** *only* expresses a notion of time.

TALKING ABOUT ACCOMMODATION

In the dialogue there are a few useful terms for talking about lodging:
• **de woning** *dwelling, residence, abode, domicile* refers to where someone lives without indicating what type of dwelling it is, a house, a flat or other.
• **het appartement** *apartment* and **de flat** are synonyms, but the latter has a less luxury connotation. The word for *house* is **het huis**.

Although **flat** is a loanword from English, the vowel sound is a bit more like a short 'e' in Dutch [fleht]. It can also refer to an apartment building, the full word for which is **het flatgebouw** *apartment building.*

106

DESCRIBING AN INTERIOR

Many of the rooms in a dwelling are described with compound words that include the term **de kamer** *room*: e.g. **de woonkamer** *living room*, **de eetkamer** *dining room*, **de slaapkamer** *bedroom* and **de badkamer** *bathroom*. Some other useful terms include: **de keuken** *kitchen*, **de douche** *shower*, **de wc** or **het toilet** *the toilet*. Often, apartments have a *storage room, storeroom* **de berging** to keep bikes or other bulky objects.

 GRAMMAR

THE DEMONSTRATIVE ADJECTIVES *DEZE, DIT* THIS; *DIE, DAT* THAT

There are four forms of singular demonstrative adjectives: two for neuter nouns and two for common nouns. The forms **dat** and **die** (*that*) are more common than the forms **dit** and **deze** (*this*), as the latter are employed <u>only</u> if there is a clear proximity between the person and the indicated object, for example, if you're holding an object in your hand or it's within reach: **deze flat** *this apartment* (when you are in it), **deze maand** *this month* (the current month).

If this is not the case, the other form is used: **die andere woning** *that* ('other') *dwelling*, or **dat andere** *that other*. Note that in the last example, the noun is implied but not actually stated.

Neuter noun	Common noun	
dit + singular noun	**deze** + singular noun	*this (here)*
dat + singular noun	**die** + singular noun	*that (there)*

As plural nouns in Dutch all take the article **de**, the plural demonstrative adjectives are the same for both neuter and common nouns: **deze woningen** *these dwellings*, **die woningen** *those dwellings*.

Neuter and common nouns	
deze + plural noun	*these (here)*
die + plural noun	*those (there)*

MORE ON FORMING THE PLURAL

We've seen that in Dutch, some nouns form the plural by adding **-en**, and others by adding **-s**. A noun with several syllables and ending in an unstressed final **-el** ends in **-s**: **appel** *apple* → **appels** *apples*. The same is true for nouns with several syllables that end in an unstressed **-er** or **-en**: **kamer** *room* → **kamers** *rooms*; **keuken** *kitchen* → **keukens** *kitchens*.

Nouns ending in an unstressed **-e** also add an **-s** in the plural: **het biertje** *beer* (diminutive) → **de biertjes** *beers*; **de dame** *lady* → **de dames** *ladies*; **het berichtje** *message* (diminutive) → **de berichtjes** *messages*.

THE COMPARATIVE (MORE ..., -ER)

As in English, the comparative is formed by adding the ending **-er** to an adjective. But note that an adjective ending in **-r** takes the comparative ending **-der**:
groot *big, large, great* → **groter** *bigger, larger, greater*
mooi *pretty* → **mooier** *prettier*
duur *costly, expensive* → **duurder** *costlier, more expensive*.

● EXERCISES

1. PUT THE SENTENCES BELOW IN THE RIGHT COLUMN: USE THE DEMONSTRATIVE ADJECTIVE TO HELP YOU.

a. Ik vind dit huis mooier.

b. Dat huis heeft meer kasten.

c. Die rode wijn is goedkoop.

d. Deze witte wijn is duur.

e. Dit balkon is groot.

f. Dat balkon is klein.

g. Die computers zijn oud.

h. Deze formulieren zijn nieuw.

Clear proximity between the person and the object?	
YES	NO

● VOCABULARY

op zoek naar *in search of, looking for*
de flat *apartment*
het appartement *apartment*
het flatgebouw *apartment building*
de makelaar / de makelaarster
  estate agent (m./f.)
vinden *to find*
vinden van *to think of, to find*
  (opinion about something)
deze *this (here)*
die *that (there)*
dit *this*
dat *that*
er is *there is*
er zijn *there are*
ruim *spacious, roomy*
de keuken *kitchen*
de open keuken *open kitchen*
de kamer *room*
de woonkamer *living room*
de badkamer *bathroom*
de slaapkamer *bedroom*
de eetkamer *dining room*
de douche *shower*
de wc / het toilet *toilet*
de kast *closet*
de berging *storeroom*
inderdaad *indeed*
ander *other* (adj.)
de woning *dwelling, residence*
meer *more*
Tja ... *Well ...*
het voordeel *advantage*

extra *extra*
de begane grond *ground floor*
de grond *ground*
Eh ... *Hmm ..., Um ...*
het balkon *balcony*
op het zuiden *south-facing*
het uitzicht *view*
mooi *pretty, beautiful*
de huurprijs *rental price*
huren *to rent*
erin (kunnen) *(to be able to) move in*
wat *somewhat, a bit*
Natuurlijk. *Of course.*
vrijkomen *to be available, to be free*
december (de) *December*
pas *only*
te *too*
eind (+ month) *end of the* (+ month)
het eind *end*
de maand *month*
verhuizen *to move house*
het huis *house*
er *there*
open *open*

2. GIVE THE COMPARATIVE FOR EACH ADJECTIVE AND THEN TRANSLATE IT.

a. schattig .... / ....

b. ver .... / ....

c. vers .... / ....

d. laat .... / ....

e. leuk .... / ....

f. ruim .... / ....

g. duur .... / ....

h. lief .... / ....

3. MAKE THESE NOUNS PLURAL.

a. de badkamer ....

b. de grootouder ....

c. het bericht ....

d. de groet ....

e. de jongen ....

f. het nummer ....

g. de dochter ....

h. de tunnel ....

i. de postcode ....

j. het meisje ....

k. de keuken ....

l. de visboer ....

4. LISTEN TO THE AUDIO, REPEAT EACH SENTENCE AND THEN WRITE IT OUT.

13

a. ....

b. ....

c. ....

d. ....

e. ....

12.
ASKING THE WAY

DE WEG VRAGEN

AIMS	TOPICS

- ASKING FOR AND GIVING DIRECTIONS
- SAYING THANK YOU

- SOME VOCABULARY FOR DIRECTIONS
- ORDINAL NUMBERS
- HOW TO ASK 'WHERE TO/ FROM' ETC.

ASKING THE WAY

– Good afternoon, are you from here *(are you here known)*? I don't know *(anymore)* where I am. Is this the way to the bus stop?

– Yes, indeed. Where do you want to go?

– I want to go to Keukenhof *(I want direction Keukenhof)*.

– There's a bus that goes there directly *(There goes a bus directly towards)* from the stop across from *(opposite)* the hospital.

– How do I get *(How come I)* there?

– You walk *(here)* straight on until the stoplights. There, you go *(go you towards)* right, and then it's the first street on the left.

– Thank you so much *(Heartily thank)*!

– May I ask you where you come from? Because you have *(You have namely)* a light northern accent.

– I come from a village to the *(at)* northeast of Groningen, from Appingedam.

– From where? Oh, here *(there)* comes the bus. Hurry *(Go you so quickly)*!

– Thank you again.

– You're welcome *(Gladly done)*!

– Goedemiddag, bent u hier bekend? Ik weet niet meer waar ik ben. Is dit de weg naar de bushalte?

– Jazeker. Waar wilt u heen?

– Ik wil richting Keukenhof.

– Daar gaat een bus rechtstreeks naartoe vanaf de halte tegenover het ziekenhuis.

– Hoe kom ik daar?

– U loopt hier rechtdoor tot de stoplichten. Daar gaat u naar rechts en dan is het de eerste straat links.

– Hartelijk dank!

– Mag ik u vragen waar u vandaan komt? U heeft namelijk een licht noordelijk accent.

– Ik kom uit een dorp ten noordoosten van Groningen, uit Appingedam.

– Waarvandaan? O, daar komt de bus aan. Gaat u maar snel!

– Nogmaals dank!

– Graag gedaan!

■ UNDERSTANDING THE DIALOGUE

→ **Goedemiddag.** *Good afternoon.* This can be used until about 6:00 p.m.

→ **Bent u hier bekend?** *Are you from around here?* ('Are you here known?') Note that **bekend** *known* is the past participle of the verb **kennen** *to know.*

→ **Waar wilt u heen?** *Where do you want to go?* The verb 'to go' is not needed here because **heen** indicates movement towards something when used with **waar**: **Waar ... heen?** *Where ... to?* Another expression to indicate movement is **daar ... naartoe** *there* ('there ... towards'), although the verb 'to go' is included in the sentence: **Daar gaat een bus rechtstreeks naartoe.** *There's a bus that goes directly there.* Another example is **Waar ... vandaan?** *From where?* in **Waar u vandaan komt?** *Where are you from?* See the section on the next page for these types of constructions for asking 'where to/from'.

→ **Hoe kom ik** ('come I') **daar?** *How do I get there?*

→ **Daar komt de bus aan.** *Here* ('There') *comes the bus.* This sentence includes the separable-prefix verb **aankomen** *to arrive.*

→ The expression **graag gedaan** *you're welcome, with pleasure* is synonymous with **tot uw dienst** *at your service,* although the latter is more formal.

CULTURAL NOTE

De Keukenhof ('the kitchen-garden') is a famous flower garden located in Lisse in the province of **Zuid-Holland** *South Holland.* In the 15th century, herbs were cultivated there for the castle kitchen of Jacqueline, Countess of Hainaut, who ruled Holland, Zeeland and Hainaut at the time. In 1949, a flower show was organized at the estate, which by then had become a park. This show is now an annual event that is held during the period when the flowers bloom in April and May.

The Dutch are known for their love of **bloemen** *flowers,* and you can buy **boeketten** *bouquets* everywhere at affordable prices. Here are some of the flowers you might see in a flower shop or stand: **de anjer** *carnation,* **de gladiool** *gladiolus,* **de lelie** *lily,* **de roos** *rose,* **de tulp** *tulip.*

◆ GRAMMAR
SOME VOCABULARY FOR DIRECTIONS

The compass directions in Dutch are **het noorden** *north,* **het zuiden** *south,* **het oosten** *east* and **het westen** *west.* To say *to the north/south/east/west of ... ,* you use the prepositions **ten ... van**: **ten noorden/zuiden/oosten/westen van ...** The combinations of the compass directions are: **noordoosten** *northeast*, **noordwesten** *northwest*, **zuidoosten** *southeast* and **zuidwesten** *southwest*. To form the adjective of the compass points, add the ending **-lijk**: **noordelijk** *northern*, **zuidelijk** *southern*, **oostelijk** *eastern*, **westelijk** *western*.

In Dutch, there are two ways to say *to the left*: **naar links** and **linksaf**. The same goes for *to the right*: **naar rechts** and **rechtsaf**. But don't confuse the word for *right* with the word **rechtdoor** *straight on, straight ahead*.

ORDINAL NUMBERS

14

To form the ordinal numbers, you just add the ending **-de** or **-ste** to the cardinal number. Up to 19th, the ending is **-de**, except for 1st (**eerste**) and 8th (**achtste**). From 20th, the ending is **-ste**.

1st	eerste*	11th	elfde
2nd	tweede	12th	twaalfde
3rd	derde*	13th	dertiende
4th	vierde	14th	veertiende
5th	vijfde	15th	vijftiende
6th	zesde	16th	zestiende
7th	zevende	17th	zeventiende
8th	achtste	18th	achttiende
9th	negende	19th	negentiende
10th	tiende	20th	twintigste

* Note the variation in spelling of these ordinal numbers compared to the corresponding cardinal number.

HOW TO ASK 'WHERE TO/FROM?' ETC.

• We've seen **Waar?** *Where?* used on its own.
• To ask about a destination, i.e. where someone is headed to, you ask **Waar ... heen?** or **Waar ... naartoe?** *Where to?*
• To ask where someone comes from or is coming from, you ask **Waar ... vandaan?** *Where from?*

• To say where you're going, you use **daar ... naartoe, daar ... heen** ('there towards'). And to say where you're coming from, you can use **daar ... vandaan** ('there from').

• You can also use these constructions with **hier** *here*, as in coming here or coming from: **hier ... naartoe / hier ... heen** ('here towards') and **hier ... vandaan** ('here from').

Note that in questions or statements using these constructions, the second element indicating the direction of movement is placed at the end:

Waar gaat u straks naartoe/heen?
Where are you going later? ('Where go you later to?')
Waar komt u eigenlijk vandaan?
Where do you actually come from? ('Where come you actually from?')
Daar gaat een bus rechtstreeks naartoe.
There's a bus that goes directly there. ('There goes a bus directly to.')

The elements can also be combined to form a single word if no extra information is needed: **Waarnaartoe?, Waarheen?, Waarvandaan?, daarnaartoe, daarheen, daarvandaan, hiernaartoe, hierheen, hiervandaan**.

Ik ga naar Utrecht. *I'm going to Utrecht.* **Waarnaartoe? / Waarheen?** *To where?* **Daarnaartoe! / Daarheen!** *To there!*

Ik kom uit Utrecht. *I come from Utrecht.* **Waarvandaan?** *From where?* **Daarvandaan!** *From there!* **Hiervandaan!** *From here!*

Waar ga je heen? *Where are you going?* **Hiernaartoe! / Hierheen!** *To here!*

● VOCABULARY

de weg vragen to ask the way
de weg way, road
vragen to ask
Goedemiddag. Good afternoon.
Bent u hier bekend? Do you come
from around here? (formal)
de bushalte bus stop
de bus bus
de halte stop
Waar ... heen? / Waarheen?
Where to? (destination)
Waar ... naartoe? / Waarnaartoe?
Where to? (destination)
daar ... naartoe / daarnaartoe
to there
daar ... heen / daarheen to there
hier ... naartoe / hiernaartoe
to here
hier ... heen / hierheen to here
Waar ... vandaan? /
Waarvandaan? Where from?
hier ... vandaan / hiervandaan
from here
de richting direction
rechtstreeks directly
vanaf from
tegenover across from, opposite
het ziekenhuis hospital
komen to come
aankomen to arrive
lopen to walk
het stoplicht stoplight
rechtdoor straight on/ahead
naar rechts / rechtsaf to the right
naar links / linksaf to the left

dan then
eerste first
namelijk namely
licht light
het accent accent
Hartelijk dank! Thank you so much!
Nogmaals dank! Thanks again!
Graag gedaan! You're welcome!
With pleasure!
Tot uw dienst. At your service.
kennen to know
het boeket bouquet
de anjer carnation
de gladiool gladiolus
de lelie lily
de roos rose
de tulp tulip
het noorden north
het zuiden south
het oosten east
het westen west
ten noordoosten van to the
northeast of
ten noorden van to the north of
ten zuiden van to the south of
ten oosten van to the east of
ten westen van to the west of
noordwesten northwest
zuidoosten southeast
zuidwesten southwest
noordelijk northern
zuidelijk southern
oostelijk eastern
westelijk western

● EXERCISES

1. LINK THE QUESTIONS TO THE CORRECT ANSWERS.

a. Waar komen ze vandaan? •

b. Waar ga je eind deze maand naartoe? •

c. Waar gaat hij heen? •

• 1. Hij gaat naar de markt.

• 2. Daarvandaan!

• 3. Dan ga ik naar Nijmegen.

2. PUT THE WORDS IN THE SENTENCES IN THE RIGHT ORDER, BEGINNING WITH THE WORD THAT STARTS WITH A CAPITAL LETTER.

a. Daar / een / over / heen / gaat / drie / tram / minuten.

→ ....

b. U / de / rechtdoor / tot / hier / stoplichten / loopt.

→ ....

c. Dan / rechts / straat / is / tweede / het / de.

→ ....

3. GIVE THE ORDINAL NUMBER FOR EACH CARDINAL NUMBER. THEN LISTEN TO THE AUDIO AND PRONOUNCE THEM OUT LOUD.

14

a. een → ....

b. drie → ....

c. zevenentwintig → ....

d. acht → ....

e. veertien → ....

4. LISTEN TO EACH SENTENCE AND THEN SELECT THE CORRECT MEANING.

14

a. ❏ She comes from the northeast of the country.
    ❏ They come from the northwest of the country.

b. ❏ Good afternoon, are you known here?
    ❏ Good afternoon, are you from around here?

c. ❏ He has a southern accent.
    ❏ She has an eastern accent.

d. ❏ Where are you going? – To there!
    ❏ Where do you come from? – From here!

13.
SHALL WE ... ?

ZULLEN WE ...?

AIMS

- **MAKING AND REPLYING TO SUGGESTIONS**
- **SHARING AN IDEA**
- **SPECIFYING DIFFERENT TIMES OF THE DAY**

TOPICS

- **TIME WORDS**
- **GREETINGS**
- **HOW TO SUGGEST SOMETHING**
- **MORE ON FORMING THE NEGATIVE**
- **CONJUNCTIONS AND WORD ORDER IN A COMPLETE CLAUSE**

WHAT SHALL WE DO TODAY?

<u>Rob</u>: Shall we go to the beach this morning *(Shall we this-morning to the beach go)*?

<u>Mirjam</u>: No, let's stay in *(let we indoors stay)*, as I don't feel like going out *(I have not-any desire to towards outside to go)*.

<u>Rob</u>: Or do you want to go to the cinema then maybe *(then maybe to the film)*?

<u>Mirjam</u>: Let's do that this evening *(Let we that this-evening do)*!

<u>Rob</u>: Okay, so shall we invite Jasper over for a tea this afternoon *(shall we then this-afternoon Jasper for the tea invite)*?

<u>Mirjam</u>: Yes, that's fine.

***

<u>Mirjam</u>: Hey Jasper, come in! Do you want tea or coffee?

<u>Jasper</u>: Ah, Mirjam. Give me a cup of tea, please, because I'm thirsty *(I have thirst)*.

<u>Mirjam</u>: Do you fancy coming with us to see a film tonight *(this-evening along to the film to go)*?

<u>Jasper</u>: Oh, unfortunately *(shame)* I can't, I'm skint! But what do you think of the idea that I stay to eat?

<u>Mirjam</u>: Oh yes, that would suit you, wouldn't it *(there have you well desire in, eh)* ?

Rob: Zullen we vanochtend naar het strand gaan?

Mirjam: Nee, laten we binnen blijven, want ik heb geen zin om naar buiten te gaan.

Rob: Of wil je dan misschien naar de film?

Mirjam: Laten we dat vanavond doen!

Rob: Oké, zullen we dan vanmiddag Jasper voor de thee uitnodigen?

Mirjam: Ja, dat is goed.

***

Mirjam: Hé Jasper, kom binnen! Wil je thee of koffie?

Jasper: Ha Mirjam. Geef maar een kop thee, want ik heb dorst.

Mirjam: Heb je zin om vanavond mee naar de film te gaan?

Jasper: Hè jammer, ik kan niet, ik ben blut! Maar wat vinden jullie van het idee dat ik blijf eten?

Mirjam: Ja, daar heb je wel zin in, hè!

■ UNDERSTANDING THE DIALOGUE

→ **Wat zullen we vandaag gaan doen?** *What shall we do today?* **Zullen we vanochtend naar het strand gaan?** *Shall we go to the beach this morning?* **Laten we binnen blijven!** *Let's stay in!* Apart from the word order, these ways of suggesting things to do are similar to English. See the section on the next page to find out more about making suggestions.

→ Note the useful words **binnen** *inside, indoors* and **buiten** *outside* and how they are used in Dutch where in English we tend to just say *in* or *out*.

→ **Of wil je dan misschien naar de film?** *Or do you want to go to the cinema then maybe?* The noun **de film** can be used both for *film* and *cinema, movie theatre*. Another word for the latter is **de bioscoop**. In some contexts, as here, the verb **gaan** *to go* is implied but not actually stated.

→ **Hé Jasper** *Hey Jasper,* **Ha Mirjam** *Ah, Mirjam:* **hé** *hey* and **ha** *ah* can both be used as greetings. The **é** accent of **hé** indicates a long **e** [hay]. The **è** accent in **Hè!** indicates a short vowel [heh]. Note also the expression **Jammer!** *Shame! What a pity!*

→ **Ja, daar heb je wel zin in, hè!** *Oh yes, that would suit you, wouldn't it?* ('there have you well desire in, eh?'). The interjection **hè** at the end of a statement can work like a question tag in English, with the meaning *isn't that right?* We'll come back to the structure **daar** + preposition in lesson 19.

SOME USEFUL TIME WORDS

Here is some useful vocabulary to talk about different times of the day according to the 24-hour clock. You already know some of these words.

Time of day				Formal greeting
06:00 – 24:00	**de dag** *day*	**vandaag** *today*		**Goede(n)dag.** *Good day.*
06:00 – 12:00	**de ochtend/ de morgen***** *morning*	**vanochtend/ vanmorgen** *this morning*	**'s ochtends / 's morgens** *in the morning*	**Goedemorgen.** *Good morning.*
12:00 – 18:00	**de middag** *afternoon*	**vanmiddag** *this afternoon*	**'s middags** *in the afternoon*	**Goedemiddag.** *Good afternoon.*
18:00 – 24:00	**de avond** *evening*	**vanavond** *this evening*	**'s avonds** *in the evening*	**Goedenavond.** *Good evening.*
24:00 – 06:00	**de nacht** *night*	**vannacht** *tonight*	**'s nachts** *in the/at night*	**Goedenacht.** *Good night.*

* Be careful not to confuse **de morgen** *morning* with the adverb **morgen** *tomorrow*.

There are a variety of more casual ways to greet someone, for example: **Dag!**, **Hallo!**, **Hoi!** *Hello!* To say goodbye when you're leaving, you can use **Dag!** – pronounced with a long **a** [daakh] – or **Doei!** *Bye!* – pronounced [doh-ee].

◆ GRAMMAR
MAKING SUGGESTIONS

• **Wat zullen we gaan doen?** *What shall we do?* The auxiliary verb **zullen** *will, shall* indicates the future and is always used with an infinitive, which is placed at the end of the sentence. As in this dialogue, it can be used to make suggestions to do something. This is the case in a question when **zullen** is followed by **we** *we*. In the question **Wat zullen we gaan doen?** the verb **gaan** also appears ('What shall we go do?'), which is unnecessary in English. Here are some *Shall we...?* examples:
Zullen we naar de film gaan? *Shall we go to the cinema?*
Zullen we Eva uitnodigen? *Shall we invite Eva?*

• It is also possible to make suggestions with **willen** *to want* or with **zin hebben om te** + infinitive *to feel like* + infinitive:
Of wil je naar de film? *Or do you want to go to the cinema?*
Heb je zin om naar de film te gaan? *Do you feel like going to the cinema?*

• Another option is to use **Laten we** *Let's* ('Let we') + infinitive, which is placed at the end of the sentence:
Laten we hier blijven! *Let's stay here!* ('Let we here stay!)
Laten we dat doen! *Let's do that!* ('Let we that do!')

• The response might be **Ja.** *Yes.* **Oké.** *Okay.* **Dat is goed.** *That's fine.* **Nee.** *No.* **Ik kan niet.** *I can't.* **Ik heb geen zin.** *I don't feel like it. / I don't fancy it.*

MORE ON FORMING THE NEGATIVE

• **geen** *no, none, not any* is used before an indefinite noun:
Ik heb honger. *I'm hungry.* → **Ik heb geen honger.** *I'm not hungry* ('have no hunger').
Ik zie een bus. *I see a bus.* → **Ik zie geen bus.** *I don't see a bus.*
Ik zie bussen. *I see buses.* → **Ik zie geen bussen.** *I don't see any buses.*

• **niet** *not* is used with a definite noun:
Ik zie de bus. *I see the bus.* → **Ik zie de bus niet.** *I don't see the bus.*
Ik zie de bussen. *I see the buses.* → **Ik zie de bussen niet.** *I don't see the buses.*

CONJUNCTIONS AND WORD ORDER IN THE MAIN CLAUSE

The conjunctions (coordinating conjunctions) **maar** *but*, **of** *or*, **en** *and*, **dus** *so* and **want** *because* can introduce a complete clause, in which the conjugated verb must be in the second position.

So because the conjunction is in the first position, the structure is:

conjunction + conjugated verb + subject/object

Ik ben niet thuis <u>maar</u> spreek een boodschap in! *I'm not at home, but leave a message!* ('but speak a message into')

Zij stopt met de studie <u>en</u> gaat een bedrijf starten. *She is stopping her studies and is going to start a business.* ('and is-going a business to-start')

Wil je thee <u>of</u> wil je koffie? *Do you want tea or do you want coffee?* ('or want you')

However, if you add an element after the conjunction, this then counts as the element in the first position in the clause, and the conjugated verb is placed directly after it:

conjunction + first element + conjugated verb + complement

Geef maar thee, <u>want ik</u> heb dorst. *Give me a tea, please, because I'm thirsty.*

Het is een risico, <u>maar ze</u> wil het een kans geven. *It's a risk, but she wants to give it a chance!*

Deze flat is duurder <u>en hij</u> komt vrij in december. *This flat is more expensive, and it will be* ('comes') *free in December.*

● EXERCISES

1. MAKE THE SENTENCES NEGATIVE USING EITHER *NIET* OR *GEEN*.

a. Hij heeft zin in een kop koffie.

→ ....

b. Ze hebben dorst en honger.

→ ....

c. Deze flat is duurder dan die andere.

→ ....

d. Ze stopt met de studie want ze gaat een bedrijf starten.

→ ....

● VOCABULARY

Zullen we ...? *Shall we ...?*
vandaag *today*
vanochtend / vanmorgen
  this morning
vanmiddag *this afternoon*
vannacht *tonight*
het strand *beach*
laten *to let, to allow*
Laten we ...! *Let's ... !*
binnen *inside, indoors*
buiten *outside, outdoors*
geen *no, none, not any* (with an
  indefinite noun)
misschien *maybe, perhaps*
de film *film*, also *cinema,*
  movie theatre
de bioscoop *cinema, movie theatre*
Dat is goed. *That's fine.*
Hé. *Hey.*
Ha. *Ah.*
Hè? *Eh? Isn't that right?*
binnenkomen *to come in*
de thee *tea*
de koffie *coffee*
de kop *cup*
de dorst *thirst*
dorst hebben *to be thirsty* ('to have
  thirst')
Jammer! *Shame! What a pity!*
eten *to eat*, also *meal, food*
de dag *day*
Goedendag! / Goededag!
  Good day! Hello!

Goedenavond! *Good evening!*
Goedenacht! *Good night!*
Dag! *Hello! Bye!*
Doei! *Bye!*

e. Mijn buurvrouw heeft een fiets.

→ ....

f. Heb je kinderen of huisdieren?

→ ....

2. TRANSLATE THESE SENTENCES INTO DUTCH.

a. Shall we invite Emma? – Yes, that's a good idea.

→ ....

b. I feel like going to the cinema. – No, let's stay here!

→ ....

c. What do you *(pl.)* think about the idea of going to the market? – OK, let's do that!

→ ....

d. Do you *(informal)* want a beer? – Yes, gladly! I'm thirsty.

→ ....

3. COMPLETE THE SENTENCES WITH THE CORRECT CONJUNCTION.

a. We kunnen vanavond thuisblijven .... naar het café gaan.

b. Waar kom je vandaan, ... je hebt een licht accent?

c. Zij werkt in Zaandam .... hij werkt in Maastricht. (2 possibilities)

d. Ze hebben geen honger, ... ze willen niet blijven eten.

e. Ik noteer de datum .... geef u vast het formulier.

4. LISTEN TO THE AUDIO AND COMPLETE THE SENTENCES. THEN READ THEM OUT LOUD AND LISTEN TO THE AUDIO AGAIN TO CHECK YOUR ANSWERS.

15

a. ...., ... Mariska. Hoe gaat het met je?

b. Hebben jullie .... geen zin om te werken?

c. ....! Wilt u een glas wijn of een biertje?

d. .... Marc! .... Ben, ik kan niet blijven hoor! ....

e. .... jammer! Ik kan .... niet met je meegaan. Oké, nou ....!

14.
THE HOROSCOPE

DE HOROSCOOP

AIMS	TOPICS

AIMS

- **DESCRIBING CHARACTER TRAITS**

- **GIVING ADVICE**

- **TALKING ABOUT HOW OFTEN**

TOPICS

- **SHORTENED FORMS OF WORDS**

- **INDEFINITE PRONOUNS (SOMEONE, SOMETHING, NOTHING, ETC.)**

- **ADVERBS EXPRESSING FREQUENCY**

- **THE CONJUNCTION *OM* TO, IN ORDER TO, FOR**

- **THE IMPERATIVE**

HOROSCOPE

ARIES *(ram)* **You are never afraid to express your opinion, but don't get angry** *(but make you not angry)*!

TAURUS *(bull)* **Although you are strong, it's time to show your feelings** *(becomes it time your emotion to show)*!

GEMINI *(twins)* **You are clever enough. So believe** *(Believe so)* **in yourself!**

CANCER *(lobster)* **No one is as hard a** *(such hard)* **worker as you, but sometimes it is really too much!**

LEO *(lion)* **You want to decide for everyone. Yet you can't always be the boss!**

VIRGO *(virgin)* **Generally, you lead a healthy life** *(Usually live you healthy)*. **Don't be too hard on yourself** *(Make it yourself not too difficult)*!

LIBRA *(scales)* **You always seek** *(seek constantly)* **balance. Learn for once to take decisions** *(decisions to take)*!

SCORPIO *(scorpion)* **Making money** *(Money to-earn)* **is important, but don't forget your friends!**

SAGITTARIUS *(bow-shooter)* **You can't wait** *(You want not until tomorrow to-wait)*. **Be patient** *(Have patience)*!

CAPRICORN *(ibex)* **You are cautious. Take some risks!**

AQUARIUS *(water-carrier)* **With you it's all or nothing. Try for once to compromise** *(Seek once the compromise)*!

PISCES *(fishes)* **You love** *(of)* **your freedom. Don't be** *(Be not)* **so idealistic!**

RAM Je bent nooit bang je mening te uiten, maar maak je niet kwaad!

STIER Hoewel je sterk bent, wordt het tijd je gevoel te tonen!

TWEELING Je bent slim genoeg. Geloof dus in jezelf!

KREEFT Niemand is zo'n harde werker als jij, maar soms is het echt te veel!

LEEUW Je wilt voor iedereen beslissen. Toch kun je niet altijd de baas zijn!

MAAGD Gewoonlijk leef je gezond. Maak 't jezelf niet te moeilijk!

WEEGSCHAAL Je zoekt steeds 't evenwicht. Leer eens om besluiten te nemen!

SCHORPIOEN Geld verdienen is belangrijk, maar vergeet je vrienden niet!

BOOGSCHUTTER Je wilt niet tot morgen wachten. Heb geduld!

STEENBOK Je bent voorzichtig. Neem 'ns risico's!

WATERMAN Bij jou is het alles of niets. Zoek 's het compromis!

VISSEN Je houdt van je vrijheid. Wees niet zo idealistisch!

UNDERSTANDING THE DIALOGUE

→ **Je bent nooit bang je mening te uiten.** *You are never afraid to express your opinion.* This sentence has a lot of useful vocabulary: **bang zijn** *to be afraid*, **nooit** *never*, **de mening** *opinion* and **uiten** *to express, to voice, to utter.* Throughout this dialogue, notice how **te** is used before certain infinitives in a similar way to the English *to.*

→ **(...) wordt het tijd je gevoel te tonen.** *it's time to show your feelings* ('becomes it time your emotion to show'). The verb **worden** *to become* indicates a change in situation.

→ **Je bent slim genoeg.** *You are clever enough.* The adverb **genoeg** *enough, sufficiently* is always placed after the adjective.

→ **Niemand is zo'n harde werker als jij, maar soms is het echt te veel!** *No one is as hard a worker* ('such hard worker') *as you, but sometimes it is really too much!* The word **zo'n** *such* is a contraction of **zo een** ('so a') – it only exists in this contracted form. Here, **te** means *too, in excess.*

→ **Toch kun je niet altijd de baas zijn!** *Yet you can't always be the boss!* After **toch** *still, yet, nevertheless* at the beginning of a sentence, the conjugated verb comes directly after it, in second position.

→ **Maak 't jezelf niet te moeilijk!** *Don't be so hard on yourself!* ('Make it yourself not too difficult!') Here we have the very useful verb **maken** *to make* in the expression **moeilijk maken** *to make it difficult.* **Je zoekt steeds 't evenwicht.** ('You seek constantly the balance.') In both these example sentences, the unstressed **het** *it, the* is shortened to **'t**.

→ **Neem 'ns risico's!** *Take some risks!* ('Take once risks!') **Zoek 's het compromis!** *Try to compromise!* ('Seek once the compromise!') The **'ns** and the **'s** here are the shortened forms of **eens** *once.* Note also that the plural of **risico** *risk* is formed by adding **'s** to retain the pronunciation of the long vowel.

SHORTENED FORMS OF WORDS

It is very common in speech to use shortened forms of certain words in Dutch. Most of these have an unstressed **e**. The omission of letters is indicated by an apostrophe:

het → **'t** *it, the*
eens → **'s, 'ns** *once*
zo een → **zo'n** *such, such a* (this word only exists in the contracted form)

Some of the unstressed personal pronouns can also be contracted, or sometimes a pronoun, article or demonstrative adjective is contracted with the verb **is**. Remember that in Dutch, certain syllables or words are stressed when speaking. The use of contracted forms can serve to put more emphasis on other words in the sentence that are essential to the information being conveyed.

◆ GRAMMAR
INDEFINITE PRONOUNS

These are used when what you're referring to is vague rather than specific:
iemand *someone*; **niemand** *no one*; **iets/wat** *something*; **niets** *nothing*;
alles *everything*; **iedereen** *everyone*.

The indefinite pronouns **iets** and **wat** are synonyms:
Mag ik je iets/wat vragen? *May I ask you something?*

ADVERBS OF FREQUENCY

These are used to say how often an action is done:
nooit *never*; **steeds** *constantly*; **vaak** *often*; **gewoonlijk** *usually, normally*;
soms *sometimes*, **altijd** *always*.

In a main clause, the adverb of frequency either starts the sentence or comes immediately after the conjugated verb: **Gewoonlijk leef je gezond.** *Generally, you lead a healthy life.* **Je bent nooit bang.** *You are never afraid.* **Je zoekt steeds 't evenwicht.** *You constantly seek balance.*

If there is a conjunction, the adverb counts as the first element and the conjugated verb comes directly after it:
(…) maar soms is het echt te veel ('but sometimes is it really too much').

THE CONJUNCTION *OM* IN ORDER TO, TO, FOR

The conjunction **om** *in order to, to, for* is required to introduce a subordinate clause that expresses purpose:
Ze hebben hun eigen kaart nodig om naar het buitenland te kunnen reizen.
They need their own card in order to be able to travel abroad.

When **om** means *to* rather than *in order to* (i.e. purpose), it is optional, as the **te** before the infinitive conveys this meaning:

Je bent nooit bang om **je mening te uiten.**
You are never afraid to express your opinion.

(…) wordt het tijd om **je gevoel te tonen** *(…) it is time to show your sentiments*
Leer eens om **besluiten te nemen!** *Learn to take decisions!*

▲ CONJUGATION
THE IMPERATIVE

The imperative (which is used for making commands) is most commonly employed in the informal second-person singular (**je**). It is formed by removing the **-en/-n** ending of the infinitive and applying the spelling rules we've seen:

zoeken → Zoek! *Seek!*; **maken → Maak!** *Make!*; **leren → Leer!** *Learn!*;
vergeten → Vergeet! *Forget!*; **beslissen → Beslis!** *Decide!*; **hebben → Heb!** *Have!*

The imperative of the verb **zijn** is irregular: **Wees!** *Be!*

To form the formal imperative (**u**), add the ending **-t** and use the personal pronoun **u** *you* (formal): **Zoekt u!** *Seek!*; **Vergeet u!** *Forget!*; **Doet u!** *Do!*

The words we've seen that are used to soften the tone are often employed with the imperative to make it sound less like giving an order:

Zoek dus het compromis! *Try* ('so') *to compromise!*
Leer eens! *Learn* ('once')*!*
Gaat u maar snel! *Hurry!* ('Go you just quickly!')

⬣ EXERCISES

1. FOR EACH SENTENCE, INDICATE IF THE CONJUNCTION *OM* IS REQUIRED OR OPTIONAL.

a. Het wordt tijd om in jezelf te geloven!

   → ....

b. Ze heeft een fiets nodig om naar huis te gaan.

   → ....

c. Hij wil stoppen met zijn studie om een eigen bedrijf te starten.

   → ....

VOCABULARY

de horoscoop *horoscope*
de ram *ram* (Aries)
de stier *bull* (Taurus)
de tweeling *twins* (Gemini)
de kreeft *lobster* (Cancer)
de leeuw *lion* (Leo)
de maagd *virgin, maiden* (Virgo)
de weegschaal *scale, balance*
  (Libra)
de schorpioen *scorpion* (Scorpio)
de boogschutter *archer, bowman*
  (Sagittarius)
de steenbok *ibex* (Capricorn)
de waterman *water carrier*
  (Aquarius)
de vissen *fishes* (Pisces)
de vis *fish*
soms *sometimes*
nooit *never*
gewoonlijk *usually, normally*
steeds *constantly*
bang zijn *to be afraid*
de mening *opinion*
uiten *to express, to voice, to utter*
kwaad maken *to make angry*
hoewel *although*
sterk *strong*
worden *to become*
de tijd *time*
het gevoel *feeling, emotion*
tonen *to show*
slim *clever, bright, intelligent*
genoeg *enough*
geloven in zichzelf *to believe in*
  oneself

zo'n *such*
hard *strenuously, forcefully*
de werker / de werkster
  worker (m./f.)
echt *really*
te veel *too much*
beslissen *to decide*
toch *yet, still, nevertheless*
de baas zijn *to be the boss*
leven *to live*
gezond *healthy*
moeilijk maken *to make difficult*
moeilijk *difficult*
zoeken *to seek, to search, to look for*
het evenwicht *balance, equilibrium*
leren *to learn*
eens *once*
het besluit *decision*
het geld *money*
verdienen *to earn*
belangrijk *important*
vergeten *to forget*
morgen *tomorrow*
wachten *to wait*
het geduld *patience*
voorzichtig *cautious, prudent*
bij *with, by*
niets *nothing*
het compromis *compromise*
houden van *to love, to like*
de vrijheid *freedom*
Wees! *Be!*
idealistisch *idealistic*
iemand *someone*
niemand *no one*
iedereen *everyone*

d. Vergeet niet om iets van je te laten horen!

→ ....

e. Ik ben niet bang om risico's te nemen.

→ ....

2. COMPLETE THE SENTENCES WITH THE CORRECT INDEFINITE PRONOUN.

a. Zij kent geen compromis. Het is voor haar altijd .... of ....

b. Willen jullie ons .... vragen? (3 possibilities)

c. .... is zo voorzichtig als hij.

d. Niet .... vindt dat een mooie film.

3. COMPLETE THESE COMMANDS WITH THE IMPERATIVE FORM OF THE VERB.

a. (Geven) .... u mij maar een kilo peren!

b. (Laten) .... maar snel iets van je horen!

c. (Zijn) .... niet zo dom!

d. (Maken) .... u niet kwaad!

e. (Leren) .... eens je mening te uiten!

4. LISTEN TO THE AUDIO TO COMPLETE THESE SENTENCES.

16

a. Heeft zij .... honger of ....?

b. Ze heeft .... zin om .... te eten .... te drinken.

c. .... maak je .... jezelf .... moeilijk!

d. Je bent .... harde werker! Maar ....vakantie!

e. Hij wil .... de baas zijn, maar niet .... vindt dat leuk.

f. Stop .... met .... tot morgen te ....!

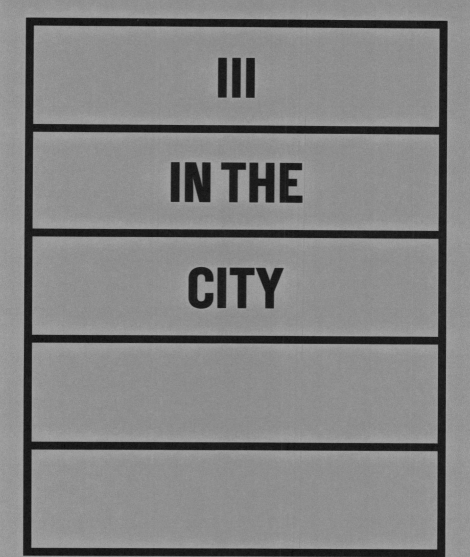

III

IN THE

CITY

15.
A NAVIGATION APP

EEN ROUTE-APP

AIMS	TOPICS

AIMS

- ASKING AND GIVING RECOMMENDATIONS

- USING VOCABULARY RELATED TO SMARTPHONE APPS

- TALKING ABOUT DIFFERENT TYPES OF TRANSPORT

TOPICS

- THE INDEFINITE PRONOUNS *ELK/ IEDER* EACH

- THE QUANTIFIER *EEN PAAR* A FEW, SOME

- UNSTRESSED OBJECT PRONOUNS

- POSSESSIVE ADJECTIVES (MY, YOUR, HIS/HER, ETC.)

A NAVIGATION APP?

Harry: Can you recommend a navigation app for my wife *(Can you me a navigation-app for my wife recommend)*?

Marieke: Does she want to use it every day *(Want she it each day to-use)* or only on the weekend?

Harry: She needs it to go to work by car *(She has of-it one need to with the car towards her work to go)*, because she doesn't want to be sitting in a traffic jam every morning anymore *(she wants not anymore each morning in the traffic-jam to-stand)*.

Marieke: The best thing *(You can the best)* is to install a few different navigation apps on her smartphone. *(The)* Most are free, but sometimes you have to pay. And for online apps, you need an internet connection.

Harry: That makes it complicated, as she doesn't have a phone with an internet connection. Is there *(Exists there)* no easy and cheap system?

Marieke: She can take the train or bus – that's called *(the)* public transport! Or the cheapest way: cycling or walking *(she goes with the bicycle or walking)*!

Harry: Kun je me een route-app voor m'n vrouw aanraden?

Marieke: Wil ze 'm elke dag gebruiken of alleen in het weekend?

Harry: Ze heeft 'r één nodig om met de auto naar d'r werk te gaan, want ze wil niet meer iedere ochtend in de file staan.

Marieke: Je kunt het beste een paar verschillende navigatie-apps op d'r smartphone installeren. De meeste zijn gratis, maar soms moet je betalen. En voor de online-apps heb je internetverbinding nodig.

Harry: Dat maakt 't lastig, want ze heeft geen telefoon met internetverbinding. Bestaat er geen gemakkelijk en goedkoop systeem?

Marieke: Ze kan de trein of bus nemen; dat heet het openbaar vervoer! Of de goedkoopste manier: ze gaat met de fiets of lopend!

■ UNDERSTANDING THE DIALOGUE

→ **Kun je me een route-app voor m'n vrouw aanraden?** *Can you recommend* ('to me') *a navigation app for my wife?* Here, **m'n** is the shortened form of **mijn** *my*. Other shortened forms of possessive adjectives in the dialogue are: **d'r werk** *her work* and **d'r smartphone** *her smartphone*, in which **d'r** is the shortened form of **haar** *her*. See the section on the forms of possessive adjectives later in this lesson.

→ **Wil ze 'm elke dag gebruiken?** *Does she want to use it every day?* ('Want she it each day to use?') Here, **'m** is the shortened, unstressed form of the object pronoun **hem** *him, it*: remember that in Dutch, **hem** can be used to refer to common nouns, not just to males.

→ The indefinite pronouns **elk** and **ieder** *each, every* are synonyms. They take a final **-e** when used as an adjective before a common noun: **elke dag** *each day, every day*, **iedere ochtend** *each morning, every morning*.

→ **Ze heeft 'r één nodig (...)** *She needs (...)* ('She has of-it one need ...') Here, **'r** is the shortened form of **er** *of it, of them*. Also note **één** *one*, which is written with two accents to distinguish it from the indefinite article **een** *a, an* and to indicate the pronunciation of the **e** as a long vowel.

→ In the phrase **in de file staan** *to be sitting in a traffic jam*, we see the verb of position **staan** *to be standing, to be upright*. It may seem an odd choice here, but this is the way you say it in Dutch! We'll come back to the different verbs of position in lesson 21.

→ **Je kunt het beste een paar verschillende navigatie-apps (...)** *The best thing is to (...) a few different navigation apps.* As in English, **je** *you* can be used with the more general meaning *one*. So **je kunt het beste** translates to the impersonal *the best thing is* or *your best bet is*.

→ Note the useful expression **het openbaar vervoer** *public transport*.

CULTURAL NOTE

As anyone who's been to the Netherlands knows, the bicycle is a very popular means of transport. In fact, the country has more bikes than people! The Dutch go to work, school or out to meet friends on bikes, sometimes travelling many kilometres, even in bad weather. Consequently, there are plentiful and wide cycle lanes and paths and extensive places to park your bike, particularly near train stations.

The abbreviation **app** comes from **de applicatie** *application*: **route-app**, **navigatie-app** *navigation app*, **online-app** *online app*. The hyphen is used only in compound words that might be difficult to recognize without it: for example, between a sequence of vowels, or in compound words made up of a Dutch word and a loanword from another language.

In Dutch, a variety of English words are used in the fields of information technology, marketing, sport, business, as well as in higher education. The everyday language of young people is dotted with many English words.

◆ GRAMMAR
UNSTRESSED OBJECT PRONOUNS

In lesson 10, we saw the stressed forms of the object pronouns. Here are the unstressed forms:

me *me*; **je** *you* (informal); **u** *you* (formal); **'m** *him, it*; **'r (d'r)*** *her*; **'t** *it*;
ons *us*; **jullie** *you* (plural); **ze** *them*.
* As **'r** on its own could lead to confusion when spoken in a string of words, this is pronounced [der] rather than [er].

Remember that in the unstressed forms, the **e** is pronounced as an unstressed **e**. Omitted letters that aren't pronounced are indicated with an apostrophe when written. However, the unstressed forms are most common in speech.

The stressed forms of the object pronouns are less frequent, as these are used essentially to emphasize the pronoun: in order to show a contrast, for example. In this case, the word stress goes on the stressed pronoun:
We houden van 'm. *We like him.*
We houden van hem **maar niet van** haar! *We like him, but not her!*
Ze zien 'r morgen. *They are seeing her tomorrow.*
Ze zien haar **morgen.** *They are seeing her tomorrow.*

POSSESSIVE ADJECTIVES

The possessive adjectives (*my, your, his, her, its, our, their*) are relatively similar in Dutch and English, apart from the difference between the stressed and unstressed forms. One exception is **ons/onze** *our*, which has two forms depending on the type of noun that follows it (what or who is 'possessed'):
ons is used before a neuter noun: **ons kind** *our child*
onze is used before a common noun: **onze dochter** *our daughter*.

Don't confuse **zijn** *his* with **zijn** *to be!* And remember that **zijn** can sometimes refer to an object with the meaning *its* (belonging to it):

zijn dochter *his daughter*; **zijn verbinding** *its connection.*

my	your (inf.)	your (formal)	his, its	her	our	your (pl.)	their
Stressed forms:							
mijn	**jouw**	**uw***	**zijn**	**haar**	**ons/ onze**	**jullie****	**hun**
Unstressed forms:							
m'n	**je**	**uw***	**z'n**	**d'r**	**ons/ onze**	**jullie****	**hun**

* To grant a level of formal respect to the possessor.

** If this refers to possessors, i.e. more than one person.

⬢ EXERCISES

1. COMPLETE THE SENTENCES WITH THE POSSESSIVE ADJECTIVE THAT CORRESPONDS TO THE PRONOUN GIVEN IN PARENTHESES.

a. (hij) .... zoon heeft geen smartphone.

b. (zij) (sing.) .... dochters staan elke dag in de file.

c. (we) .... kinderen nemen iedere ochtend de bus.

d. (we) .... huis heeft een grote woonkamer en een open keuken.

2. CHANGE THE STRESSED FORMS TO UNSTRESSED FORMS.

a. Hoe is het met hem?

→ ....

b. Ik zie jouw naam niet in mijn bestand staan.

→ ....

c. Wij houden veel van haar.

→ ....

d. Zij willen er één met internetverbinding.

→ ....

● VOCABULARY

de route-app /
  de navigatie-app *navigation app*
de online-app *online app*
aanraden *to recommend*
elk(e) *each, every*
gebruiken *to use*
alleen *only*
het weekend *weekend*
één *one* (number)
'm *him, it*
't *it*
er ('r) *of it, of them*
de auto *car*
het werk *work, job*
ieder(e) *each, every*
de file *traffic jam*
staan *to be standing, to be upright,*
  to be (position)
in de file staan *to be stuck in a*
  traffic jam
het beste *the best*
een paar (+ noun) *a few, several*
verschillend *different*
de smartphone *smartphone*
installeren *to install*
de meeste *most*
gratis *free (of charge)*
betalen *to pay*
de verbinding *connection*
de internetverbinding
  internet connection
lastig maken *to make difficult,*
  to complicate

bestaan *to exist*
gemakkelijk *easy*
goedkoop *cheap*
goedkoopste *cheapest*
het systeem *system*
de trein *train*
het openbaar vervoer
  public transport
de manier *way, manner*
lopend *walking*
m'n *my*
jouw *your* (informal)
z'n *his, its*
'r (d'r) *her*
ons/onze *our*
hun *their*

3. TRANSLATE THESE SENTENCES INTO ENGLISH.

a. Hij wil met het openbaar vervoer naar zijn werk gaan.

→ ....

b. Kun je een paar apps op m'n smartphone installeren?

→ ....

c. Er bestaat een gemakkelijk en goedkoop systeem.

→ ....

d. Ze hebben er één nodig om naar het buitenland te kunnen reizen.

→ ....

4. LISTEN TO THE AUDIO AND SELECT *WAAR* IF THE SENTENCE MATCHES AND *NIET WAAR* IF IT DOESN'T. THEN READ EACH SENTENCE OUT LOUD AND CHECK YOUR PRONUNCIATION BY LISTENING TO THE AUDIO AGAIN.

17

	WAAR	NIET WAAR
a. Heeft d'r smartphone een internetverbinding?		
b. Waar is ze? Is ze op d'r werk?		
c. Hij heeft 'r één nodig om naar 't strand te gaan.		
d. Z'n dochter gaat met de tram naar huis.		
e. Onze zoon ziet 'm niet zo vaak.		

146

16.
DOING THE SHOPPING

BOODSCHAPPEN DOEN

AIMS	TOPICS

- EMPLOYING COMMON EXPRESSIONS WHEN SHOPPING
- EXPRESSING NEEDS AND WANTS IN A SHOP

- THE NEGATION *GEEN MEER* NO MORE
- THE QUESTION WORD *WELK?* WHICH?
- SOME FOOD VOCABULARY
- SEPARABLE-PREFIX VERBS
- THE FUTURE

DOING THE SHOPPING

At the baker's

Shop assistant *(Saleswoman)*: **Whose turn is it?** *(Who is there at the turn?)*

Customer: Mine *(I)*! **Two brown breads, please.**

Shop assistant: Anything else *(Otherwise still something)*?

Customer: A rye bread.

Shop assistant: We don't have any more rye bread.

Customer: It doesn't matter *(That is not grave)*.

At the butcher's

Butcher: What will *(may)* **it be?**

Customer: 150 grams of *(1½ ounce)* **ham and a beef roast.**

Butcher: Will that be all? *(That is it?)*

Customer: And a bit of liverwurst *(a piece liver-sausage)*, **please.**

Butcher: Here you go.

At the cheeseshop

Cheesemonger: Can I help you?

Customer: Yes, what sorts of cheese do you recommend for a cheese board? And how much cheese do I need per person?

Cheesemonger: You choose first 4 or 5 cheeses with *(of)* **different tastes. Plan on perhaps about 100 grams per person. And …**

Customer: I'm in a hurry *(I have haste)*. **Put something tasty together. I'll come at 6:00 to pick it up** *(I come it at 6 o'clock to-pick-up)*. **And I'd like to pay with a card** *(I want gladly to-pin)*.

Cheesemonger: As you wish *(want)*! **The customer is king!**

Bij de bakker

<u>Verkoopster</u>: Wie is er aan de beurt?

<u>Klant</u>: Ik! Twee bruine broden alsjeblieft.

<u>Verkoopster</u>: Anders nog iets?

<u>Klant</u>: Een roggebrood.

<u>Verkoopster</u>: We hebben geen roggebrood meer.

<u>Klant</u>: Dat is niet erg.

Bij de slager

<u>Slager</u>: Wat mag het zijn?

<u>Klant</u>: Anderhalf ons ham en een runderrollade.

<u>Slager</u>: Dat is het?

<u>Klant</u>: En een stukje leverworst graag.

<u>Slager</u>: Alstublieft.

In de kaaswinkel

<u>Kaasboer</u>: Kan ik je helpen?

<u>Klant</u>: Ja, welke soorten kaas raad je me voor een kaasplankje aan? En hoeveel kaas heb ik per persoon nodig?

<u>Kaasboer</u>: Je kiest eerst 4 of 5 kazen van verschillende smaken uit. Ga maar van ongeveer 100 gram per persoon uit. En …

<u>Klant</u>: Ik heb haast. Stel maar iets lekkers samen. Ik kom het om zes uur ophalen. En ik wil graag pinnen.

<u>Kaasboer</u>: Zoals je wilt! De klant is koning!

■ UNDERSTANDING THE DIALOGUE

→ **Wie is er aan de beurt?** *Whose turn is it?* ('Who is there at the turn?') For more on this expression and others that are commonly used when shopping, see the next section.

→ **de verkoopster** *saleswoman* refers to a female shop assistant; a male shop assistant or salesman would be **de verkoper**.

→ **We hebben geen roggebrood meer.** *We don't have any more rye bread.* Remember **geen** *none, not any*, which is used before an indefinite noun. The same is true for the construction **geen … meer** *no more, not… any more*.

→ **anderhalf ons** *150 grams* ('one-and-a-half ounces'). Note the useful word **anderhalf** *one and a half*.

→ **Ja, welke soorten kaas raad je me voor een kaasplankje aan?** ('Yes, which sorts cheese recommend you to-me for a cheese-board [separable prefix]?') The question word **welk** *which* adds an **-e** before a common noun. In this question we also see the separable-prefix verb **aanraden** *to recommend*. See the section on these verbs under 'Grammar'.

→ **Ga maar van ongeveer 100 gram per persoon uit.** ('Plan but on about 100 gram per person [separable prefix].') The separable-prefix verb + preposition **uitgaan van** means *to plan on, to assume, to suppose*.

→ **Ik heb haast.** *I'm in a hurry.* ('I have haste.') Note the use of the verb **hebben** *to have* in this expression.

→ **Stel maar iets lekkers samen.** *Put something tasty together.* ('Compose but something tasty [separable prefix].') An adjective placed directly after **iets** *something* always takes an **-s**: **iets lekkers** *something tasty*. And here is another separable-prefix verb: **samenstellen** *to compose, to compile, to put together*.

→ **Ik wil graag pinnen.** ('I want gladly to-pin.') The present tense followed by **graag** *gladly* is the equivalent of the English conditional *I would like*. The verb **pinnen** is used to say *to pay by card*.

→ **Zoals je wilt!** *As you wish!* This is the present tense of **willen** *to want*.

USEFUL VOCABULARY FOR SHOPPING

Some common expressions you might hear in shops include: **Wie is er aan de beurt?** *Whose turn is it?*; **Anders nog iets?** *Anything else?* ('Otherwise still something?'); **Wat mag het zijn?** *What would you like?* ('What may it be?'); **Dat is het?** *Is that all ?* ('That is it?'); **Kan ik je helpen?** *Can I help you?*; **Ik wil graag pinnen.** *I'd like to pay with a card.*

The Dutch tend to use the informal **je** even with people they don't know, including in shops, restaurants, cafés, etc. This is not disrespectful.

The verb **pinnen** *to pay by card, to withdraw money from an ATM*, derives from **PIN: Persoonlijk Identificatie Nummer** *personal identification number*.

As in English, you can simply say **het witbrood** *white bread* and **het bruinbrood** *brown bread*. But if you want to get more specific, there are a lot of different types of bread in the Netherlands to choose from, for example: **tarwebrood** *wheat bread*, **volkorenbrood** *wholewheat bread*, **meergranenbrood** *multigrain bread* or, as in the dialogue, **roggebrood** *rye bread*.

De kaas *cheese* is omnipresent in Dutch meals. The most well-known cheeses are **de Goudse kaas** *gouda*, named after the town of Gouda, and **de Edammer** *edam*, which comes from the town of Edam. Different descriptive terms are used to indicate its age: **jong** *young* (aged for four weeks), **belegen** *mature* (aged for four months) and **oud** *old, sharp* (aged for at least one year).

◆ GRAMMAR
SEPARABLE-PREFIX VERBS

Separable-prefix verbs are very common in Dutch. They are not so different from prepositional verbs in English such as *to plan on* or *to put away*, however, in Dutch the prefix is attached to the infinitive, and then detaches when conjugated in the present tense and the imperative, usually moving to the end of the main clause:

Welke soorten kaas raad **je me voor een kaasplankje** aan**? (aanraden)**
Which sorts of cheese do you recommend for a cheese board?
Je kiest **eerst 4 of 5 kazen van verschillende smaken** uit**. (uitkiezen)**
You choose first 4 or 5 cheeses with different tastes.
Ga **maar van ongeveer 100 gram per persoon** uit**. (uitgaan)**
Plan on about 100 grams per person.
Stel **maar iets lekkers** samen**. (samenstellen)**
Put together something tasty.

The prefix can also be placed <u>in front of</u> a complement introduced by a preposition: **(...) komt** vrij **in december** *(...) becomes available in December* **(vrijkomen)**. This construction, which is considered more casual, is only possible with a complement introduced by a preposition, so it's best to get used to placing the prefix at the end of the sentence. In this case, the word order would be: **(…) komt in december** vrij *(…)* *becomes available in December.*

If the preposition **te** (which functions a bit like *to* in English) is required before the infinitive, it is placed in between the prefix and the verb stem without attaching them:
We hebben verschillende soorten kaas nodig om een lekkere kaasplank samen te stellen.
We need different types of cheese to put together a tasty cheese board.
Hij heeft zin om iets lekkers uit te kiezen.
He feels like choosing something tasty.
Heb je tijd om me een leuk café aan te raden?
Do you have time to recommend a nice café to me?

▲ CONJUGATION
THE FUTURE

We've seen that often the present tense is used in Dutch to express a future action, sometimes with a word that indicates a time in the future:
Ik kom het om zes uur ophalen. *I'll come* ('I come') *at 6:00 to pick it up.*
Hoe laat ben je terug? *What time will you be* ('How late are you') *back?*
Wanneer is ze terug? *When will she be* ('is she') *back?*

The verb **gaan** *to go* is also frequently used to express the near future:
We gaan beginnen. *We're going to begin.*
Heb je zin om vanavond mee naar de film te gaan?
Do you feel like going to the cinema with us tonight?

⬢ EXERCISES

1. LINK THE QUESTIONS AND RESPONSES THAT GO TOGETHER.

a. Wie is er aan de beurt? •   • 1. Anderhalf ons ham, alstublieft.

b. Kan ik u helpen? •   • 2. Ik! Ik wil graag een pond belegen kaas.

c. Dat is het? •   • 3. Ja graag! Kunt u me iets lekkers aanraden?

d. Wat mag het zijn? •   • 4. Nee, ik wil ook graag een meergranenbrood.

● VOCABULARY

boodschappen doen *to do the shopping*

de boodschap *shopping, message*

de bakker *baker, baker's*

de slager *butcher, butcher's*

de verkoper / de verkoopster *shop assistant (m./f.)*

de klant *customer, client*

het brood *bread*

bruin *brown*

het bruinbrood *brown bread*

het roggebrood *rye bread*

het witbrood *white bread*

het tarwebrood *wheat bread*

het volkorenbrood *wholewheat bread*

het meergranenbrood *multigrain bread*

Wie is er aan de beurt? *Whose turn is it?*

Wat mag het zijn? *What would you like?*

Alsjeblieft. *Please. / Here you are.*

Anders nog iets? *Anything else?*

Dat is het? *Is that all?*

geen ... meer *no more, not ... any more*

erg *serious, grave*

anderhalf *one and a half*

het stuk *piece, small amount*

de ham *ham*

de runderrollade *beef roast*

de leverworst *liverwurst*

de kaas *cheese*

de winkel *shop*

de kaaswinkel *cheese shop*

de kaasboer / de kaasboerin *cheesemonger (m./f.)*

de kaasplank *cheese board*

de Goudse kaas *gouda cheese*

de Edammer *edam*

jong *young*

belegen *mature (cheese)*

helpen *to help*

Welk(e)? *Which?*

de soort *sort, type, kind*

de persoon *person*

uitkiezen *to choose, to select*

de smaak *taste, flavour*

uitgaan van *to plan on, to reckon on, to assume*

haast hebben *to be in a hurry*

samenstellen *to compile, to put together*

lekker *delicious, tasty, good*

pinnen *to pay with a card, to withdraw money from an ATM*

de koning / de koningin *king / queen*

PIN Persoonlijk Identificatie Nummer *personal identification number*

2. COMPLETE EACH SENTENCE WITH THE CORRECT PREFIX AND INDICATE IF IT IS ATTACHED TO THE VERB OR SEPARATED.

a. Hij heeft haar nummer nodig om haar .... te nodigen. → ....

b. Het is niet gemakkelijk om iets leuks voor haar .... te kiezen. → ....

c. Waarom ga je niet met ons .... ? → ....

d. Je kunt na de piep een boodschap .... spreken. → ....

e. Ze stelt hem aan de buurvrouw .... → ....

f. Hoe laat wil je .... staan? → ....

g. Daar komt de trein .... → ....

3. CIRCLE THE CORRECT FORM OF THE VERB.

a. Ze wil/will de kaas om zes uur ophalen.

b. Hij heeft /hebt geen tijd, want hij heeft/is haast.

c. Zoals u wil(t) / willen.

d. Welke soorten kaas raad /raadt je me aan.

4. LISTEN TO THE AUDIO TO COMPLETE THE SENTENCES AND THEN READ THEM OUT LOUD. LISTEN TO THE AUDIO AGAIN TO CHECK YOUR ANSWERS.

18

a. .... brood hebben we .... nodig?

b. De .... is ....!

c. .... u .... van .... uit.

d. Hij wil een ...., een .... en een stuk ....

e. We hebben .... nodig om een .... te ....

154

17.
GOING TO THE RESTAURANT

NAAR HET RESTAURANT GAAN

AIMS	TOPICS

- ORDERING AT A CAFÉ OR RESTAURANT
- TALKING ABOUT DIFFERENT FOODS AND DRINKS
- SAYING YOU'RE HUNGRY OR THIRSTY

- USEFUL VOCABULARY FOR GOING OUT TO EAT
- MORE ON FORMING THE PLURAL OF NOUNS
- HOW TO EXPRESS PREFERENCES AND TASTES

THE INDONESIAN CAFÉ-RESTAURANT

Bas: Could we have a menu *(May we the menu)*?

Waitress: Here you are. Is it for here or to go *(Here to-eat-up or to-take-away)*?

Bas: For here *(Here to-eat-up)*.

Nelleke: I'm hungry: I'll have *(I take)* a starter and then *(after)* the daily special *(day-dish)*.

Bas: I'd rather have *(I have rather)* a main course and then a dessert. Or should we order an Indonesian rijsttafel *(rice-table)*?

Nelleke: Yes, delicious!

Bas: I love *(I am crazy on)* prawns with satay sauce. But I don't like it *(of)* spicy, so for me, not too much chilli paste!

Bas: I find it a bit bland. Can you pass me the salt and pepper?

Nelleke: Here you go. What should we drink with it *(What drink we there-with)*?

Bas: I'd ideally like rosé *(I have the most-preferably rosé)*.

Nelleke: I'm thirsty so I'll have *(and I-take)* tea.

Waitress: Would you like *(Want you)* a dessert?

Bas: I'd like a coffee. And she'll have a crêpe with no sugar *(a pancake without sugar for this young-lady)*. And the bill, please.

Bas: Mogen we de kaart?

Serveerster: Alsjeblieft. Hier opeten of meenemen?

Bas: Hier opeten.

Nelleke: Ik heb honger: ik neem een voorgerecht en daarna de dagschotel.

Bas: Ik heb liever een hoofdgerecht en dan een toetje. Of zullen we een rijsttafel bestellen?

Nelleke: Ja, heerlijk!

Bas: Ik ben gek op gamba's met satésaus. Maar ik houd niet van pikant, dus voor mij niet te veel sambal!

Bas: Ik vind het een beetje flauw. Kun je me het zout en de peper aangeven?

Nelleke: Alsjeblieft. Wat drinken we erbij?

Bas: Ik heb het liefst rosé.

Nelleke: Ik heb dorst en neem thee.

Serveerster: Willen jullie een dessert?

Bas: Ik wil graag een koffie. En een pannenkoek zonder suiker voor deze jongedame. En de rekening alsjeblieft.

UNDERSTANDING THE DIALOGUE

→ **het Indonesische eetcafé** *Indonesian café-restaurant* ('eat-café'). There is a large community of people of Indonesian origin in the Netherlands. The name of the country is **Indonesië** *Indonesia*: the **ë** is pronounced [yuh].

→ **Mogen we de kaart?** *Could we have the menu?* The verb **hebben** *to have* here is implied but is not explicitly stated. Another word for **de kaart** *the menu* is **de menukaart**.

→ **Hier opeten of meenemen?** *To eat here or to take away?* The verb **eten** means *to eat*, while **opeten** has the more informal meaning of *to eat up*. The verb **nemen** means *to take*, while **meenemen** means *to take with, to take along*.

→ **een voorgerecht en daarna de dagschotel** *a starter and then the daily special* ('a before-dish and after the day-dish').

→ **Ik heb liever een hoofdgerecht en dan een toetje.** *I prefer a main course and then a dessert.* ('I have rather a main-dish and then a little-after.') The term **het toetje** *dessert* is usually used at home. Did you notice that it's a diminutive? Synonyms are **het nagerecht** ('after-dish') or **het dessert** *dessert*.

→ **(…) een rijsttafel bestellen** *(…) to order a rijsttafel.* See the next section to find out about this popular dish.

→ **Ik ben gek op gamba's met satésaus.** *I love prawns with satay sauce.* Note the useful expression **ik ben gek op** ('I am crazy about'). And remember that **'s** is one of the markers of the plural in Dutch, not the possessive.

→ **Ik wil graag een koffie.** *I'd like* ('I want gladly') *a coffee.* Don't forget this useful expression for ordering: **ik wil graag** *I'd like*.

→ **En de rekening alsjeblieft.** *And the bill, please.* A tip for remembering the word for *the bill, the check* is that it resembles 'reckoning' in English.

EATING OUT IN THE NETHERLANDS

There are several types of café in the Netherlands, including **het eetcafé** *café-restaurant*, which is between a **café** and a **restaurant**, and **het bruin café** ('brown café'), which is a cosy traditional pub with smoke-darkened walls, dark wood furniture and maroon or brown carpets.

You'll also find restaurants serving a wide range of cuisine, although few offer authentic Dutch food. Traditional Dutch meals tend to be eaten at home: for example, **de boerenkoolstamppot** ('farmers'-kale-mash-pot'), which consists of mashed potatoes mixed with milk, butter, a bit of broth and finely chopped kale, and is often eaten with **de rookworst** *smoked sausage*.

Other options in the same category are **de andijviestamppot**, which is mashed potatoes and **de andijvie** *chicory, endive, escarole*, or **de hutspot**, which is mashed potatoes, carrots and onions.

One of the most popular types of cuisine in the Netherlands is Indonesian food, whose roots in the country can be traced back to the 17ᵗʰ century, when the Dutch colonized Indonesia. One of the most well-known meals is **de rijsttafel** ('rice-table'), which consists of an elaborate medley of small Indonesian dishes, rice and various sauces, as well as **nasi goreng**, Indonesian fried rice, and **saté**, brochettes of meat with a satay sauce, which is made from soy sauce, peanuts and coconut milk. All of these can be made more or less spicy with the chosen dose of **sambal** *chilli paste*. The influence of Indonesian cooking can also be seen at a **snackbar**, where you can find not only **de patat / de friet** *chips, fries*, but **de nasibal**, a deep-fried breaded Indonesian rice ball, or **de bamischijf**, a deep-fried breaded slice of Indonesian noodles.

Eet smakelijk! ('Eat tasty!') **/ Smakelijk eten!** *Enjoy your meal!*

GRAMMAR
MORE ON FORMING THE PLURAL OF NOUNS

To form the plural of nouns that end in a long **-a**, **-o**, **-i** or **-u**, an **'s** is added in order to retain the pronunciation of the long vowel. This is not to be confused with the apostrophe s in English used to mark the possessive:

de gamba *prawn* → **de gamba's** *prawns*; **de kilo** *kilo* → **de kilo's** *kilos*;
de kiwi *kiwi* → **de kiwi's** *kiwis*; **het menu** *menu* → **de menu's** *menus*.

A final **-s** is added to loanwords from other languages:
de film *film* → **de films** *films*; **de computer** *computer* → **de computers** *computers*.

EXPRESSING PREFERENCES AND TASTES

The following terms can be used after a wide range of verbs to express degrees of preference: **graag** *gladly* (I like), **liever** *rather* (I prefer) and **het liefst** *most preferably, ideally* (I most like):
Ik drink graag rosé. *I like drinking rosé.*
Ik drink liever rosé. *I prefer to drink rosé.*
Ik drink het liefst rosé. *I most like to drink rosé.*

159

Ik ga graag naar de film. *I like going to the cinema.*
Ik ga liever naar de film. *I prefer going to the cinema.*
Ik ga het liefst naar de film. *I most like going to the cinema.*

Ik heb graag thee. *I'd like tea.*
Ik heb liever thee. *I'd rather have tea.*
Ik heb het liefst thee. *I'd most like to have tea.*

Associated with **graag** *gladly*, the verbs **willen** *to want* and **hebben** *to have* express a wish, which would typically be in the conditional in English:
Ik heb/wil graag thee. *I would like tea.*

Also note the following verbs and phrases for expressing tastes and preferences:
houden van *to like*, **vinden** *to find* or **gek/dol zijn op** *to love, to be crazy about*:
Ik houd niet van pikant. *I don't like it spicy.*
Ik vind het een beetje flauw. *I find it a bit bland.*
Ik ben gek/dol op gamba's met satésaus. *I love prawns with satay sauce.*

⬡ EXERCISES

1. FIND THE ODD ONE OUT IN EACH LIST.

a. dessert / hoofdgerecht / toetje / nagerecht

b. rijsttafel / nasibal / bamischijf / kaas

c. bestellen / meenemen / ophalen / aangeven

d. eetcafé / restaurant / koffie / snackbar

e. sambal / peper / zout / pannenkoek

2. MAKE THESE WORDS PLURAL.

a. de foto → ....

b. het risico → ....

c. de flat → ....

d. de oma → ....

● VOCABULARY

Indonesisch *Indonesian* (adj.)
Indonesië (het) *Indonesia*
het eetcafé *café-restaurant*
de kaart / de menukaart /
  het menu *menu*
de serveerder / de serveerster
  server (m./f.)
hier opeten *to eat here*
meenemen *to take away*
daarna *after, afterwards, next*
de dagschotel *daily special*
het voorgerecht *starter, appetizer*
het hoofdgerecht *main course*
het toetje / het nagerecht /
  het dessert *dessert*
de rijst *rice*
de tafel *table*
bestellen *to order*
heerlijk *delicious, lovely*
de gamba *prawn*
de satésaus *satay sauce*
pikant *spicy*
de sambal *chilli paste*
een beetje *a bit*
flauw *bland*
het zout *salt*
de peper *pepper*
aangeven *to pass, to hand*
Alsjeblieft. *Please. / Here you go.*
erbij *with*
liever *rather, preferably*
het liefst *most preferably, ideally*
de rosé *rosé*
graag willen *to want* (would like)
de koffie *coffee*

de pannenkoek *pancake, crêpe*
zonder *without*
de suiker *sugar*
de jongedame *young lady*
de rekening *bill, check*
het café *café*
het restaurant *restaurant*
het bruin café *brown café, pub*
de boerenkoolstamppot
  mashed potato and kale
de rookworst *smoked sausage*
de andijvie *chicory, endive, escarole*
de andijviestamppot
  mashed potato and endive
de hutspot *mashed potato, carrots*
  and onions
de snackbar *snackbar*
de patat / de friet *chips, fries*
gek zijn op / dol zijn op *to love,*
  to be crazy about
de kiwi *kiwi*
Eet smakelijk! / Smakelijk eten!
  Enjoy your meal! Bon appétit!

3. TRANSLATE THESE SENTENCES INTO DUTCH.

a. I'd like a coffee.

→ ....

b. Do you *(informal sing.)* prefer to drink wine or beer?

→ ....

c. They most like to go to the beach.

→ ....

d. He is crazy about bread with young cheese.

→ ....

e. Enjoy your meal!

→ ....

4. LISTEN TO THESE SENTENCES. THEN WRITE THEM IN THE NEGATIVE AND LISTEN TO THE AUDIO AGAIN TO CHECK YOUR ANSWERS.

19

a. Ik houd van friet met satésaus.

→ ....

b. We vinden die toetjes lekker.

→ ....

c. Waarom zijn Nederlanders gek op gerechten uit Indonesië?

→ ....

d. Ze eten graag pannenkoeken.

→ ....

18.
AT THE DOCTOR'S

BIJ DE DOKTER

<table>
<tr><td>

AIMS

</td><td>

TOPICS

</td></tr>
<tr><td>

- TALKING ON THE PHONE
- ASKING AND SAYING WHAT'S WRONG
- DESCRIBING YOUR SYMPTOMS AND PHYSICAL CONDITION

</td><td>

- STANDARD EXPRESSIONS FOR TALKING ON THE PHONE
- SOME VOCABULARY ABOUT HEALTH AND THE HUMAN BODY
- THE IMPERSONAL SUBJECT PRONOUN *ER* THERE

</td></tr>
</table>

GENERAL PRACTITIONERS' OFFICE

Ring, ring…

<u>Assistant</u>: Hello, Wellbeing GPs' Office.

<u>Lucas</u>: Hello, this is Lucas. Can I speak to the doctor?

<u>Assistant</u>: What's bothering you *(Where have you trouble from)*?

<u>Lucas</u>: I have a headache *(head-pain)* and a 39° *(degrees)* fever.

<u>Assistant</u>: The doctor is speaking to someone *(in conversation)*. Do you want to call back or stay on the line? Oh, she just hung up *(she hangs just up)*, I'll transfer you *(I connect you through)*.

***

<u>Doctor</u>: Hello, Lucas. What are your symptoms *(complaints)* apart from the headache and fever?

<u>Lucas</u>: I have a sore throat and I ache all over *(Throat-pain and muscle-pain in my whole body)*. Moreover, I'm very tired.

<u>Doctor</u>: Do you have a cough *(Cough you)*?

<u>Lucas</u>: Yes.

<u>Doctor</u>: There are several epidemics going around, including the flu. Your symptoms sound like it *(resemble there)* in any case. I'll write *(prepare)* a prescription for a cough syrup and painkiller for you. You should also drink a lot of water *(Further much water drink)*. But if your fever gets higher *(if you more fever get)*, then you must come in. Get well soon *(Betterness)*!

<u>Lucas</u>: Thank you.

Tring, tring …

<u>Assistente</u>: Met huisartsenpraktijk Welzijn.

<u>Lucas</u>: Met Lucas. Kan ik de dokter spreken?

<u>Assistente</u>: Waar heb je last van?

<u>Lucas</u>: Ik heb hoofdpijn en 39 graden koorts.

<u>Assistente</u>: De dokter is in gesprek. Wil je terugbellen of blijf je aan de lijn? O, ze hangt net op, ik verbind je door.

***

<u>Dokter</u>: Dag Lucas. Wat zijn je klachten behalve de hoofdpijn en koorts?

<u>Lucas</u>: Keelpijn en spierpijn in m'n hele lichaam. Verder ben ik erg moe.

<u>Dokter</u>: Hoest je?

<u>Lucas</u>: Ja.

<u>Dokter</u>: Er heersen verschillende epidemieën, waaronder de griep. Je symptomen lijken er in ieder geval op. Ik leg een recept voor een hoestdrank en pijnstiller voor je klaar. Verder veel water drinken. Maar als je meer koorts krijgt, dan moet je langskomen. Beterschap!

<u>Lucas</u>: Bedankt.

UNDERSTANDING THE DIALOGUE

→ **Met huisartsenpraktijk Welzijn.** *Hello, Wellbeing GPs' Practice.* Note that **de huisartsenpraktijk** is made up of three nouns: **het huis** *house*, **artsen** *doctors* and **de praktijk** *practice, office*. The noun **de huisarts** refers to a *GP, primary care physician*.

→ **Waar heb je last van?** *What's bothering you?* ('Where have you trouble from?') The expression **last hebben van** means *to suffer from, to be bothered by*.

→ **Ik heb hoofdpijn.** *I have a headache.* Generally, to describe an ache, you just combine the word indicating the part of the body and add the word **pijn** *pain*. Since pain is uncountable, no indefinite article is needed. In this dialogue, for example, we have **de keelpijn** *sore throat* and **de spierpijn** *muscle aches*. It is also possible to say: **pijn in mijn hoofd/keel** *pain in my head/throat*, etc.

→ **ze hangt net op** *she just hung up*. The verb here is in the present tense – **net** *just* indicates that it happened in the recent past.

→ **Wat zijn je klachten?** *What are your symptoms* ('complaints')? In the next section, you'll find out more about various expressions frequently used at the doctor's office.

→ **Je symptomen lijken er (...) op.** *Your symptoms resemble it (...).* The verb **lijken** is followed by the preposition **op** to convey *to sound like, to seem like, to look like*.

→ Note the separable-prefix verb **klaarleggen** *to prepare, to get ready, to set out*, which is composed of the verb **leggen** *to lay* and **klaar** *ready*.

→ **(...) als je meer koorts krijgt, dan moet je langskomen** *(...) if your fever goes up, then you must come in* ('if you more fever get, then must you along-come'). The verb **krijgen** *to get* here indicates a change of state, as in *to begin to have*.

→ In this dialogue, there is more useful vocabulary for telephone conversations: **in gesprek zijn** *to be speaking with someone* ('in conversation to-be'); **terugbellen** *to call back* ('back-to-ring'); **aan de lijn blijven** *to stay on the line*; **ophangen** *to hang up*; **doorverbinden** *to transfer* ('through-to-connect').

GOING TO THE DOCTOR IN THE NETHERLANDS

If you need to describe your symptoms or physical condition to a health professional, some common expressions you might need include: **last hebben van** *to suffer from* ('trouble to-have from'); **klachten hebben** *to have symptoms* ('complaints to-have'); **koorts hebben** *to have a fever* (note that Celsius is used: 39°C is 102°F); **ziek zijn** *to be ill/sick*; **moe zijn** *to be tired*; **hoesten** *to cough*; **de griep hebben** *to have the flu*; **pijn hebben** *to have pain, to ache*; **pijn doen** *to hurt, to ache*.

Generally, Dutch people tend not to go to the doctor or take medication unless they really need to. This attitude is in line with the government policy of the Netherlands to keep health costs down. Doctors or medical practices charge a fee for certain services, including *phone consultations* (**het telefonisch spreekuur**) and *online consultations* (**het e-consult**).

Typically, phone consultations are offered every day during a certain time period (**het spreekuur** *consultation hours* → **spreek** *speak* + **uur** *hour*) and allow patients to ask simple health questions or for a prescription to be renewed (**het herhaalrecept** *refill* → **herhalen** *to renew, to repeat* + **het recept** *prescription*). Online appointments with a doctor are possible if you need to discuss a medication (**het medicijn**) or a non-threatening illness such as a common cold (**verkouden zijn** *to have a cold*).

PARTS OF THE BODY

Here is some vocabulary for parts of the body:

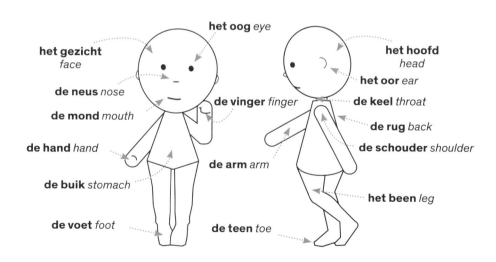

het oog *eye*

het gezicht
face

het hoofd
head

de neus *nose*

het oor *ear*

de mond *mouth*

de keel *throat*

de vinger *finger*

de rug *back*

de hand *hand*

de schouder *shoulder*

de arm *arm*

de buik *stomach*

het been *leg*

de voet *foot*

de teen *toe*

167

◆ GRAMMAR
THE IMPERSONAL PRONOUN *ER* THERE

We saw the construction **er is** *there is,* **er zijn** *there are* in lesson 11:
Er is een ruime woonkamer en er zijn twee slaapkamers.
There is a spacious living room, and there are two bedrooms.

The pronoun **er** can also be used with other verbs. In this case, the verb always conjugates according to the noun that follows it:
Er heerst een epidemie. *There is an epidemic going around.* ('There reigns an …')
Er heersen epidemieën. *There are epidemics going around.* ('There reign …')
Er loopt een hond op straat. *There is a dog walking in the street.* ('There walks a …')
Er lopen honden op straat. *There are dogs walking in the street.* ('There walk …')

⬢ EXERCISES

1. COMPLETE THESE SENTENCES WITH THE CORRECT CONJUGATION OF THE VERB IN PARENTHESES.

a. Er .... (staan) geen fiets in de berging.

b. Er .... (komen) een auto aan.

c. Er .... (wonen) veel makelaars in dat flatgebouw.

d. Er .... (lopen) een paar mannen op het strand.

2. TRANSLATE THESE SENTENCES INTO DUTCH.

a. They are very tired, and they are coughing.

→ ....

b. She has stomach pain and back pain, but she does not have a sore throat.

→ ....

c. Your symptoms resemble it in any case.

→ ....

d. My feet and toes hurt.

→ ....

● VOCABULARY

de huisartsenpraktijk *GPs' practice, primary care practice*
de arts *doctor, physician*
de huisarts *family doctor, GP*
de dokter *doctor*
de praktijk *practice*
de assistent / de assistente *assistant (m./f.)*
het welzijn *well-being, wellness*
last hebben van *to suffer from, to be bothered by*
de graad *degree*
de koorts *fever*
in gesprek *speaking to, in conversation*
terugbellen *to call back*
aan de lijn blijven *to stay on the line*
ophangen *to hang up*
doorverbinden *to transfer a call, to connect to*
net *just, only just*
de klacht *complaint*
klachten hebben *to have complaints*
behalve *except, apart from*
heel *whole, entire*
het lichaam *body*
verder *further, moreover, in addition*
moe *tired*
hoesten *to cough*
de hoestdrank *cough syrup*
heersen *to go around* (illness), *to reign, to rule*
de epidemie *epidemic*
waaronder *including*
de griep *flu*
het symptoom *symptom*
lijken op *to resemble, to seem like*
het water *water*

in ieder geval *in any case*
het geval *case*
klaarleggen *to prepare, to ready*
als *if*
krijgen *to get, to receive*
langskomen *to come by*
Beterschap! *Get well soon!*
de pijn *pain*
pijn hebben *to have pain, to hurt*
pijn doen *to hurt*
de hoofdpijn *headache*
de keelpijn *sore throat*
de spierpijn *muscle aches*
de pijnstiller *painkiller*
het hoofd *head*
het gezicht *face*
het oog *eye*
het oor *ear*
de neus *nose*
de mond *mouth*
de keel *throat*
de schouder *shoulder*
de arm *arm*
de hand *hand*
de vinger *finger*
de buik *stomach*
de rug *back*
het been *leg*
de voet *foot*
de teen *toe*
het telefonisch spreekuur *phone consultation*
het e-consult *online consultation*
het recept *prescription*
herhalen *to repeat, to renew*
het herhaalrecept *prescription refill/renewal*
het medicijn *medicine, drug*
ziek zijn *to be ill/sick*
verkouden zijn *to have a cold*
Wat erg! *How awful! What a shame!*

3. COMPLETE EACH SENTENCE WITH THE CORRECT SEPARABLE-PREFIX VERB.

a. We .... straks wel even .... (*to call back*)

b. Ze hebben geen zin om .... te .... (*to hang up*)

c. Hij .... haar met de dokter .... (*to connect, to transfer*)

d. .... je vanavond even ....? (*to come by*)

4. WRITE THE WORDS FOR THE PARTS OF THE BODY IN THE CORRECT PLACE, ADDING THE DEFINITE ARTICLE.

arm; been; buik; hand; hoofd; keel; mond; neus; oog; oor; rug; schouder; teen; vinger; voet

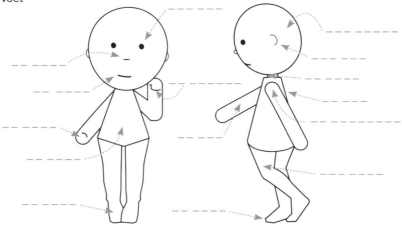

5. LISTEN TO EACH SENTENCE, REPEAT IT OUT LOUD AND WRITE IT DOWN.

20

a. ....

b. ....

c. ....

d. ....

e. ....

f. ....

19.
THE ROUTINE

DE ROUTINE

AIMS	TOPICS

- **TALKING ABOUT YOUR DAILY ROUTINE**

- **MAKING SUGGESTIONS FOR CHANGES**

- **DESCRIBING A TYPICAL WORK DAY**

- **THE TERMS *ZO'N* AND *ZULK(E)* SUCH**

- **THE DEMONSTRATIVE ADJECTIVES *DEZELFDE* AND *HETZELFDE* THE SAME**

- **MORE ON *ER/DAAR* THERE**

THE ROUTINE

Kees: It's Monday again *(It is again Monday)*! Awful! Especially the thought that the alarm will go off at 6:00 *(the alarm at 6 o'clock goes-off)*.

Maartje: You always have such negative thoughts *(ideas)*! Just go to bed early on Sunday *(Go simply on Sunday early to bed)* and start your morning with some exercise.

Kees: And at the office, always the same grind *(rut)*: at 9:00 turning on the laptop *(the laptop on)*, then a meeting, at 12:00 having lunch *(to-lunch)*, at 1:00 typing letters *(letters to-type)*, at 2:00 updating spreadsheets *(spreadsheets to-update)* and in between making phone calls *(to-telephone)*, making photocopies *(photocopies to-make)* and so on *(and goes so more on)*.

Maartje: Stop moaning and make some changes! *(Stop really with that whining and dare to change!)* Start the day with a smile and get out at lunchtime *(go there between the midday awhile between-out)* to break *(break-through)* the routine.

Kees: It's easy for you to say *(You have easy to-talk)*: you work only *(but)* two days a week!

Maartje: What's wrong with that *(What is there wrong about)*?

Kees: Het is weer maandag! Vreselijk! Vooral de gedachte dat de wekker om 6 uur afgaat.

Maartje: Jij hebt altijd zulke negatieve ideeën! Ga gewoon op zondag vroeg naar bed en begin je ochtend met wat sport.

Kees: En op kantoor altijd dezelfde sleur: om 9 uur de laptop aan, dan vergadering, om 12 uur lunchen, om 1 brieven typen, om 2 spreadsheets bijwerken en tussendoor telefoneren, fotokopieën maken en ga zo maar door.

Maartje: Houd toch op met dat gezeur en durf te veranderen! Begin de dag met een lach en ga er tussen de middag even tussenuit om de routine te doorbreken.

Kees: Je hebt makkelijk praten: jij werkt maar twee dagen per week!

Maartje: Wat is daar verkeerd aan?

■ UNDERSTANDING THE DIALOGUE

→ **dat de wekker om 6 uur afgaat** *that the alarm goes off at 6:00*. Here we see **afgaan** *to go off*, a separable-prefix verb.

→ **Jij hebt altijd zulke negatieve ideeën!** *You always have such negative thoughts* ('ideas')*!* For more on the term **zulk(e)** *such*, see the 'Grammar' section. Note the spelling of **ideeën** *ideas*: we'll come back to forming the plural of nouns ending in **-ee** and **-ie** in lesson 28.

→ **En op kantoor altijd dezelfde sleur: om 9 uur de laptop aan (…)** *And at the office, always the same grind: at 9:00 turning on the laptop (…)*. Here the stem (**doen**) of the separable-prefix verb **aandoen** *to start up, to turn on* is implied rather than explicitly stated: **om 9 uur de laptop aandoen** *at 9:00 starting up the laptop*. In phrases like **laptop aandoen** and **brieven typen** ('letters to type') and **spreadsheets bijwerken** ('spreadsheets to update'), the infinitive is used to describe the action, whereas in English we would tend to use the *-ing* form of the verb. See the 'Grammar' section for more on the term **dezelfde** *the same*.

→ **en ga zo maar door** *and so on, and so forth* ('and goes so more on') contains the separable-prefix verb **doorgaan** *to continue, to go on*. Another useful term with a similar meaning is **enzovoort(s)** *etcetera*, which is often abbreviated to **enz.** *etc.*

→ **Begin de dag met een lach.** *Start the day with a smile*. The noun **de lach** can mean *laugh* or *smile*. The noun **de glimlach** specifically means *smile*.

→ **en ga er tussen de middag even tussenuit** *and take a break at lunchtime.* This slightly complicated phrase contains the expression **tussen de middag** *at lunchtime* ('between the midday') as well as **er tussenuit gaan** *to take a break, to get out, to get away* ('there between-out to-go'). Here the term **toch** in the initial exclamation is used to express exasperation, something like *really*!

→ **Je hebt makkelijk praten: jij werkt maar twee dagen per week!** *It's easy for you to say* ('You have easy to talk')*: you only work two days a week!* The adjective/adverb **makkelijk** is synonymous with **gemakkelijk** *easy, easily*. The adverb **maar** in combination with a quantity means *only*.

→ **Wat is daar verkeerd aan?** *What's wrong with that?* ('What is there wrong on?') See the 'Grammar' section for more about **daar** *there* used with a preposition.

CULTURAL NOTE

Until the 1980s, the number of women in the Dutch workforce was quite low. Over the decades since then, the mentality has significantly changed, and today the majority of women without children have full-time jobs outside the home.

However, when parents have children, they often – especially the mother – go part time. This can be partly explained by the fact that traditionally the Dutch have placed a lot of importance on the home and the family; the feeling that parents should, to the extent possible, look after their children themselves is still prevalent.

Another contributing factor is that while structures such as pre-school or after-school facilities are on the rise, they can still be difficult for some families to access and are also fee-paying, so parents that work have to find childcare options that are both available and affordable.

◆ GRAMMAR
ZO'N AND *ZULK(E)* SUCH

• We saw **zo'n** *such* in lesson 14. It is used with <u>countable</u> nouns in the singular:
Niemand is zo'n harde werker als jij. *No one is such a hard worker as you.*
Ik heb zo'n buikpijn! *I have such a stomachache!*
Het is zo'n vrolijk meisje! *She is such a cheerful girl!*

• The term **zulk** also means *such*, but it is used with <u>uncountable</u> neuter nouns in the singular:
Het is zulk lekker bier! *It is such good beer!*
Waarom eet je zulk hard brood? *Why do you eat such hard bread?*

• The form **zulke** is used with plural nouns:
Jij hebt altijd zulke negatieve ideeën! *You always have such negative thoughts!*
Dat zijn zulke goede medicijnen! *These are such good medicines!*

THE DEMONSTRATIVE ADJECTIVES *DEZELFDE* AND *HETZELFDE* (THE SAME)

The demonstrative adjective **dezelfde** *the same* is written as one word. It is used before a common noun or before a plural noun:
dezelfde sleur *the same routine*
dezelfde aarde *the same Earth*
dezelfde ideeën *the same ideas*

The demonstrative adjective **hetzelfde** *the same* is used before a neuter noun or as an adverb:

hetzelfde idee *the same idea*

Dat is precies hetzelfde. *That is exactly the same.*

MORE ON *ER/DAAR* THERE

The combination **er** *there* + preposition refers to an object or a concept that is not specifically named in the sentence. The stressed variant **daar** *there* is emphasized when speaking and is often found at the beginning of the sentence. These terms can be attached to the preposition or used as separate words. Generally, they are placed as near as possible to the conjugated verb, and the preposition is placed at the end of the sentence:

Wanneer kan ik in de woning? *When can I move into the residence?*

→ **Wanneer kan ik erin?** *When can I move in?* ('When can I there-in?')

Wat is verkeerd aan twee dagen per week werken?
What's wrong with working two days a week?
→ **Wat is daar verkeerd aan?** *What's wrong with that?* ('What is there wrong on?')

Je hebt wel zin om te blijven eten, hè! *You fancy staying to eat, don't you?*
→ **Daar heb je wel zin in, hè!** *That would suit you, wouldn't it?*
('There have you well desire in, eh!')

⬡ EXERCISES

1. COMPLETE THE SENTENCES WITH *ZO'N, ZULK* OR *ZULKE.*

a. Hij vindt de zondag .... fijne dag!

b. Ze hebben .... lieve kinderen!

c. .... lekkere broodjes vind je alleen in Nederland.

d. Zij heeft .... grappige achternaam!

e. Waarom drink je .... koud *(cold)* water?

● VOCABULARY

de routine routine
weer again
vreselijk awful, terrible, horrible
vooral especially
de gedachte thought
de wekker alarm, alarm clock
afgaan to go off
zulk(e) such
zo'n such
negatief negative
vroeg early
naar bed gaan to go to bed
de sport sport
het kantoor the office
op kantoor at the office
dezelfde / hetzelfde the same
de sleur grind, rut, routine
de laptop laptop
de vergadering meeting
lunchen to have lunch
de brief letter
typen to type
het spreadsheet spreadsheet
bijwerken to update
tussendoor in between
telefoneren to telephone
fotokopieën maken to make
   photocopies
de fotokopie photocopy
en ga zo maar door and so on
ophouden met to stop
het gezeur moaning, whining,
   whingeing, complaining

durven to dare
veranderen to change
de lach smile, laugh
de glimlach smile
er tussenuit gaan to take a break,
   to get out
tussen de middag at midday
doorbreken to break through
makkelijk praten to be easy to say
makkelijk easy, easily
praten to talk
maar only, but
de week week
verkeerd wrong
doorgaan to continue, to go on
enzovoort(s) etcetera
enz. etc.
precies exact, exactly
koud cold

2. REWRITE EACH OF THESE SENTENCES, REPLACING THE UNDERLINED WORDS:
   - FIRST, USING *ER*
   - NEXT, USING *DAAR*.

a. Ze heeft zin in <u>een glas rode wijn</u>.

   → ....

   → ....

b. Kan ik over een maand in <u>het appartement</u>?

   → ....

   → ....

c. Wat is leuk aan <u>hard werken</u>?

   → ....

   → ....

3. ADD THE CORRECT FORM: *DEZELFDE* OR *HETZELFDE*.

a. .... bushalte

b. .... herhaalrecept

c. .... jongedame

d. .... personen

e. .... systeem

4. LISTEN TO THE SENTENCES AND THEN SELECT THE CORRECT MEANING FROM THE PAIR.

21

a. ❑ She begins by typing letters on her laptop.   ❑ He begins by typing letters on his laptop.

b. ❑ We are going to take a break this morning.   ❑ We are going to take a break at lunchtime.

c. ❑ She has a negative attitude!   ❑ He has such negative thoughts!

d. ❑ I don't like making photocopies.   ❑ I can't stop making photocopies.

20.
THE JOB INTERVIEW

HET SOLLICITATIEGESPREK

AIMS	TOPICS

AIMS

- **RESPONDING TO QUESTIONS IN A JOB INTERVIEW**

- **DESCRIBING YOUR EXPERIENCE AND SKILLS**

- **EXPRESSING MOTIVATION**

- **SAYING WHEN YOU'RE AVAILABLE**

TOPICS

- **SOME VOCABULARY FOR JOB HUNTING**

- **SOME FREQUENT IRREGULAR VERBS IN THE PRESENT TENSE: *WILLEN* TO WANT, *KUNNEN* TO BE ABLE TO (CAN), *MOGEN* TO HAVE PERMISSION TO (MAY)**

- **THE DIFFERENCE BETWEEN *WANT* AND *OMDAT* BECAUSE**

- **SUBORDINATE CLAUSES**

THE JOB INTERVIEW

Peter: In our job post *(vacancy)* it says that we are looking for an administrative employee (f.). I see in your CV that you have absolutely no work experience. Don't you think that would be *(is)* a problem?

Ans: I am studying media and communications *(communication-sciences)*, and despite the fact that I have little experience, I have *(have-at-my-disposal I)* many skills of interest *(many interesting skills)* for this job.

Peter: Why do you want to come work with us?

Ans: Because you are an innovative organization.

Peter: Why are you a suitable candidate (f.)?

Ans: If I understand correctly *(I it good understand)*, I would be assisting the web editor *(go I the web-editor* [f.] *to-assist)*. I have great social skills *(I am socially wholly skilled)*, and in addition I can use *(can I good handle with)* different software including word processing packages.

Peter: Even though you don't have much experience, I still want to hire you. When can you start?

Ans: Right away *(Now immediately)*.

Peter: In onze vacature staat dat we een administratief medewerkster zoeken. Ik zie in je cv dat je helemaal geen werkervaring hebt. Denk je niet dat dat een probleem is?

Ans: Ik studeer communicatiewetenschappen, en ondanks het feit dat ik weinig ervaring heb, beschik ik over veel interessante competenties voor deze baan.

Peter: Waarom wil je bij ons komen werken?

Ans: Omdat jullie een innoverende organisatie zijn.

Peter: Waarom ben jij een geschikte kandidate?

Ans: Als ik het goed begrijp, ga ik de webredactrice assisteren. Ik ben sociaal heel vaardig en bovendien kan ik goed overweg met verschillende software waaronder tekstverwerkers.

Peter: Al heb je niet veel ervaring, ik wil je toch aannemen. Wanneer kun je beginnen?

Ans: Nu meteen.

■ UNDERSTANDING THE DIALOGUE

→ **dat we een administratief medewerkster zoeken** *that we're looking for an administrative employee* (f.). As you may have noticed in previous lessons, certain names of professions have a masculine and a feminine form: **de medewerker** *employee* is used for a male employee, and **de medewerkster** for a female.

→ **helemaal geen werkervaring** *absolutely no work experience*: **helemaal** combined with a negation such as **geen** or **niet** means *absolutely no*; on its own **helemaal** means *totally, completely* (it is made up of the words **heel** *whole, entire, intact* and **maal** *time*).

→ **Denk je niet …?** *Don't you think …?* The frequently used verb **denken** means *to think, to consider, to reckon*.

→ **communicatiewetenschappen** ('communication-sciences'): **de wetenschap** in the singular is *science* (**weten** is the verb *to know*). Also note the verb + preposition **beschikken over**, which means *to have* in the sense of *to have at one's disposal, to have access to*.

→ **Omdat jullie een innoverende organisatie zijn.** *Because you are an innovative organization.* The conjunction **omdat** is similar to **want** *because*, but it has some important differences. See the 'Grammar' section for more on this and on the word order of subordinate clauses.

→ **Waarom ben jij een geschikte kandidaat?** *Why are you a suitable candidate?* This is another case where there are masculine and feminine forms of the noun: **de kandidaat / de kandidate** *candidate* (m./f.).

→ **Ik ben sociaal heel vaardig.** *I have great social skills.* ('I am socially wholly skilled.') Adjectives such as **vaardig** *accomplished, skilful* and **geschikt** *suitable, qualified, apt* are useful in job interviews.

→ **kan ik goed overweg met …** *I can use …* ('can I good handle with'). This is another useful construction to remember.

APPLYING FOR JOBS IN THE NETHERLANDS

In a CV, **de sollicitatiebrief** *cover letter* or **het sollicitatiegesprek** *job interview* (**de sollicitatie** *job application*), common terms include **de competentie** *skill, competence* and **de vaardigheid** *proficiency, mastery, professional aptitude*. Note that the suffix **-heid** is used to turn an adjective into a noun. The plural of a noun ending in **-heid** is formed with **-heden**: **de vaardigheden** *skills, capabilities*.

As seen in the dialogue, Dutch people don't necessarily use the formal *you* (**u**) in job interviews. This can depend on the type of job and the sector, or in some cases, on the person conducting the interview. In the dialogue, the context is informal, between a student looking for a job in the media sector and a professional working in a new organization such as a start-up.

SOME VOCABULARY FOR JOB HUNTING

Some useful terms include: **de advertentie** *advertisement*; **de vacature** *vacancy, opening, job post*; **solliciteren naar een functie van** *to apply for a post of*; **solliciteren bij een bedrijf** *to apply to a company*; **solliciteren op een vacature** *to apply for an opening*; **de opleiding** *training*; **stage lopen** *to do an internship/work placement*; **de ervaring** *experience*; **geschikt** *suitable*; **het beroep** *profession*; **de baan** *job, position*; **beschikbaar zijn** *to be available*.

▲ CONJUGATION
SOME COMMON IRREGULAR VERBS IN THE PRESENT TENSE: *WILLEN* TO WANT, *KUNNEN* CAN, *MOGEN* MAY

The present tense conjugation of the verb **willen** *to want, to wish* is very simple, as its conjugated form in the singular (*I, you, he, she*) is **wil** and its conjugated form in the plural (*we, they*) is **willen**. But you might see an optional form in the second-person singular that ends in **-t**: **je wilt** *you want* (informal) or **u wilt** *you want* (formal).

When used with another verb, **willen** is considered a modal verb. These are auxiliary verbs used with an infinitive to express an opinion, a possibility, an ability, an obligation or, as with **willen**, a desire or a wish:
Ik wil je even voorstellen ... *I just want to introduce you ...*
Ik wil haar uitnodigen ... *I want to invite her ...*
Waarom wil je dat weten? *Why do you want to know that?*

To soften a request, **willen** is often used with **graag** *gladly*:
Ik wil graag pinnen. *I would like to pay with a card.* ('I want gladly to-pay ...')

The verb **kunnen** *to be able to, can* is another modal verb. It is used with another verb to convey a possibility or an ability. Its singular present tense (*I, you, he, she, it*) is **kan** and its plural (*we, they*) is **kunnen**. There is also an optional form in the second-person singular: **je kunt** *you can* (informal) or **u kunt** *you can* (formal). (The **-t** is dropped when the subject and verb are inverted.)
(...) kan ik goed overweg met (...) *I can easily cope with*
Wanneer kun je beginnen? *When can you begin?*

The modal verb **mogen** *to have permission to, may* is used to ask for authorization. The singular present tense is **mag**, and the plural present tense is **mogen**.

Mogen we de kaart? *May we have the menu?*

Mag ik je iets vragen? *May I ask you something?*

◆ GRAMMAR
THE DIFFERENCE BETWEEN *WANT* AND *OMDAT* BECAUSE

• **want** *because* is a coordinating conjunction that explains a previous statement. The conjugated verb is in the second position: subject – verb – object.

• **omdat** *because* is a subordinating conjunction. Its use inverts the word order to subject – object – verb (it can also start a sentence, unlike **want**):

Hij heeft geen baan, want hij heeft geen ervaring.

He has no job because he has no experience.

Hij heeft geen baan, omdat hij geen ervaring heeft.

He has no job ('because he no experience has').

SUBORDINATE CLAUSES

A subordinating conjunction links a dependent clause to an independent clause to add more information to the sentence's main idea. A few common subordinating conjunctions include **als** *if*, *when*, *as*; **dat** *that*; **hoewel** *although*, *however*; **sinds** *since*; **terwijl** *while*; **toen** *then*, *when*; **zodat** *so that, in order to*. In Dutch, in a subordinate clause, the word order is subject – object – verb, with the subject directly after the conjunction and the conjugated verb at the end of the clause:

Als ik het goed begrijp ... ('If I it good understand')

Als je meer koorts krijgt ... ('If you more fever get')

Denk je niet dat dat een probleem is? ('Think you not that that a problem is?')

Wat fijn dat jullie er allemaal zijn! ('How nice that you there all are!')

Hoewel je sterk bent ... ('However you strong are').

⬡ EXERCISES

1. COMPLETE THE SENTENCES WITH THE CORRECT MODAL VERB IN THE CORRECT FORM.

a. .... je goed overweg met computers?

b. Ze .... niet wachten en .... meteen beginnen.

c. .... ik de kaart?

d. We .... graag hier blijven.

● VOCABULARY

het sollicitatiegesprek
  job interview
de sollicitatiebrief *cover letter*
solliciteren naar een functie van
  to apply for the post of
solliciteren bij een bedrijf *to apply*
  to a company
solliciteren op een vacature
  to apply for a job opening
de vacature *vacancy, opening*
administratief *administrative*
de medewerker / de
  medewerkster *employee* (m./f.)
het cv *CV*
denken *to think, to consider*
het probleem *problem*
studeren *to study*
de communicatiewetenschappen
  media and communications
de wetenschap *science*
ondanks *despite*
het feit *fact*
weinig *little*
de ervaring *experience*
de werkervaring *work experience*
beschikken over *to have at one's*
  disposal, to have access to
interessant *interesting*
de competentie *competence*
de baan *job, position*
omdat *because*
innoverend *innovative*
de organisatie *organization*
geschikt *suitable*
de kandidaat / de kandidate
  candidate (m./f.)
begrijpen *to understand*

de webredacteur / de
  webredactrice *web editor* (m./f.)
assisteren *to assist*
sociaal vaardig *good social skills*
sociaal *social*
vaardig *accomplished, skilful*
de vaardigheid *profiency, mastery,*
  aptitude
bovendien *in addition, moreover*
overweg kunnen met *to be able to*
  use, to be able to handle
de software *software*
de tekstverwerker
  word processing
al *even if, though*
veel *a lot, much*
toch *still, nevertheless*
aannemen *to hire, to take on*
meteen *immediately*
helemaal *completely, totally*
helemaal geen *absolutely no*
helemaal niet *absolutely not,*
  not at all
de advertentie *advertisement*
de opleiding *training*
stage lopen *to do an internship/*
  work placement
het beroep *profession*
beschikbaar zijn *to be available*
als *if, when*
hoewel *although, however*
sinds *since*
terwijl *while*
toen *then, when*
zodat *so that, in order to*
blij *happy, glad*

2. COMPLETE THE SENTENCES WITH EITHER *WANT* OR *OMDAT*.

a. Ze neemt een glas wijn .... ze heeft dorst.

b. Hij eet een broodje .... hij honger heeft.

3. TRANSLATE THESE SENTENCES INTO DUTCH.

a. He has absolutely no work experience.

→ ....

b. I am not available at the moment.

→ ....

c. She is going to apply for an interesting job opening.

→ ....

4. COMPLETE THESE SENTENCES WITH THE MOST SUITABLE SUBORDINATING CONJUNCTION.

a. Je bent sociaal heel vaardig .... ik het goed begrijp.

b. Waarom studeer je communicatiewetenschappen? .... ik dat een leuke studie vind!

c. .... hij met zijn werk begint, drinkt hij eerst een kop koffie.

d. .... ze geen werkervaring heeft, neemt hij haar toch aan.

e. Ze zijn blij (*glad*) .... ze niet meer iedere ochtend in de file staan.

5. LISTEN TO THE AUDIO TO COMPLETE EACH SENTENCE. THEN READ THE SENTENCES OUT LOUD AND LISTEN TO THE AUDIO AGAIN TO CHECK YOUR ANSWERS.

🔊 **22**

a. Ik .... over .... baan.

b. Jullie .... goed ....!

c. Hij is .... want hij is ....

d. Wat .... is ....!

e. Ik ....

f. Het is ....

21.
AT THE OFFICE

OP KANTOOR

<table>
<tr><td>

AIMS

</td><td>

TOPICS

</td></tr>
<tr><td>

- **SHOWING SOMEONE AROUND AN OFFICE**

- **FINDING YOUR WAY AROUND A BUILDING**

- **DESCRIBING VARIOUS OFFICE TASKS**

- **EXPRESSING AN IDEA**

</td><td>

- **VERBS OF POSITION**

- **SOME USEFUL OFFICE VOCABULARY**

- **THE MONTHS OF THE YEAR**

- **FORMING THE FEMININE OF NOUNS**

- *ER* **THERE + NUMBER**

- **THE MODAL VERBS *MOETEN* TO HAVE TO (MUST) AND *HOEVEN* TO NEED TO**

</td></tr>
</table>

AT THE OFFICE

Mr Jansen: You must be the new assistant (f.). Our offices are found *(find themselves)* on the first floor.

This is your desk. Here in this cupboard are *(lie)* envelopes, pens and pencils. Rolls of tape and paperclips are *(sit)* in this box. Over there by the copier is *(lies the)* paper, and the ink cartridges are *(lie)* next to the printer.

Ms van Dijk: Where is *(stands)* the printer?

Mr Jansen: There is *(stands there)* one next to your desk lamp, but we try to print as little as possible *(so little possible to print)*. You must save *(store)* the emails that you receive and send on a USB flash drive. So you don't need to keep *(compile)* a paper file. In January and June, we order all the office supplies.

Good, now we just have *(have we just still but)* to wait for the new boss (m.).

Ms van Dijk: Hm, I believe that you are mistaken *(you yourself err)*: I am the new boss (f.)!

Meneer Jansen: U moet de nieuwe assistente zijn. Onze kantoren bevinden zich op de eerste verdieping.

Dit is uw bureau. Hier in deze kast liggen enveloppen, pennen en potloden. Rolletjes plakband en paperclips zitten in die doos. Daar bij de kopieermachine ligt het papier en de inktpatronen liggen naast de printer.

Mevrouw van Dijk: Waar staat de printer?

Meneer Jansen: Er staat er één naast uw bureaulamp, maar we proberen zo min mogelijk te printen. U moet de mails die u binnenkrijgt en verzendt, op een USB-stick opslaan. U hoeft dus geen papieren dossier samen te stellen. In januari en juni bestellen we alle kantoorbenodigdheden.

Goed, nu hoeven we alleen nog maar te wachten op de nieuwe baas.

Mevrouw van Dijk: Eh, ik geloof dat u zich vergist: ik ben de nieuwe bazin!

UNDERSTANDING THE DIALOGUE

→ **Onze kantoren bevinden zich ...** *Our offices are found ...* The verb **zich bevinden** *to be found* ('itself to find') is a slightly formal register. Note that this is a reflexive verb. These are verbs that include a pronoun (here, the third-person **zich**) to indicate that the subject is also the object of the action of the verb. We'll come back to this in lesson 24.

→ **Dit is uw bureau.** *This is your desk.* The noun **het bureau** can mean *desk* or *office*. The noun **het kantoor** *office* refers only to the place.

→ **zitten in die doos** ('sit in this box'); **ligt het papier** ('lies the paper'); **staat de printer** ('stands the printer'). See the next section on verbs of position.

→ **Er staat er één ...** *There is one ...* ('there stands there one'). See the 'Grammar' section for more about the construction **er** + verb + **er** + number.

→ Note the useful expression **zo min mogelijk** as *little as possible*.

→ **U hoeft dus geen papieren dossier samen te stellen.** ('You need so no paper file together to put'). The verb **hoeven** *to need to* is very often used with a negative in the sense of *don't have to*. More on this in the 'Grammar' section.

→ In the comment **nu hoeven we alleen nog maar te wachten** ('now have we just still but to wait'), **alleen nog maar** means *only, just*.

→ **dat u zich vergist** *that you are mistaken* ('you yourself err'): **zich vergissen** *to be mistaken* is another example of a reflexive verb.

VERBS OF POSITION

In English, to say where something is located, we just use *to be*. However, in Dutch, the verb describes the position of the object: **staan** *to be standing*, **liggen** *to be lying*, **hangen** *to be hanging* or **zitten** *to be sitting*.

• **staan** *to stand* conveys a vertical position, but is also used for things that are written or printed, as well as for objects on wheels:
De lamp staat op het bureau. *The lamp is on the desk.*
De auto staat buiten. *The car is outside.*

• **liggen** *to lie* conveys a horizontal position, but is also used for round objects and objects whose functional position is horizontal:
De enveloppen liggen in de kast. *The envelopes are in the cupboard.*
De bloemkool ligt op tafel. *The cauliflower is on the table.*

• **hangen** *to hang* is used for anything hanging:
De lamp hangt aan de muur. *The lamp is mounted on the wall.*

190

• **zitten** *to sit* is used for anything sitting, as well as for objects whose position is not obvious to describe or are found in a small space:

De paperclips zitten in de doos. *The paperclips are in the box.*
De nietjes zitten in de nietmachine. *The staples are in the stapler.*

SOME OFFICE VOCABULARY

Here are some useful computer-associated terms: **het scherm** *screen, display*; **het toetsenbord** *keyboard*; **de muis** *mouse*; **de enter-toets** *enter key*; **de spatiebalk** *space bar*; **de foutmelding** *error message*; **wissen** *to delete*; **kopiëren** *to copy*; **knippen** *to cut*; **plakken** *to paste*; **dubbel klikken** *to double-click*; **scannen** *to scan*; **de cursor** *cursor*; **de delete-toets** *delete key*; **de startpagina** *home page*; **downloaden** *to download*; **de bijlage** *attachment*; **het apenstaartje** '*at*' *sign @* (literally, 'monkey's-tail' in the diminutive: **de aap** *monkey*, **de apen** *monkeys*, **de staart** *tail*).

THE MONTHS OF THE YEAR

Note that months are not capitalized in Dutch: **januari** *January*; **februari** *February*; **maart** *March*; **april** *April*; **mei** *May*; **juni** *June*; **juli** *July*; **augustus** *August*; **september** *September*; **oktober** *October*; **november** *November*; **december** *December*.

◆ GRAMMAR
THE FEMININE FORM OF NOUNS

Certain nouns that describe a person's profession or status have a masculine and a feminine form, depending on the person's gender. In most cases, the feminine form simply adds a final **-e** to the masculine form. This occurs, for example, with loanwords from another language in which the final syllable is stressed:

de assis<u>tent</u>* *assistant* (m.) → **de assis<u>tent</u>e** *assistant* (f.)
de stu<u>dent</u> *student* (m.) → **de stu<u>dent</u>e** *student* (f.)

* The underlined syllable receives the stress when spoken.

However, some nouns form the feminine with the suffixes **-ster**, **-ice**, **-es** or **-in**. Try to memorize the examples of this as you come across them. The suffixes **-es** and **-in** receive the stress when speaking:

de <u>werk</u>nemer *employee* (m.) → **de <u>werk</u>neemster** *employee* (f.)
de redac<u>teur</u> *editor* (m.) → **de redac<u>tr</u>ice** *editor* (f.)

de <u>zanger</u> *singer* (m.) → **de zanger<u>es</u>** *singer* (f.)

de <u>boer</u> *farmer* (m.) → **de boer<u>in</u>** *farmer* (f.)

ER THERE + NUMBER

In lesson 19, we saw **er** *there* + preposition used to refer to an object or concept not explicitly named in the sentence (often referring to something previously mentioned). We see something similar with **er** + verb + **er** + number:

de printer *printer* → **Er staat** er **één op uw bureau.** *There's one on your desk.*

Hoeveel dozen **zijn er?** *How many boxes are there?* → **Er zijn** er **vijf.** *There are five.*

toetsen *keys* → **Ik ken** er **tien.** *I know ten of them.* ('I know there ten.')

THE MODAL VERBS *MOETEN* TO HAVE TO (MUST) AND *HOEVEN* TO NEED TO

• The modal verb **moeten** *to have to, must* conveys an obligation, a necessity or a duty. Remember that modal verbs are auxiliary verbs (which are conjugated) that are used with another verb (in the infinitive). The singular present tense conjugation (*I, you, he, she, it*) is **moet**, and the plural (*we, they*) is **moeten**:

U moet de nieuwe assistente zijn. *You must be the new assistant.*

U moet de mails opslaan. *You have to archive emails.*

• The verb **hoeven** *to need to* has a similar meaning. Most of the time it is used in the negative to convey what doesn't have to be done or what isn't needed. It has a regular present tense conjugation:

U hoeft geen dossier samen te stellen. *You don't have to compile a file.*

Je hoeft niet meer te komen. *You don't need to come anymore.*

⬡ EXERCISES

1. FILL IN THE SENTENCES WITH THE CORRECT VERB OF POSITION.

a. Het bureau .... in de woonkamer.

b. De fietsen .... voor het huis.

c. Het dossier .... op de grond.

d. De lamp .... aan de muur.

e. De delete-toets .... op het toetsenbord.

● VOCABULARY

zich bevinden *to be found/located*
zich *itself, himself, herself, oneself, themselves*
liggen *to lie, to be lying*
zitten *to sit, to be sitting*
hangen *to hang, to be hanging*
de verdieping *floor, storey*
het bureau *desk, office*
de envelop *envelope*
de pen *pen*
het potlood *pencil*
de rol *roll*
het plakband *sellotape, scotch tape*
de paperclip *paperclip*
de doos *box* (**de dozen** *boxes*)
de kopieermachine *photocopier*
het papier *paper*
papieren *paper (adj.), made of paper*
het inktpatroon *ink cartridge*
naast *next to*
de printer *printer*
printen *to print*
de bureaulamp *desk lamp*
proberen *to try*
zo min mogelijk *as little as possible*
binnenkrijgen *to receive*
verzenden *to send*
opslaan *to store, to archive*
samenstellen *to compile, to put together*
hoeven *to need to*
het dossier *file*
de kantoorbenodigdheden *office supplies*
alleen nog maar *only*
wachten op *to wait for*
de baas / de bazin *boss* (m./f.)

geloven *to believe*
zich vergissen *to be mistaken*
het nietje *staple*
de nietmachine *stapler*
het scherm *screen, display*
het toetsenbord *keyboard*
de muis *mouse*
de enter-toets *enter key*
de spatiebalk *space bar*
de foutmelding *error message*
wissen *to delete*
kopiëren *to copy*
knippen *to cut*
plakken *to paste*
dubbel klikken *to double-click*
scannen *to scan*
de cursor *cursor*
de delete-toets *delete key*
de startpagina *home page*
downloaden *to download*
de bijlage *attachment*
het apenstaartje *'at' sign, @*
de USB-stick *USB flash drive*
januari (de) *January*
februari (de) *February*
maart (de) *March*
april (de) *April*
mei (de) *May*
juni (de) *June*
juli (de) *July*
augustus (de) *August*
september (de) *September*
oktober (de) *October*
november (de) *November*
december (de) *December*
de student / de studente *student* (m./f.) (university)
de zanger / de zangeres *singer* (m./f.)

2. REWRITE THE SENTENCES USING *ER* + NUMBER FOLLOWING THE EXAMPLE.

Example: Ze geeft me twee peren. → Ze geeft me er twee.

a. Ik neem geen risico's.
→ ....

b. Er staan drie fietsen in de berging.
→ ....

c. We hebben vijf formulieren nodig.
→ ....

d. Er liggen twee formulieren op tafel.
→ ....

e. Hij kent vier bakkers.
→ ....

3. WRITE THE FEMININE FORMS OF THESE NOUNS, USING A DICTIONARY TO HELP YOU. THEN LISTEN TO THE AUDIO AND REPEAT THEM OUT LOUD.

23

a. de redacteur → ....

b. de kandidaat → ....

c. de baas → ....

d. de medewerker → ....

e. de vriend → ....

f. de docent → ....

g. de leerling → ....

h. de vertaler → ....

i. de koning → ....

j. de student → ....

4. LISTEN TO THE AUDIO AND THEN COMPLETE THESE SENTENCES.

23

a. We .... een ....

b. Het is te laat! Je ....te komen.

c. Je moet eerst .... en dan .... en ....

d. Hij bestelt .... in .... en ....

e. .... je niet wat .... is?

f. Hoe spel je ...., ... en ....?

194

IV

FREE

TIME

22.
HOLIDAYS

DE FEESTDAGEN

AIMS	TOPICS

- TALKING ABOUT WINTER HOLIDAYS
- WISHING SOMEONE A HAPPY BIRTHDAY OR HOLIDAY
- OFFERING GIFTS AND SAYING THANK YOU

- *HEEL* AND *ERG* VERY
- COMPOUND ADJECTIVES
- THE PRONOUN *HET* IT
- MORE ON THE DIMINUTIVE

SAINT NICHOLAS DAY

Bart: Ah, at last, Saint Nicholas Day *(little-package-evening)*! Oh, come and look! There are so many packages in front of the door.

Johanna: I just have to put on my glasses. Well, there are really a lot *(it are there very very many)*. So open them, but first recite the little poem and sing a little Saint Nicholas song, right?

Bart: Look, a watch. And a book and a ball …

Johanna: You'll get *(become)* spoiled. Thank the saint quickly!

Bart: Thank you very much, Saint Nicholas!

Johanna: Oh look, for me a game of Ludo *(a human-vex-you-not game)*! Thank you so much, Saint Nicholas!

Bart: And tonight it's a double celebration: Happy Birthday *(congratulations with your birthday)*! **Here's your little gift.**

Johanna: Oh, a jumper! It goes well with my trousers, and it's nice and warm *(This fits good with my long trousers and it is nicely warm)*.

Bart: Don't you want to put it on *(Put you it not on)*? It is after all five degrees below zero.

Johanna: Good idea, because I'm freezing *(I have it ice-cold)*.

<u>Bart</u>: Ha, eindelijk pakjesavond! O, kom 's kijken! Er staan zoveel pakjes voor de deur.

<u>Johanna</u>: Ik moet even m'n bril opzetten. Nou, het zijn er heel erg veel. Maak ze maar open, maar wel eerst het gedichtje voorlezen en een sinterklaasliedje zingen, hè.

<u>Bart</u>: Kijk, een horloge. En een boek en een bal…

<u>Johanna</u>: Je wordt verwend. Bedank de Sint maar snel!

<u>Bart</u>: Dank je wel Sinterklaas!

<u>Johanna</u>: O kijk, voor mij een mens-erger-je-niet spel! Dank je wel Sinterklaas!

<u>Bart</u>: En vanavond is het dubbel feest: gefeliciteerd met je verjaardag! Alsjeblieft, je cadeautje.

<u>Johanna</u>: O, een trui! Die past goed bij m'n lange broek en hij is lekker warm.

<u>Bart</u>: Trek je hem niet aan? Het is tenslotte vijf graden onder nul.

<u>Johanna</u>: Goed idee, want ik heb het ijskoud.

■ UNDERSTANDING THE DIALOGUE

→ **Ha, eindelijk pakjesavond!** *Ah, at last, Saint Nicholas Day!* The name **de pakjesavond** ('little package evening') refers to the fact that people give gifts on the eve of Saint Nicholas Day (see the next section).

→ **m'n bril opzetten** *to put on my glasses.* Note that **de bril** *pair of glasses, spectacles* is singular in Dutch. The verb **opzetten** *to put on* is used specifically for glasses and hats.

→ **het gedichtje voorlezen** *to recite the little poem.* The separable-prefix verb **voorlezen** *to read out loud, to recite* contains the verb **lezen** *to read.*

→ **Bedank de Sint maar snel!** ('Thank the Saint but quickly!') invites the person who receives the present to say loudly: **Dank je wel Sinterklaas!** *Thank you very much, Saint Nicholas!* It's a tradition.

→ **het mens-erger-je-niet spel** *Ludo* ('the human-vex-you-not game'). The name of this game contains **het mens** *person, human, individual*, the negation **niet** *not* and the verb **ergeren** *to irritate, to vex, to exasperate, to annoy.*

→ Remember the expression **Gefeliciteerd (met je/uw verjaardag)!** *Happy Birthday!* ('Congratulations with your birthday!')

→ **en hij is lekker warm** *and it is nice and warm*; **Trek je hem niet aan?** *Don't you want to put it on?* Note the masculine pronouns **hij** and **hem** used here to refer to the jumper (**de trui**), in this case meaning *it.* The separable-prefix verb **aantrekken** *to put on* is used for clothes.

→ **Ik heb het ijskoud.** *I'm freezing.* As with describing hunger and thirst, in Dutch **hebben** is used to say you're cold.

DUTCH HOLIDAYS

In the Netherlands, **Sinterklaas** (or **pakjesavond**) *Saint Nicholas Day* is celebrated on the eve of 6 December. It's the occasion for singing Saint Nicholas songs: in the dialogue, **O, kom 's kijken!** *Oh, come and look!* alludes to one of them: **O kom er eens kijken wat ik in m'n schoentje vind, alles gekregen van die goede Sint.** *Oh come have a look at what I found* ('find') *in my shoe, all received from the good Saint.*

In the evening, people offer each other gifts, along with a humorous little poem, **het sinterklaasgedicht** *Saint Nicholas poem*, as well as **de surprise** *surprise presents*, which are often handmade and have something to do with the real gift.

In fact, Saint Nicholas is more popular than Santa Claus, the occasion for a family celebration for all ages. Legend has it that Saint Nicholas arrives in the country from

Spain a few weeks before the holiday, when Dutch children can put out a *shoe* (**de schoen**) – traditionally a clog – in front of the *chimney* (**de schoorsteen**) so that Saint Nicholas can put some little treats inside when he visits during the night. In fact, 6 December was the day of his death, and this marks the end of the festivities.

Another popular holiday is one celebrated around the world: 31 December or New Year's Eve. But in Dutch, this is known as **de oudejaarsavond** ('old year's evening'). Like revellers all over the planet, at midnight Dutch people send off the old year and bring in the new with *fireworks* (**het vuurwerk**), wishing each other **Gelukkig nieuwjaar!** *Happy New Year!*

◆ GRAMMAR
HEEL AND *ERG* VERY

The adverbs **heel** and **erg** can both mean *very*:
heel veel / erg veel *a lot, very many*
Hij is heel/erg moe. *He is very tired.*

They can be used together, with **heel** emphasizing **erg** *very*:
heel erg veel *really a lot, very very much*
Het zijn er heel erg veel! *There are really a lot!*
Hij is heel erg moe. *He is completely exhausted.*

COMPOUND ADJECTIVES

We've already seen a number of compound nouns, made up of more than one noun, but adjectives can also be used together to form compound words:
ijskoud *ice cold*
doodstil *dead calm, deathly quiet*
dolblij ('delirious-happy') *overjoyed*
peperduur ('pepper-dear') *extremely expensive*

THE PRONOUN *HET* IT

The pronoun **het** *it* is used to refer to singular neuter nouns:
Het pakje/biertje staat op tafel. *The package/beer is on the table.* →
Het staat op tafel. *It is on the table.*

It is also used as an impersonal pronoun in certain contexts:

Het is koud/warm. *It is cold/warm.*

Het is vijf graden onder nul. *It is five degrees below zero.*

Ik heb het ijskoud. *I'm freezing.* ('I have it ice-cold.')

THE DIMINUTIVE

As we've seen, the diminutive is very frequent in Dutch. It can convey a range of meanings: to show affinity with or affection for something (**het gedichtje** *poem*; **het sinterklaasliedje** *Saint Nicholas song*), soften a request, minimize something or indicate a small size. In the last case, it can be preceded by **klein** *small*:

Mag ik een klein stukje kaas? *May I have a small piece of cheese?*

Ik wil graag een klein beetje water. *I'd like a little bit of water.*

Wat een schattig klein hondje! *What a cute little doggy!*

It is also used to quantify an uncountable substance, which allows it to be employed as a countable or plural noun: **Ze nemen drie ijsjes.** *They take three ice creams.*

To form the diminutive, most of the time the suffix **-je** is added to the end of the noun. But certain nouns take the suffixes **-tje**, **-etje**, **-kje** or **-pje**:

bos → **bosje** *small bouquet*

mobiel → **mobieltje** *mobile/cell (phone)*

spel → **spelletje** *little game*

koning → **koninkje** *little king* (note that the **-g** in the base noun disappears)

boom → **boompje** *little tree*

While there are rules about how to form the diminutive of different nouns, the simplest thing is to try to learn them as you come across them: for example, **pakje** *little package, gift* in the dialogue of this lesson.

● EXERCISES

1. LINK THE FIRST PART OF THE WORD TO THE SECOND.

a. peper •   • 1. stil

b. ijs •   • 2. blij

c. dood •   • 3. duur

d. dol •   • 4. koud

● VOCABULARY

de sint / Sinterklaas
  saint / Saint Nicholas
de pakjesavond *Saint Nicholas Eve*
  ('little packages evening')
het pak *package*
het cadeau *gift, present*
eindelijk *at last, finally*
de deur *door*
de bril *glasses, spectacles* (singular)
opzetten *to put on* (glasses, hat)
aantrekken *to put on* (clothes)
openmaken *to open*
voorlezen *to recite, to read out loud*
het sinterklaasgedicht *Saint*
  Nicholas poem
het gedicht *poem*
het sinterklaasliedje *Saint*
  Nicholas song
het lied *song*
zingen *to sing*
het horloge *watch*
het boek *book*
de bal *ball*
verwend worden *to become*
  spoiled
bedanken *to thank*
het mens-erger-je-niet spel *Ludo*
het mens *person, human,*
  individual
zich ergeren *to get annoyed,*
  to get irritated, to be vexed
het spel *game*
dubbel *double*
het feest *party, celebration*
Gefeliciteerd! *Congratulations!*
Gefeliciteerd met je/uw
  verjaardag! *Happy Birthday!*
de verjaardag *birthday*
de trui *jumper, sweater*

die *it*
het *it*
passen bij *to go with, to suit*
de lange broek *trousers* (singular)
lekker *nice, pleasant*
warm *warm*
tenslotte *after all*
onder *under, below*
de nul *zero*
ijskoud *ice cold*
het ijs *ice*
het ijsje *ice cream*
wat *what*
de schoen *shoe* (**de schoenen**
  shoes)
de surprise *surprise, present*
de schoorsteen *chimney*
de oudejaarsavond *New Year's Eve*
het vuurwerk *firework*
Gelukkig nieuwjaar!
  Happy New Year!
gelukkig *happy*
het nieuwjaar *new year*
zoveel *so much, so many*
heel veel / erg veel *very many*
heel erg *really, extremely*
heel erg veel *really a lot, very much*
doodstil *dead calm, deathly quiet*
dood *dead*
de dood *death*
stil *silent, quiet*
dolblij *overjoyed*
peperduur *extremely expensive*
de boom *tree*

2. TURN THESE NOUNS INTO DIMINUTIVES.

a. bier → ....

b. ui → ....

c. vis → ....

d. mobiel → ....

e. bos → ....

f. kroket → ....

g. kwartier → ....

h. patat → ....

i. kaasplank → ....

j. stuk → ....

k. rol → ....

l. gedicht → ....

3. TRANSLATE THESE SENTENCES INTO DUTCH.

a. Just thank her quickly!

→ ....

b. There are really a lot of packages in front of the door.

→ ....

c. Happy Birthday!

→ ....

d. It is seven degrees below zero and I'm freezing.

→ ....

24

4. LISTEN TO THE AUDIO AND SELECT *WAAR* IF IT MATCHES THE SENTENCE OR *NIET WAAR* IF IT DOESN'T. THEN READ EACH SENTENCE OUT LOUD AND LISTEN TO THE AUDIO AGAIN.

	WAAR	NIET WAAR
a. Hij moet even z'n bril opzetten.		
b. Kijk, een horloge, een spelletje en een bal!		
c. Die lange broek past goed bij m'n trui.		
d. Ze worden verwend.		
e. We lezen eerst het gedichtje voor.		

23.
HOBBIES

DE HOBBY'S

AIMS	TOPICS
• **TALKING ABOUT YOUR FREE TIME AND HOBBIES** • **DISCUSSING DIFFERENT SPORTS** • **SPECIFYING DIFFERENT MUSICAL INSTRUMENTS** • **EXPRESSING AGREEMENT**	• **TIME SEQUENCES** • **THE COMPARATIVE AND SUPERLATIVE** • **COMPOUND WORDS** • **THE PRESENT PARTICIPLE (-ING VERBS)**

HOBBIES

Beja: What are doing on your day off *(free day)* tomorrow?

Alfred: First thing in *(In the beginning of)* the morning I'm going to play *(go I to the)* football, because nothing's more fun *(I find nothing funner)* than that! Mid-morning, I'm taking my son to go horse riding *(Halfway of morning bring I my little-son to horse-ride)*, and last thing in the morning I'll go back *(at the end go I again back)* to the football pitch.

Beja: I don't understand why you like that so much *(that that you so amuses)*. These days you are almost required to do sport, but I get more enjoyment from, for example *(I entertain myself more with for-example the)*, listening to music or playing the piano.

Alfred: Playing sports is better for your health than sitting on the sofa or playing an instrument.

Beja: I agree with you on that *(That am I with you agreed)*, but I get my exercise *(movement)* from my weekly walk in the park.

Alfred: Ha ha, and I get mine from walking back and forth *(I with the away and again to-walk)* in the football stands!

<u>Beja</u>: Wat doe jij op je vrije dag morgen?

<u>Alfred</u>: In het begin van de morgen ga ik naar het voetbal, want ik vind niks leuker dan dat! Halverwege de ochtend breng ik m'n zoontje naar paardrijden en aan het einde ga ik weer terug naar het voetbalveld.

<u>Beja</u>: Ik begrijp niet dat dat je zo amuseert. Tegenwoordig ben je bijna verplicht om aan sport te doen, maar ik vermaak me meer met bijvoorbeeld het luisteren naar muziek of met piano spelen.

<u>Alfred</u>: Sporten is beter voor je gezondheid dan op de bank zitten of een instrument bespelen.

<u>Beja</u>: Dat ben ik met je eens, maar m'n beweging krijg ik door m'n wekelijkse wandeling in het park.

<u>Alfred</u>: Ha ha, en ik met het heen en weer lopen op de voetbaltribune!

■ UNDERSTANDING THE DIALOGUE

→ **Wat doe jij morgen?** *What are you doing tomorrow?* **In het begin van de morgen …** *First thing in the morning …*. Note that in Dutch you describe the part of the day by saying 'in the beginning of', 'middle of' or 'end of'. Also, be careful not to confuse the time adverb **morgen** *tomorrow* with the noun **de morgen** *morning*.

→ **ik vind niks leuker dan dat** *nothing's more fun than that* ('I find nothing funner than that'): in everyday speech, **niks** is often used instead of **niets** *nothing*. In this phrase, **leuker** *more fun* is the comparative of **leuk** *fun*. See the 'Grammar' section for more on forming the comparative and superlative.

→ In Dutch, you say **pianospelen** *to play the piano* and **spelen** *to play a game or sport*, but **een instrument bespelen** *to play an instrument*.

→ **Dat ben ik met je eens.** *I agree with you on that.* ('That am I with you agreed.') The expression is **het eens zijn met iemand** *to agree with someone* or **het niet eens zijn met iemand** *not to agree with someone*.

→ **het heen en weer lopen** *walking back and forth* ('the away and again to-walk'). As we've mentioned, in Dutch the infinitive sometimes translates to an English *-ing* verb. The expression **heen en weer** means *back and forth*.

POPULAR HOBBIES

Sports are a common leisure activity in the Netherlands. One of the most popular sports to watch and to play is **het voetbal** *football* (i.e. soccer), but other frequently practised activities are **de fitness** *fitness*, **het tennis** *tennis*, **het vissen** *fishing*, **het golf** *golf*, **de gymnastiek** *calisthenics*, **het hockey** *hockey*, **het paardrijden** *horse riding*, **de atletiek** *athletics*, **het zwemmen** *swimming* and **het volleybal** *volleyball*.

In terms of musical instruments, among the most commonly played are: **de piano** *the piano*, **het drumstel** *the drums*, **de fluit** *the flute*, **de gitaar** *the guitar*, **de viool** *the violin*, **de mondharmonica** *the harmonica*, **de saxofoon** *the saxophone*, **de klarinet** *the clarinet* and **de trompet** *the trumpet*.

◆ GRAMMAR
CONVEYING TIME SEQUENCES

To talk about the order in which something happens, some useful words and phrases are: **in/aan het begin** *in the beginning*; **in het midden**, **halverwege** *in the middle,* *halfway*; **aan het einde** *at the end*; **eerst** *first*; **dan** *then*; **vervolgens** *subsequently*; **tot slot** *finally, lastly*; **ten eerste** *firstly, in the first place*; **ten tweede** *secondly, in the second place*; **ten slotte** *finally, in conclusion*. For a reminder on forming ordinal numbers, check back to lesson 12.

THE COMPARATIVE AND SUPERLATIVE

We first looked at how to form the comparative (to express that something is *more* or *less*) in lesson 11: you just add the ending **-er/-der** to the adjective. If you want to say what something is more or less than, you introduce this with **dan** *than*:

Ik vind niks leuker dan dat. *Nothing's funnier than that.*
Sporten is beter voor je gezondheid dan op de bank zitten.
Playing sports is better for your health than sitting on the sofa.

To say *as ... as* (a comparison of equality), you use the construction **net zo** or **even** + adjective + **als** *as ... as*:

Piano spelen is net zo/even leuk als gitaar spelen.
Playing the piano is as fun as playing the guitar.
Hij is net zo/even groot als ik.* *He is as tall as I (am).*
* Here, **ben** *am* is implied though not stated: **Hij is even groot als ik ben.**

The negative form is **niet zo** + adjective + **als** *not as ... as*:
Hij is niet zo groot als ik. *He is not as tall as I (am).*

The superlative (to express that something is *the most*) is formed by adding the ending **-st** to the adjective, or if the adjective already ends in an **-s**, you just add a **-t**:
groot *large* → **grootst** *largest*
klein *small* → **kleinst** *smallest*
vers *fresh* → **verst** *freshest*

As in English, there are a few very common adjectives that have an irregular comparative and superlative form:
goed *good* → **beter** *better* → **best** *best*
graag *gladly* → **liever** *preferably* → **liefst** *most preferably*
veel *much* → **meer** *more* → **meest** *most*
weinig *little, few* → **minder** *less, fewer* → **minst** *least, fewest*

COMPOUND WORDS

Compound words made up of two or three nouns are common in Dutch. It is also possible to form compound words with an adjective, a number or a verb. Typically, the word stress falls on the first word, but the last word in the construction determines whether it is a common or neuter noun:

de televisie *television* + **het programma** *programme* → **het televisieprogramma** *televison programme*

oud *old* + **het jaar** *year* + **de avond** *evening* → **de oudejaarsavond** *New Year's Eve*

twee *two* + **de kamer** *room* + **de woning** *dwelling* → **de tweekamerwoning** *two-room flat*

roken *to smoke* + **de worst** *sausage* → **de rookworst** *smoked sausage*

 ## CONJUGATION
THE PRESENT PARTICIPLE

In English, the present participle is the form of the verb ending in *-ing*. It is used to convey an ongoing or continuous action. In Dutch, the present participle is usually formed by adding a final **-d** to the infinitive:

lopen *to walk* → **lopend** *walking*

helpen *to help* → **helpend** *helping*

The present participle can be used with another verb to show that the two actions are happening at the same time:

Hij komt het kantoor lachend binnen. *He comes into the office laughing.*

It can also function as an adjective: **een helpende hand** *a helping hand*; **een rijdende trein** *a moving* ('riding') *train*.

However, it is used much less frequently in Dutch than in English. Most of the time what would be expressed in English with an *-ing* verb is constructed in another way in Dutch: for example, with a preposition followed by a verb functioning as a noun (a verbal noun), or **door te** + infinitive:

Ik vermaak me met het luisteren naar muziek. *I enjoy listening to music.* ('I entertain myself with the to-listen of music.')

bij het lachen *while laughing* ('by the to-laugh')

door te hoesten *by coughing* ('due to to-cough')

● VOCABULARY

de hobby hobby
vrij free, open, unoccupied
de vrije dag day off
in/aan het begin in/at the
  beginning, first thing
halverwege / in het midden
  halfway, in the middle, mid-
aan het einde at the end, last thing
het voetbal football, soccer
het veld field/pitch
het voetbalveld football field/pitch
de voetbaltribune football stands
niks nothing
leuk fun, nice, tasty, pleasant
brengen to bring
het paardrijden horse riding
het paard horse
teruggaan to go back, to return
weer again
zich amuseren / zich vermaken
  to enjoy oneself, to have fun
tegenwoordig these days,
  nowadays
bijna almost, nearly
verplicht zijn to be obliged to,
  to be required to
aan sport doen to play sports
bijvoorbeeld for example
luisteren naar to listen to
de muziek music
piano spelen to play the piano
spelen to play
de piano piano
een instrument bespelen to play
  an instrument
bespelen to play (an instrument)
het instrument instrument
sporten to exercise, to do sports
de gezondheid health

de bank couch, sofa, bench
het (niet) eens zijn met iemand
  (not) to agree with someone
de beweging movement, exercise
wekelijks weekly
de wandeling walk
het park park
het heen en weer lopen to walk
  back and forth
de fitness fitness
het tennis tennis
het vissen fishing
het golf golf
de gymnastiek calesthenics
het hockey hockey
de atletiek athletics
het zwemmen swimming
het volleybal volleyball
het drumstel drums
de fluit flute
de gitaar guitar
de viool violin
de mondharmonica harmonica
de saxofoon saxophone
de klarinet clarinet
de trompet trumpet
vervolgens subsequently
tot slot finally, lastly
ten eerste firstly
ten tweede secondly
ten slotte finally, in conclusion
dan than (comparison)
als as (comparison)
net zo/even … als just as … as
niet zo … als not as … as
meest most
minder less
minst least
het programma programme
de tweekamerwoning two-room
  flat

● EXERCISES

1. GIVE THE COMPARATIVE AND SUPERLATIVE FORMS OF THESE ADJECTIVES.

a. belangrijk → ....   e. lekker → ....   i. weinig → ....

b. gelukkig → ....   f. veel → ....   j. graag → ....

c. goed → ....   g. slim → ....   k. duur → ....

d. kort → ....   h. warm → ....   l. mooi → ....

2. COMPLETE THESE SENTENCES USING *ALS* OR *DAN*.

a. Haar dochter is jonger .... zijn zoon.

b. Deze kaas is net zo lekker .... die andere.

c. Zij sporten meer .... wij.

d. Hij gaat liever naar de bioscoop .... naar het restaurant.

e. Deze vis is niet zo vers .... die daar.

3. TRANSLATE THESE SENTENCES INTO ENGLISH.

a. Ze loopt te zingen.

→ ....

b. Laten we lopend naar het strand gaan!

→ ....

c. Wanneer krijg je buikpijn? - Bij het lachen.

→ ....

d. Als u goed naar me luistert, zult u het begrijpen.

→ ....

25   ### 4. FORM COMPOUND WORDS BY LINKING A WORD IN THE LEFT COLUMN WITH ONE IN THE RIGHT COLUMN, THEN LISTEN TO THE AUDIO. REPEAT THE COMPOUND WORDS OUT LOUD, EMPHASIZING THE WORD STRESS.

a. de televisie •   • 1. het brood

b. de telefoon •   • 2. het programma

c. volkoren •   • 3. de brief

d. de sollicitatie •   • 4. het nummer

24.
GOING SHOPPING

WINKELEN

AIMS	TOPICS

- TALKING ABOUT GOING SHOPPING

- ASKING FOR SIZES

- DISCUSSING CLOTHES

- CONVERSING WITH SALES ASSISTANTS

- SOME VOCABULARY ABOUT SHOPS AND CLOTHES

- REFLEXIVE VERBS AND PRONOUNS

GOING SHOPPING

Claudia: Next month Eline and Michiel are getting married *(Following month marry Eline and Michiel)*, so I'm going to buy new clothes. I wonder if *(ask myself whether)* that clothes shop near *(in the area of)* the bank is open yet.

Frans: I think it's *(This is according-to me)* still closed, but there's one in the centre.

Claudia: Oh, you mean the one by the hairdresser.

At the fashion boutique

Claudia: Do you have this dress in size 38?

Shop assistant: Absolutely, do you want to try it on?

Claudia: Yes, and I'm looking for a coat to go with it *(I search a coat this there-with it-fits)*. And ankle boots with high heels, size 40.

Shop assistant: Why don't you try on this coat?

Claudia: It is really *(especially)* pretty. I'll just take a look in the mirror *(Just in the mirror to-look)*.

Shop assistant: It's a rather simple model, but you can wear it with anything *(it anywhere by to-wear)*. And it looks good on you *(it stands you good)*.

Claudia: Hmm, I see that it's on sale *(discounted)*. Oh, there's a hole in it *(there sits a little-hole in)*!

Claudia: Volgende maand trouwen Eline en Michiel, dus ik ga nieuwe kleren kopen. Ik vraag me af of die kledingwinkel in de buurt van de bank al open is.

Frans: Die is volgens mij nog gesloten, maar er zit er één in het centrum.

Claudia: O, je bedoelt die bij de kapper.

In de modewinkel

Claudia: Heeft u deze jurk in maat 38?

Verkoper: Jazeker, wilt u hem passen?

Claudia: Graag, en ik zoek een jas die erbij past. En laarsjes met hoge hakken, maat 40.

Verkoper: Probeert u deze jas maar!

Claudia: Hij is bijzonder mooi. Even in de spiegel kijken.

Verkoper: Het is een tamelijk eenvoudig model, maar u kunt hem overal bij dragen. En hij staat u goed.

Claudia: Hmm, ik zie dat hij is afgeprijsd. O, er zit een gaatje in!

UNDERSTANDING THE DIALOGUE

→ **(…) trouwen, dus ik ga nieuwe kleren kopen** *(…) are getting married, so I'm going to buy new clothes.* The verb **trouwen** *to marry* is used rather than *to get married*: 'they marry'. The noun **de kleren** *clothes* is plural, whereas **de kleding** *clothing, garment* is singular.

→ **Ik vraag me af of …** *I wonder if …* ('I ask myself whether …'): here the verb is **zich afvragen of** *to wonder if*, which is a reflexive separable-prefix verb. See the 'Grammar' section for more on reflexive verbs.

→ **in de buurt van** *near, nearby* ('in the neighbourhood of') is synonymous with **bij** *near, close, by*.

→ **die is volgens mij …** *I think it's …* ('this is according-to me …'). Note this way of stating something you're not 100% sure about.

→ **die is (…) nog gesloten** *it's still closed (…).* The word **gesloten** *closed* is the past participle of **sluiten** *to close, to shut.* Another word for *closed* is **dicht**.

→ **Heeft u deze jurk in maat 38?** *Do you have this dress in size 38?* The Dutch for *size* is **de maat**. And did you notice the diminutive **laarsjes** ('little-boots'), from **de laars** *boot* (**de laarzen** *boots*)? Careful, the noun **de boot** means *boat*!

→ **Wilt u hem passen?** *Do you want to try it on?* The verb **passen** can mean *to try on* (used only for clothes), as well as *to fit, to go with*, as we see in the next line of the dialogue. The verb **proberen** has the more general sense of *to try, to try out*.

→ **bijzonder mooi** *especially pretty*: the 'ij' in **bijzonder** *special, particular, unique* is pronounced with a long **i** [ee].

→ **En hij staat u goed.** *And it looks good on you.* The verb **staan** can mean *to suit*.

→ **(…) is afgeprijsd** *(…) is on sale* ('discounted'). This is the past participle of the verb **afprijzen** *to mark down* ('down-price'). The related noun is **de prijs** *price*.

→ **O, er zit een gaatje in!** *Oh, it has a hole in it!* ('there sits a little-hole in!') Note that the **a** in the noun **het gat** *hole* is pronounced like [aah], whereas the **aa** in the diminutive **het gaatje** is pronounced more like the [a] in 'hat'.

SHOPPING IN THE NETHERLANDS

In Dutch towns, **de binnenstad** *the town centre* has one or several streets with a range of shops. Sometimes this area is **autovrij** *car-free, pedestrianized*, making it easy for shoppers to stroll along and window-shop. Alongside clothes shops and boutiques, you'll find welcoming cafés and tea rooms, or markets selling flowers, antiques or books. Some well-known cities where you can spend many a pleasant hour poking into shops include **Amsterdam, Maastricht, Haarlem, Utrecht, Delft, Alkmaar, Leiden** and **Den Haag** *The Hague*.

Don't be surprised to see road signs indicating **'s-Gravenhage** ('the count's-hedge') for *The Hague* (**Den Haag** is in fact the abbreviated form of the city's name), and **'s-Hertogenbosch** ('the duke's-wood') for **Den Bosch** (its colloquial name). Note that today the word for *wood, forest* is **het bos** and not **bosch**.

USEFUL CLOTHES VOCABULARY

Some useful terms concerning **de garderobe** *wardrobe*: **de bloes** *blouse*, **het overhemd** *shirt, dress shirt*, **de stropdas** *necktie*, **de sjaal** *scarf*, **de kousen** *stockings, tights*, **de sokken** *socks*, **de rok** *skirt*, **de korte broek / de short** *shorts* (singular), **de onderbroek / de slip** *underpants* (singular), **de beha** *bra* (short for **de bustehouder** 'bust-holder'), **het hemd** *undershirt, vest*.

◆ GRAMMAR
REFLEXIVE VERBS AND PRONOUNS

A reflexive verb is a verb used with a pronoun to indicate that the performer of the action is also the receiver. Examples in English include *to hurt oneself, to convince oneself, to apply oneself,* etc. Some verbs that are reflexive in Dutch are also reflexive in English: **zich amuseren / zich vermaken** *to enjoy oneself*; **zich schamen** *to be ashamed of oneself.*

However, there are many verbs that are reflexive in Dutch that are not in English: **zich bewust zijn** *to know, to be aware*; **zich bevinden** *to be found, to be located*; **zich ergeren** *to be annoyed*; **zich vergissen** *to make a mistake.*

In some languages, reflexive verbs can also be used to show interaction, with the meaning *each other*. However, in Dutch as in English, this meaning is conveyed with a pronoun: **elkaar** *each other, one another.*
Ze houden van elkaar. *They like/love each other.*

Here are the reflexive pronouns in Dutch, shown with the present tense conjugation of **zich ergeren** *to be annoyed*. The pronoun must be included when the verb is used: don't leave it out!
ik erger me/mij *I am annoyed* (myself); **je ergert** je *you are annoyed* (yourself); **u ergert** u/zich *you are annoyed* (yourself); **hij / ze ergert** zich *he/she is annoyed* (himself, herself), **we ergeren** ons *we are annoyed* (ourselves), **jullie ergeren** je *you are annoyed* (yourselves), **ze ergeren** zich *they are annoyed* (themselves).

In the first-person singular, it is possible to use **me** or the stressed form **mij**:
Ik erger mij **echt aan die man.** *That man really annoys me.*
('I am-annoyed myself really with that man.')

Likewise, there are two possible reflexive pronouns in formal address: **u** *yourself* or **zich** *oneself*.

After **u hebt / u bent** (second-person singular), it is preferable to use **u**:
U hebt u vergist. *You have made a mistake.* ('You have yourself erred.')
U bent u bewust ... *You are* ('yourself') *aware ...*

After **u heeft** (third-person singular) it is preferable to use **zich**:
U heeft zich vermaakt. *You have enjoyed yourself.*

To avoid the awkward juxtaposition of the subject pronoun **u** and the reflexive pronoun **u**, usually **zich** is used:
Amuseert u zich? *Are you enjoying yourself?*

Aside from its use in polite address, **zich** is used for all third-person reflexive pronouns: *himself, herself, itself, oneself, themselves.*

You can also add the suffix **-zelf** *-self* to reinforce the pronoun:
Geloof dus in jezelf! *So believe in yourself!*
Maak 't jezelf niet te moeilijk! *Don't be so hard on yourself!*
('Make it yourself not too difficult!')

⬢ EXERCISES

1. COMPLETE THE SENTENCES WITH THE CORRECT PRONOUN.

a.   Hij gelooft in ....zelf.

b.   Ze wassen (*wash*) .... niet vaak. (2 possibilities)

c.   Vermaakt u ....hier wel?

d.   Ik erger .... aan die verkoopster. (2 possibilities)

e.   Je vergist ....

2. GIVE THE ENGLISH EQUIVALENT OF THESE VERBS.

a. zich schamen → ....   e. heten → ....

b. zich vergissen → ....   f. zich bewust zijn → ....

c. zich vermaken → ....   g. houden van → ....

d. trouwen → ....   h. zich ergeren → ....

● VOCABULARY

winkelen *to go shopping*
de winkel *shop, boutique*
de modewinkel *fashion boutique*
de kledingwinkel *clothes shop*
de kleding (sing.) *clothing, garment*
de kleren (pl.) *clothes*
volgend *next, following*
trouwen *to marry, to get married*
kopen *to buy*
zich afvragen of *to wonder if*
in de buurt van *near, in the area of*
de buurt *neighbourhood*
volgens *according to*
gesloten / dicht *closed*
sluiten *to close, to shut*
bedoelen *to mean, to intend*
bij *near, close, by*
de kapper / de kapster
  hairdresser (m./f.)
de verkoper / de verkoopster
  sales assistant (m./f.)
passen *to try on clothes, to fit,*
  to go with
staan *to suit, to look good on*
erbij *with it*
de maat *size*
hoog *high*
de hak *heel*
bijzonder *special, particular, unique,*
  especially, particularly
de spiegel *mirror*
tamelijk *rather, quite*
eenvoudig *simple, plain*
het model *model*
overal *everywhere, anywhere*
dragen *to wear*
afgeprijsd *on sale, discounted*
afprijzen *to mark down*
de prijs *price*

het gaatje *little hole*
het gat *hole*
het centrum *centre, town centre*
de binnenstad *town centre*
autovrij *car-free, pedestrianized*
Den Haag/'s-Gravenhage
  The Hague
Den Bosch/'s-Hertogenbosch
  Den Bosch
het bos *wood, forest*
de garderobe *wardrobe*
de jurk *dress*
de jas *coat*
het laarsje(s) *ankle boot(s)*
de laars *boot* (**de laarzen** *boots*)
de bloes *blouse*
het overhemd *shirt, dress shirt*
de stropdas *necktie*
de sjaal *scarf*
de kous *stocking* (**de kousen**
  stockings, tights)
de sok *sock* (**de sokken** *socks*)
de rok *skirt*
de korte broek / de short
  shorts (sing.)
de onderbroek / de slip
  underpants (sing.)
de beha / de bustehouder *bra*
het hemd *undershirt, vest*
elkaar *each other, one another*
zich schamen *to be ashamed of*
  oneself
zich bewust zijn *to be aware,*
  to know
zich *himself, herself, itself, oneself*
  themselves
-zelf *-self*
houden van *to like, to love,*
  to care for
wassen *to wash*
wakker worden *to wake up*

3. TRANSLATE THESE SENTENCES INTO DUTCH.

a. Where is my shirt/blouse?

→ ....

b. Those high-heeled ankle boots look good on you *(formal)*.

→ ....

c. May I try on this skirt?

→ ....

d. Do you *(formal)* have these shoes in size 42?

→ ....

e. He is looking for a clothes shop.

→ ....

4. TURN THESE STATEMENTS INTO QUESTIONS. THEN LISTEN TO THE AUDIO TO CHECK YOUR ANSWERS AND REPEAT THE STATEMENTS AND QUESTIONS OUT LOUD.

26

a. De binnenstad van Den Bosch is autovrij.

b. Er zit een gaatje in die jas.

c. U vindt dat eenvoudige model bijzonder mooi.

d. Je bedoelt die bank in de buurt van de kapper.

25.
A WEEKEND AWAY

EEN WEEKEND WEG

AIMS	TOPICS
• **TALKING ABOUT WHAT HAPPENED IN THE PAST**	• **SOME VOCABULARY AROUND MEALS**
• **ASKING AND GIVING THE MEANING OF A WORD**	• **THE RELATIVE PRONOUNS *DIE* AND *DAT* THAT, WHICH**
• **SAYING WHAT YOU PLAN TO DO**	• **THE DEMONSTRATIVE PRONOUNS *DIE* AND *DAT* IT**
	• **THE PRESENT PERFECT (HAVE ... -ED) AND THE SIMPLE PAST**

A WEEKEND AWAY

Floor: Did you have a nice weekend *(Have you a nice weekend had)*?

Edwin: Lovely, I went to the seaside *(I have [am] to sea been)*. On Saturday, I took *(have .... made)* a cruise on the Eastern Scheldt, and yesterday I *(have)* visited a museum in Zierikzee.

Floor: Did you have *(Had you)* nice weather?

Edwin: It was quite cold, but it didn't rain *(has not rained)*.

Floor: Is there also a 'horeca'-boat where you can eat *(Have you there also that horeca-boat that service does as eat-house)*? It seems that you can have a delicious brunch there *(you there scrumptious can brunch)*!

Edwin: 'Horeca'? What does that mean?

Floor: It is a portmanteau *(an abbreviation)* of the words 'hotel', 'restaurant' and 'café'.

Edwin: Ah! No, I didn't see a boat like that *(such sort boat have I not seen)*.

Floor: Well, next weekend I will probably go to Den Burg on Texel. I want to see the church tower there and go to the swimming pool.

Edwin: Good idea *(Reason have you)*, as the weather will be nice *(as it becomes beautiful weather)*!

Floor: Heb je een prettig weekend gehad?

Edwin: Heerlijk, ik ben naar zee geweest. Op zaterdag heb ik een rondvaart op de Oosterschelde gemaakt en gisteren heb ik in Zierikzee een museum bezocht.

Floor: Had je mooi weer?

Edwin: Het was nogal koud, maar het heeft niet geregend.

Floor: Heb je daar ook die horecaboot die dienst doet als eethuis? Het schijnt dat je daar verrukkelijk kunt brunchen!

Edwin: Horeca? Wat betekent dat?

Floor: Dat is een afkorting van de woorden 'hotel', 'restaurant' en 'café'.

Edwin: Ah! Nee, zo'n soort boot heb ik niet gezien.

Floor: Nou, ik ga volgend weekend waarschijnlijk naar Den Burg op Texel. Ik wil daar de kerktoren zien en naar het zwembad.

Edwin: Gelijk heb je, want het wordt mooi weer!

▨ UNDERSTANDING THE DIALOGUE

→ **Een weekend weg** *A weekend away.* The word **weg** means *away*, and is also part of the separable-prefix verb **weggaan** *to go away, to leave.*

→ **Heb je een prettig weekend gehad?** *Did you have a good weekend?* ('Have you a nice weekend had?'). Here we see the past participle **gehad** *had* of **hebben** *to have.* You'll have noticed that in Dutch the present perfect is used in certain contexts in which the simple past is used in English. More on this in 'Grammar'. The adjectives **prettig** and **fijn** *pleasant, enjoyable* are both options here.

→ **Ik ben naar zee geweest.** *I went to the seaside.* ('I have [am] to sea been.') This is also the present perfect, but formed with **zijn** *to be* as the auxiliary rather than **hebben** *to have* because the action concerns movement: **ik ben geweest** *I have been.* See 'Grammar' for more about this.

→ **Had je mooi weer?** *Did you have nice weather?* ('Had you pretty weather?'): **had** *had* is the simple past of **hebben** *to have.* This tense is used for describing something that was ongoing in the past rather than a one-off event.

→ **Het schijnt dat je daar verrukkelijk kunt brunchen!** *It seems that you can have a delicious brunch there!* ('It seems that you there scrumptious can brunch!')

→ **Wat betekent dat?** *What does that mean?* This is the verb **betekenen** *to mean, to signify, to denote,* not to be confused with **bedoelen** *to mean, to intend, to get at.*

→ **volgend weekend** *next weekend*: two useful adjectives for talking about the future or the past are **volgend** *next* and **vorig** *last, previous.*

→ **Gelijk heb je.** ('Reason have you.') This is how you say *You're right.* or *Good idea.*

→ **het wordt mooi weer** *it's going to be nice* ('it becomes beautiful weather').

CULTURAL NOTE

The town of **Zierikzee** is in **Zeeland** in the south of the Netherlands. After the catastrophic flooding of a large part of the province in 1953, **het Deltaplan** was conceived. It is a system of dykes and dams, the most well known of which is the **Oosterscheldekering** *Eastern Scheldt Storm Surge Barrier.*

The island of **Texel** is one of the five inhabited **Waddeneilanden** *Wadden Islands* between **de Noordzee** *the North Sea* and **de Waddenzee** *the Wadden Sea* to the north of the country. At low tide, you can – with a guide – walk to the islands, whose name is made up of the plurals of **het wad** *mudflat* and **het eiland** *island.* These islands have a rich diversity of flora and fauna. **Texel** is in the province of **Noord-Holland** *North Holland.* The other islands, **Vlieland**, **Terschelling**, **Ameland** and **Schiermonnikoog**, are part of the province of **Friesland**.

Generally speaking, the Dutch eat one hot meal a day, usually in the evening: **het avondeten** *dinner* (**eten** is the verb *to eat*, as well as the noun *food, meal*). The other meals, **het ontbijt** *breakfast* (**bijten** means *to bite*) and **het middageten** *lunch*, are usually cold meals, consisting of cereal and/or bread with cheese, cold meats and spreads such as **de pindakaas** *peanut butter* ('peanut-cheese') or sweet toppings such as **de hagelslag** *chocolate sprinkles*.

The terms **de lunch** and **het diner** exist, but they are more formal.

While in English we say to have breakfast/lunch/dinner, in Dutch they say: **ontbijten** *to breakfast*, **lunchen** *to lunch*, **dineren** *to dine* and **brunchen** *to brunch*.

◆ GRAMMAR
THE RELATIVE PRONOUNS *DIE* AND *DAT* THAT, WHICH

The pronouns **die** and **dat** can be used to mean *that, which*. In this case, **die** refers to a singular common noun or to a plural noun, and **dat** to a neuter noun:
de man die *the man* that; **de jassen** die *the coats* that
het huis dat *the house* that

THE DEMONSTRATIVE PRONOUNS *DIE* AND *DAT* IT

It is very common to use **die** or **dat** with the meaning of *it/they* or even *he/she* rather than the personal pronoun. Again, **die** refers to a singular common noun or to a plural noun, and **dat** is used for a singular neuter noun. This usage emphasizes the pronoun, particularly if it is at the beginning of the sentence:
de winkel *the shop* → **Die is gesloten.** *It is closed.*
de winkels *the shops* → **Die zijn open.** *They are open.*
het brood *the bread* → **Dat ligt op tafel.** *It is on the table.*
het inktpatroon *the ink cartridge* → **Dat ligt op mijn bureau.** *It is on my desk.*

▲ CONJUGATION
TALKING ABOUT THE PAST

In the dialogue there are several examples of differences in tense usage between English and Dutch. In Dutch, very often the present perfect (i.e. *I have gone, you have eaten, he has visited*, etc.) is used to describe an action in the past that in English would be conveyed with the simple past. The rule in Dutch is that the present perfect is used to talk about an isolated event that happened in the past whose results or consequences have an impact on the present.

With most verbs, as in English, the present perfect is formed with the auxiliary verb **hebben** *to have* conjugated in the present + the past participle of the main verb. But in Dutch the past participle is usually placed at the end of the clause:

Gisteren heb ik een museum bezocht. *Yesterday I visited a museum.*
('Yesterday have I a museum visited.')
(**bezocht** *visited* is the irregular past participle of **bezoeken** *to visit*)
Het heeft niet geregend. *It didn't rain.*
('It has not rained.')
(**geregend** *rained* is the regular past participle of **regenen** *to rain*)

However, with verbs that indicate movement or a change of state, the present perfect is formed with the auxiliary verb **zijn** *to be* conjugated in the present tense + past participle of the main verb.

Ik ben naar zee geweest. *I went to the seaside.*
('I have to sea been.')
(**geweest** *been* is the irregular past participle of **zijn** *to be*)

The simple past tense in Dutch is used to narrate something or describe an ongoing situation in the past (as opposed to a specific, one-off event).

Het was nogal koud. *It was quite cold.*
(**was** *was* is the irregular third-person simple past of **zijn** *to be*)

We'll come back to how to form the present perfect, the past participle and the simple past in lessons 27 and 29.

⬡ EXERCISES

1. COMPLETE THESE PHRASES WITH THE DEFINITE ARTICLE (THE) AND *DIE* OR *DAT* THAT.

a. .... rondvaart ....

b. .... zwembad ....

c. .... boten ....

d. .... broden ....

● VOCABULARY

weg *away*
weggaan *to go away, to leave*
prettig / fijn *pleasant, enjoyable*
heerlijk *lovely, wonderful*
de zee *sea*
de rondvaart *cruise*
een rondvaart maken
  to take a cruise
het museum *museum*
bezoeken *to visit*
het weer *weather*
nogal *quite, rather*
regenen *to rain*
de horecaboot *boat used as a*
  restaurant (horeca: hotel
  restaurant café *hospitality*)
het hotel *hotel*
de boot *boat, ship*
die *that, which*
dienst doen als *to serve as*
het eethuis *restaurant*
schijnen *to seem, to appear*
verrukkelijk *scrumptious,*
  delectable, mouthwatering
betekenen *to mean, to signify,*
  to denote
bedoelen *to mean, to intend,*
  to get at
de afkorting *abbreviation*
het woord *word*
zo'n soort *that kind of, like that*
  ('such sort')
waarschijnlijk *probably, likely*

de kerktoren *church spire, steeple*
de kerk *church*
de toren *tower*
het zwembad *swimming pool*
gelijk hebben *to be right*
Gelijk heb je. *You're right.*
het gelijk *reason*
volgend *next, following*
vorig *last, previous*
Zeeland (het) *Zeeland*
 de Oosterscheldekering *Eastern*
   Scheldt Storm Surge Barrier
de Waddenzee *Wadden Sea*
de Waddeneilanden
  Wadden Islands
het wad *mudflat, tidal flat*
het eiland *island*
de Noordzee *North Sea*
Noord-Holland (het)
  North Holland
Friesland (het) *Friesland*
eten *to eat* (verb); *food, meal* (noun)
bijten *to bite*
het ontbijt *breakfast*
de brunch *brunch*
het middageten / de lunch *lunch*
het avondeten / het diner *dinner*
ontbijten *to have breakfast*
brunchen *to have brunch*
lunchen *to have lunch*
dineren *to have dinner*
de pindakaas *peanut butter*
de pinda *peanut*
de hagelslag *chocolate sprinkles*
herinneren *to remember, to recall*

2. COMPLETE THESE SENTENCES WITH *DIE* OR *DAT* INSTEAD OF A SUBJECT PRONOUN.

a. de zee → .... is nogal koud.

b. de kaas → .... is heerlijk!

c. haar gezicht → .... herinner *(remember)* ik me niet meer.

d. onze zoon → .... woont in Haarlem.

3. COMPLETE THESE SENTENCES WITH *BEGRIJPEN, BETEKENEN, BEDOELEN* OR *BEDANKEN* IN THE CORRECT CONJUGATION.

a. Wat .... dat woord?

b. Ze .... niet waarom dat belangrijk is. (2 possibilities)

c. Hij .... haar voor het cadeau.

d. .... je die winkel in de buurt van de bank?

4. LISTEN TO EACH SENTENCE, PAYING ATTENTION TO THE INTONATION. WRITE THEM DOWN AND THEN REPEAT THEM OUT LOUD.

27

a. ....

b. ....

c. ....

d. ....

e. ....

f. ....

26.
AT THE TOURIST OFFICE

BIJ HET VVV-KANTOOR

AIMS	TOPICS

AIMS

- ORGANIZING A TRIP OR OUTING
- TALKING ABOUT DIFFERENT TYPES OF ACCOMMODATION
- EXPRESSING PREFERENCES

TOPICS

- SOME TRAVEL VOCABULARY
- THE VERBS *BEVALLEN* TO PLEASE, TO SUIT, *VINDEN* TO FIND AND *LIJKEN* TO BE LIKE, TO RESEMBLE
- THE EXPRESSION *WAT VOOR SOORT?* WHAT KIND?
- THE PREPOSITIONS *OP* ON AND *MET* WITH
- THE USE OF THE IMPERSONAL PRONOUN *MEN* ONE

AT THE TOURIST OFFICE

Huib: Hi, I would like some information about a tour in the month of May. Last year I went *(have ... gone)* to a number of Hanseatic cities, but this time I would like to go somewhere else *(would I gladly somewhere different towards to-want)*.

Olga: How do you want to travel? By *(With the)* car?

Huib: I know that people these days usually take their car *(that one nowadays easily the car takes)*, but I like to cycle *(I cycle gladly)*.

Olga: And what sort of holiday accommodation do you prefer *(goes your preference out-to)*?

Huib: Last time, I had a nice spot in *(on)* a campsite, and I liked that *(that has well pleased)*, so something similar.

Olga: How about *(What thought you of)* a cycling holiday around Lake IJssel? You cycle through gorgeous natural areas and pass through *(you come along)* well-known historical villages with bustling medieval streets.

Huib: Yes, that sounds good *(that seems to-me well very)*. And with a bicycle, I can stop *(dismount)* wherever I want.

Huib: Hallo, ik wil graag inlichtingen over een rondreis voor in de maand mei. Vorig jaar ben ik naar een aantal Hanzesteden gegaan, maar ditmaal zou ik graag ergens anders naartoe willen.

Olga: Hoe wil je reizen? Met de auto?

Huib: Ik weet dat men tegenwoordig makkelijk de auto neemt, maar ik fiets graag.

Olga: En naar wat voor soort vakantieaccommodatie gaat je voorkeur uit?

Huib: De vorige keer had ik een leuke plek op een camping en dat is goed bevallen, dus iets dergelijks.

Olga: Wat dacht je van een fietsvakantie rond het IJsselmeer? Je fietst door schitterende natuurgebieden en je komt langs bekende historische dorpjes met gezellige middeleeuwse straatjes.

Huib: Ja, dat lijkt me wel wat. En met de fiets kan ik afstappen waar ik wil.

UNDERSTANDING THE DIALOGUE

→ **het VVV-kantoor** *tourist office*: the acronym **VVV** stands for **Vereniging voor Vreemdelingenverkeer** ('organization for **vreemdelingen** *foreigners* **verkeer** *circulation/traffic*').

→ **inlichtingen over een rondreis voor in de maand mei** *information about a tour in the month of May.* The word **de inlichtingen** *enquiries* is the plural of **de inlichting** *enquiry.* Both are used to mean *information.*

→ **(...) ben ik naar een aantal Hanzesteden gegaan** *(...) I went to a number of Hanseatic cities* ('have I to .... gone'). This is the present perfect, using **zijn** *to be* as the auxiliary because the main verb indicates movement: **gegaan** *gone* is the past participle of **gaan** *to go.* Note also the irregular plural of **de stad** *city*: **de steden** *cities.* (The Hanseatic League was a confederation of medieval merchant guilds and market towns in northern and central Europe.)

→ **ditmaal zou ik graag ergens anders naartoe willen** *this time I would like to go somewhere else* ('this-time would I gladly somewhere different towards want'). Both **maal** and **keer** mean *time*: **ditmaal** *this time* is written as one word. The phrase **ergens anders** means *somewhere else.* The verb **zou** *would* is the singular simple past of **zullen** *will, shall* – here it expresses the conditional.

→ **En naar wat voor soort vakantieaccommodatie gaat je voorkeur uit?** *And what type of holiday accommodation do you prefer?* The verb here is **uitgaan** *to go out*; **de voorkeur** means *preference, liking.* Remember this construction: possessive adjective + **voorkeur uitgaan naar** *to prefer,* (my/your/his/her, etc.) *preference is for.*

→ **dat is goed bevallen** *I liked that* ('that has well pleased'). This is another example of the present perfect using **zijn** *to be* as the auxiliary, this time because the main verb indicates a change of state or mood. The main verb is **bevallen** *to please, to suit*, whose past participle is **bevallen** *pleased, suited.*

→ **Wat dacht je van ...?** *How about ...?* ('What thought you of ...'). The verb **dacht** *thought* is the singular simple past of **denken** *to think.*

USEFUL ACCOMMODATION VOCABULARY

If you're going on holiday in the Netherlands, here are some terms that might come in handy: **vakantieaccommodaties** *holiday accommodation*, **de camping** *camping, campsite, camp pitch*, **de tent** *tent*, **de caravan** *caravan, travel trailer*, **de stacaravan** *mobile home, motor home*, **de jeugdherberg** *youth hostel*, **het vakantiehuisje** *holiday home, holiday cottage*, **het bungalowpark** *holiday village*, **het hotel** *hotel*, **het appartement** *apartment*.

Note that the first and last **a** in **caravan** are pronounced as in English, as is the **a** in **camping**. However, the verb **kamperen** *to camp* is written with a **k**, and the **a** is pronounced [ah].

CULTURAL NOTE

The term **gezellig** is difficult to translate as it doesn't have an exact equivalent in English. In the dialogue it is best conveyed with *bustling, buzzing*, but it is often used to mean *cosy, snug, sociable*. You will hear it frequently in Dutch to describe a convivial, warm, comfortable atmosphere, somewhere that gives you a pleasant feeling, usually in the company of others.

About one-quarter of the Netherlands is below sea level (hence the historic name **de Nederlanden**, 'low countries', for the region), which involves a constant struggle against the encroachment of water. Effective water management has required a variety of organizations* to work closely together. Over the years, entire lakes have been transformed into **de polder** (a low-lying tract of land enclosed by **de dijken** *dykes*). The most famous dyke is **de Afsluitdijk** ('closure-dyke'), which has turned **de Zuiderzee**, a former shallow bay of the North Sea, into the freshwater lake **het IJsselmeer** *Lake IJssel*.

* Various government agencies and ministries, as well as regional and local governments, environmental protection organizations and public sector flood control engineers with expertise in the prevention of water encroachment.

The key role of water in the history and culture of the Netherlands has left its mark on the Dutch language, as well as on place names. We find the word **de dam** *dam* in city names such as **Amsterdam** and **Rotterdam**. Other words related to water include **de waterkering** *flood defence* ('water-barrier'), **het waterschap**** *the water authority*, **de gracht** *canal*, **de sloot** *dyke, ditch*, **het kanaal** *channel*, **de haven** *harbour, port* and **de ophaalbrug** *drawbridge*.

** This is a regional body that is one of the institutions responsible for monitoring and managing water in a given region. The first of these dates back to the 13th century.

THE VERBS *BEVALLEN* TO PLEASE, TO SUIT *VINDEN* TO FIND AND *LIJKEN* TO SEEM LIKE, TO RESEMBLE

The verb **bevallen** *to please, to suit* is usually used with an object:
Dat bevalt me goed/niet. *I like/don't like that.* ('That pleases me well/not.')

Other verbs used to show your approval or disapproval of something are **vinden** *to find* and **lijken** *to be like, to seem like, to resemble*:

Dat vind ik leuk. *I like that.* ('That find I nice.')

Ik vind dat niks. *I don't like that.* ('I find that nothing.')

Dat lijkt me wat. *That sounds good.* ('That seems-like to-me very.')

Dat lijkt me geen goed idee. *That doesn't seem like a good idea to me.*

GRAMMAR

THE EXPRESSION *WAT VOOR SOORT?* WHAT KIND?

Remember the useful expression **Wat voor soort … ?** *What kind of…?* The answer might include: **iets dergelijks** *something like* or **zo'n soort** *of that kind, like that*.

THE PREPOSITIONS *OP* ON AND *MET* WITH

You will have noticed that the usage of prepositions can vary in different languages. For instance, in this dialogue we see that **op** *on* and **met** *with* are used in the sense of *by* for means of transport <u>on</u> which you're seated: **fiets** *bicycle*, **motor** *motorcycle*, etc. But note that only **met** can be used for means of transport <u>in</u> which you're seated:

met/op de fiets, de motor, de brommer *by bicycle, motorcycle, moped*

met de auto, het vliegtuig, de boot, de trein, de tram, de bus *by car, plane, boat, train, tram, bus/coach.*

Also note the verbs used for getting on/off or in/out of different types of transport:

fiets, **motor** etc. → **opstappen** *to get on, to mount*, **afstappen** *to get off, dismount*

auto, **vliegtuig** etc. → **instappen** *to get in, to board*, **uitstappen** *to get out/off, to disembark*.

THE USE OF THE IMPERSONAL PRONOUN *MEN* ONE

Similar to its English equivalent *one*, the pronoun **men** is considered relatively formal today. It is used in the general sense of 'people', but the verb conjugates in the singular. As we saw in lesson 15, it is more common to use the personal pronoun **je** *you* in these contexts, which in this case has the general meaning of *one*.

● VOCABULARY

het VVV-kantoor *tourist office*
de vereniging *organization*
de vreemdeling / de vreemdelinge *foreigner* (m./f.)
het verkeer *circulation, traffic*
de inlichting *information, enquiry*
de rondreis *tour*
rond *around*
de reis *journey, voyage, trip*
een aantal *a number*
het aantal *number*
de Hanzestad *Hanseatic city*
de stad *city*
ditmaal *this time*
de maal / de keer *time*
ergens anders *somewhere else*
men *one, people*
Wat voor soort ...?
  What kind of ... ?
de vakantieaccommodatie
  holiday accommodation
... voorkeur uitgaan naar
  ... preference for, to prefer
de plek *place, spot*
bevallen *to please, to suit*
iets dergelijks *something similar*
de fietsvakantie *cycling holiday*
het IJsselmeer *Lake IJssel*
het meer *lake*
door *through, by*
schitterend *gorgeous*
het natuurgebied *natural area*
de natuur *nature*
het gebied *zone, area, region*
langs *along*
bekend *well known*

historisch *historic*
gezellig *cosy, convivial, sociable, bustling, homey*
middeleeuws *medieval*
lijken *to seem like, to resemble*
de tent *tent*
de caravan *caravan, travel trailer*
de stacaravan *mobile home, motor home*
de jeugdherberg *youth hostel*
het vakantiehuisje *holiday home, holiday cottage*
het bungalowpark *holiday village*
de camping *camping, campsite, camp pitch*
kamperen *to camp*
de dijk *dyke*
afsluiten *to close, to occlude, to lock*
de dam *dam*
de waterkering *water defence*
het waterschap *water authority*
de gracht *canal*
de sloot *dyke, ditch*
het kanaal *channel*
de haven *harbour, port*
de ophaalbrug *drawbridge*
de brug *bridge*
de motor *motorcycle*
de brommer *moped*
het vliegtuig *airplane*
de bus *bus, coach*
opstappen *to get on, to mount*
afstappen *to get off, to dismount*
instappen *to get in, to board*
uitstappen *to get off/out, to disembark*

⬡ EXERCISES

1. COMPLETE THESE SENTENCES USING *OP* AND/OR *MET*.

a. Hij gaat .... de brommer naar het strand.

b. Ik ga het liefst .... het vliegtuig.

c. .... de fiets kunnen ze stoppen waar ze willen.

d. Ga je .... de boot naar Engeland of .... de trein?

2. GIVE THE DUTCH VERB CORRESPONDING TO THE WORD IN PARENTHESES.

a. motor (*to get off*) → ....   c. tram (*to board*) → ....

b. bus (*to disembark*) → ....   d. fiets (*to get on*) → ....

3. TRANSLATE THESE SENTENCES INTO ENGLISH.

a. Ditmaal zou ze graag ergens anders naartoe willen.

→ ....

b. Naar wat voor soort vakantieaccommodatie gaat zijn voorkeur uit?

→ ....

c. Ze willen graag inlichtingen over een fietsvakantie voor in de maand maart.

→ ....

d. Een leuke plek op een camping? Ja, dat lijkt haar wel wat.

→ ....

🔊 4. LISTEN TO THE AUDIO AND WRITE DOWN THE SENTENCES. WHAT DO THEY MEAN?

28

a. ....

b. ....

c. ....

d. ....

e. ....

27.
THE ONLINE BANK

DE INTERNETBANK

AIMS	TOPICS

- ASKING OR EXPLAINING WHAT HAS HAPPENED
- EXPRESSING DISAGREEMENT
- RELATING EVENTS IN THE PAST
- TALKING ABOUT ISSUES REGARDING A BANK ACCOUNT

- SOME VOCABULARY ABOUT MONEY
- QUANTITIES AND MEASUREMENTS
- THE SIMPLE PAST OF *HEBBEN* TO HAVE AND *ZIJN* TO BE
- HOW TO FORM THE PAST PARTICIPLE OF REGULAR VERBS

ONLINE SHOPPING?

Ina: What's going on *(What is there by the hand)*?

Fred: My bank account is blocked!

Ina: Oh, how did that happen *(has that happened)*?

Fred: I wanted to shop *(go shopping)* online yesterday, but I didn't have an account yet. When I wanted to create one at an online bank, I had to come up with a user name and a password and specify when I was born *(have been born)*. When I had done that, I received a code by text message that I had to enter *(input)*.

Ina: That's more secure, so that seems logical to me.

Fred: I don't agree with that! *(There am I it not with agreed!)* Why do they want to know all these things? Anyway, after I had done that, I could finally log in. But when I wanted to shop online and needed a code again *(again a code need had)*, I typed in the *(have ... typed in a)* wrong code three times.

Ina: Well, after the third time, of course everything is *(becomes)* blocked!

Fred: How are you supposed to know that *(can you that well know)*?

Ina: Wat is er aan de hand?

Fred: Mijn bankrekening is geblokkeerd!

Ina: O, hoe is dat gebeurd?

Fred: Ik wilde gisteren online gaan shoppen, maar ik had nog geen account. Toen ik er één wilde aanmaken bij een internetbank, moest ik een gebruikersnaam en wachtwoord bedenken en aangeven wanneer ik ben geboren. Toen ik dat had gedaan, ontving ik per sms een code, die ik moest invoeren.

Ina: Dat is veiliger, dus dat lijkt me logisch.

Fred: Daar ben ik het niet mee eens! Waarom willen ze al die dingen weten? Afijn, nadat ik dat had gedaan, kon ik eindelijk inloggen. Maar toen ik online wilde gaan shoppen en opnieuw een code nodig had, heb ik drie keer een foute code ingetypt.

Ina: Tja, na de derde keer wordt natuurlijk alles geblokkeerd!

Fred: Hoe kan jij dat nou weten?

UNDERSTANDING THE DIALOGUE

→ **Wat is er aan de hand?** *What's going on?* ('What is there by the hand?') is a very common expression you'll hear a lot.

→ **ik had nog geen account** *I didn't have an account yet* ('I had yet no account'). It is common in Dutch to make the noun negative rather than the verb.

→ **Toen ik er één wilde aanmaken …** *When I wanted to create one ….* Here, **wilde** *wanted* is the singular simple past of the verb **willen** *to want*.

→ **ik ben geboren** *I was* ('am') *born.* This is actually the present perfect ('I have been born'), with **zijn** as the auxiliary verb as the main verb conveys a change of state. You'll also hear **geboren worden** *to be* ('become') *born* (**geboren** is the past participle of **baren** *to give birth, to bear*).

→ **Toen ik dat had gedaan, ontving ik een code, die ik moest invoeren.** *When I had done that, I received a code that I had to enter.* Here we have the past perfect **had gedaan** *had done*: **gedaan** is the past participle of **doen** *to do*. There are also two verbs in the simple past: **ontving** *received* (from **ontvangen** *to receive*) and **moest** *had to* (from **moeten** *to have to, must*).

→ **Daar ben ik het niet mee eens!** *I don't agree with that!* ('That am I it not with agreed.') You could also say: **Dat ben ik niet met je eens!** *I don't agree with you!*

→ **nadat ik dat had gedaan, kon ik (…) inloggen** *after I had done that, I could (…) log in.* After **nadat** *after*, the past perfect is required. The verb **kon** *could, was able to* is the singular simple past of **kunnen** *to be able to, can*.

→ **(…) wordt (…) alles geblokkeerd** *everything is* ('becomes') *blocked.* Note the use of **worden** *to become* here.

→ **Hoe kan jij dat nou weten?** *How are you supposed to know that?* In this useful expression, we see another example of *you* with the meaning *one, a person*.

MONEY AND BANKING

Online banking (**internetbankieren** *to bank online*) is increasingly common in the Netherlands, and secure apps allow customers to check their balance, transfer money, pay bills and confirm purchases when online shopping.

Here is some vocabulary related to money and banking: **het biljet** *bill, banknote*, **de munt** *coin*, **de cent** *cent*, **contant betalen** *to pay in cash*, **overmaken** *to transfer, to remit*, **de pincode** *PIN code*, **de bankpas** *bank/debit card*, **de spaarrekening** *savings account*, **geld opnemen** *to withdraw money*, **het saldo inzien** *to view one's bank balance*, **rekeningen betalen** *to pay bills* (**de rekening** *bill, invoice, expense*), **de kosten** *fees*, **uitgeven** *to spend*, **(be)sparen** *to save*.

◆ GRAMMAR
QUANTITIES AND MEASUREMENTS

A noun can be countable or uncountable. A countable noun is a noun that can be modified by a quantity and exists in singular and plural forms:

een dorp *one village* → **twee dorpen** *two villages*.

An uncountable noun, or a 'mass noun', denotes something that can't be counted – often a substance or a quality – so they have no plural form: **het water** *water*, **het bier** *beer*. To indicate the quantity of an uncountable noun, you have to use another term such as a container or a unit of measurement: **een fles water** *a bottle of water*, **een liter melk** *a litre of milk*. In Dutch, some uncountable nouns can be made countable using the diminutive: **twee ijsjes** *two ice creams*.

Generally, in Dutch, when a quantity or measurement of something is given, there is no preposition: **de maand mei** *the month of May*; **een kilo peren** *a kilo of pears*; **40 graden koorts** *40°* ('degrees') *fever*; **de bos bloemen** *bouquet of flowers*.

As we've seen, units of money, measurements (except for **graad** *degree*), units of time such as **uur** *hour* and **jaar** *year*, and terms such as **de keer / de maal** *time* (as in *instance*) are in the singular when they are preceded by a number, by **hoeveel** *how much, how many* or by **een paar** *a few*. For example:

zes cent *six cents*; **twee meter/gram** *two metres/grams*; **vijf uur/jaar** *five hours/years*; **drie keer/maal** *three times*; **Hoeveel euro?** *How many euros?*; **een paar keer/maal** *a few times*.

▲ CONJUGATION
THE SIMPLE PAST OF *HEBBEN* TO HAVE AND *ZIJN* TO BE

The simple past of **hebben** *to have* is very simple, with one form in the singular (**had** *I/you/he/she/it had*) and one form in the plural (**hadden** *we/they had*). The same is true for **zijn** *to be* (**was** *I/he/she/it was, you were* / **waren** *we/they were*).

HOW TO FORM THE PAST PARTICIPLE OF REGULAR VERBS

The past participle (the equivalent of the *-ed* form in English, as in *have blocked*) is formed for regular verbs in Dutch by placing **ge-** before the verb stem and adding the ending **-t** or **-d** after the verb stem. The ending to use depends on the last letter of the verb stem (i.e. the last letter after removing the final **-en** of the infinitive). If the verb stem ends in **-t**, **-k**, **-f**, **-s**, **-ch** or **-p**, the past participle takes the ending **-t** (but if the stem already ends in **-t**, an extra **-t** is not added). A mnemonic to help you remember this is **'t kofschip**, or the 'soft ketchup' rule — verb stems ending in any of the consonants in this mnemonic take a **-t**:

fietsen *to cycle* → **ge-** + verb stem **fiets** + **-t** = ge**fiets**t *cycled*
brunchen *to brunch* → **ge-** + verb stem **brunch** + **-t** = ge**brunch**t *brunched*

If the verb stem ends in any other letter, the past participle ends in **-d**:
dineren *to dine* → **ge-** + verb stem **diner*** + **-d** = ge**dineer**d *dined*
* Don't forget to double the vowel if it is long.

BUT: verbs starting with **be-**, **ge-**, **(h)er-**, **ont-** and **ver-** don't add the prefix **ge-**:
betalen *to pay* → verb stem **betal** + **-d** = **betaal**d *paid*

If the last letter of the verb stem is **-v** or **-z**, the past participle is formed with **-d**. But remember that **-v** turns into **-f** at the end of a word, and **-z** into **-s**.
geloven *to believe* → verb stem **gelov** + **-d** = ge**loof**d *believed*

With separable-prefix verbs, the past participle marker **ge-** is inserted between the separable prefix and the verb stem:
intypen *to type in* → prefix **in** + **-ge-** + verb stem **typ** + **-t** = **in**ge**typ**t *typed in*

⬡ EXERCISES

1. INDICATE IF THE NOUN IS COUNTABLE OR UNCOUNTABLE, THEN TRANSLATE THE PHRASES.

a. bier   ❑ countable   ❑ uncountable
    een liter bier →..
    een paar biertjes →...

b. cent   ❑ countable   ❑ uncountable
    drie cent →..
    Hoeveel cent? →..

c. graad   ❑ countable   ❑ uncountable
    37 graden koorts →..
    een paar graden →...

d. keer   ❑ countable   ❑ uncountable
    zes keer →...
    de zesde keer →..

VOCABULARY

online shoppen *to shop online*
Wat is er aan de hand?
What's going on?
blokkeren *to block*
gebeuren *to happen, to occur*
gisteren *yesterday*
het/de account *user account*
aanmaken *to create*
bij *at*
de internetbank *online bank*
internetbankieren *to bank online*
de gebruikersnaam *user name*
de gebruiker *user*
gebruiken *to use*
het wachtwoord *password*
de wacht *guard, sentry*
bedenken *to think of, to contrive,*
to concoct, to come up with
aangeven *to indicate, to specify*
geboren worden *to be born*
geboren *born* (past participle of
baren)
baren *to give birth, to bear*
ontvangen *to receive*
de sms *text message*
de code *code*
invoeren *to enter, to input*
inloggen *to log in*
intypen *to type in*
veilig *secure, safe*
lijken *to seem like*
logisch *logical*
mee *along*
eens *agreed*
het ding *thing*
nadat *after*

opnieuw *again*
fout *wrong, incorrect*
natuurlijk *of course, naturally*
het biljet *bill, banknote*
de munt *coin*
de cent *cent*
overmaken *to transfer, to remit*
de pincode *PIN code*
de bankpas *bank/debit card*
de bankrekening *bank account*
de spaarrekening *savings account*
(be)sparen *to save*
geld opnemen *to withdraw money,*
to take out money
het saldo *bank balance*
inzien *to view*
contant betalen *to pay in cash*
rekeningen betalen *to pay bills*
de rekening *bill, invoice*
de kosten *fees*
de kost *fee, cost*
uitgeven *to spend*
de fles *bottle*
de liter *litre*
de melk *milk*
de meter *metre*
daarom *therefore, for that reason,*
that's why

e. uur   ❑ countable   ❑ uncountable

een paar uur → ....

vijf uur → ....

f. wijn   ❑ countable   ❑ uncountable

een glas wijn → ....

twee wijntjes → ....

2. COMPLETE THESE SENTENCES WITH THE PAST PARTICIPLE OF THE VERB GIVEN IN PARENTHESES.

a. Ze heeft een foute code .... (gebruiken) en daarom (*therefore*) is haar spaarrekening .... (blokkeren).

b. Hij heeft gisteren eerst een account .... (aanmaken) en daarna een code .... (invoeren).

c. Ze hebben haar .... (feliciteren) met haar verjaardag.

d. Ik heb op een leuke vacature .... (solliciteren).

e. Heb je veel geld .... (verdienen)?

f. Ze zijn al zes keer .... (verhuizen)!

3. PUT THE WORDS IN THE CORRECT ORDER TO FORM A SENTENCE. THE FIRST WORD SHOULD BE THE ONE STARTING WITH A CAPITAL LETTER.

a. Na / wordt / de / alles / keer / geblokkeerd / derde → ....

b. Waarom / geld / je / op / zoveel / neem → ....?

c. Daar / niet / eens / ben / het / mee / ik → ....!

d. Ik / goed / bedenken / kon / wachtwoord / geen → ....

e. In / mei / niets / de / ik / maand / uitgegeven / heb → ....

4. LISTEN TO THE AUDIO, THEN WRITE OUT EACH SENTENCE. READ THEM OUT LOUD AND LISTEN TO THE AUDIO AGAIN TO CHECK YOUR ANSWERS.

🔊 29

a. ....?   d. ....?

b. ....   e. ....?

c. ....   f. ....

28.
MOVING HOUSE

DE VERHUIZING

AIMS	TOPICS

AIMS

- TALKING ABOUT WHERE THINGS ARE

- SPECIFYING HOUSEHOLD ITEMS

- EXPRESSING SATISFACTION

TOPICS

- SOME VOCABULARY FOR FURNITURE, APPLIANCES AND KITCHEN ITEMS

- CONTAINERS AND CONTENTS

- FORMING THE PLURAL OF NOUNS ENDING IN *-IE* AND *-EE*

- FORMING THE NEGATIVE WITH *MEER* MORE

- MORE ON VERBS OF POSITION

A NEW PLACE

Max: Let's load the heavy furniture first and *(already)* drive to the new place *(dwelling)*!

Sophie: What brilliant ideas you *(still)* always have! Then Chris can quickly put the kitchen stuff in boxes *(can Chris the kitchen's-little-things still soon in boxes put)*.

Max: Do you want to bring *(along-take)* the two televisions?

Sophie: No, the one from upstairs *(above)* goes to the neighbours.

Two hours later

Max: Everything is empty! Great, it's going nice and fast!

In the new residence

Sophie: The fridge *(cool-cupboard)* can be put *(set)* in the corner against the wall, and the dishwasher next to it, under the window.

Max: We're almost done *(clear)*! Who wants *(of-them)* coffee and *(with)* cake?

Sophie: First a glass of lemonade!

Max: I can't find the lemonade glasses and the coffee cups anywhere *(can ... nowhere more find)*.

Sophie: They are in the hallway. Did you put the little cake forks in the drawer *(Have you ... in the drawer laid)*?

Max: Hm, I can't find those either *(can I also not more find)* ... but here's a plant cutting for our new place!

Max: Laten we eerst de zware meubels inladen en vast naar de nieuwe woning rijden!

Sophie: Wat heb jij toch altijd briljante ideeën! Dan kan Chris de keukenspulletjes nog gauw in dozen stoppen.

Max: Wil je de twee televisies meenemen?

Sophie: Nee, die van boven gaat naar de buren.

Twee uur later

Max: Alles is leeg! Geweldig, het gaat lekker vlug!

In de nieuwe woning

Sophie: De koelkast kan in die hoek tegen de muur gezet en de afwasmachine ernaast, onder het raam!

Max: We zijn bijna klaar! Wie wil er koffie met gebak?

Sophie: Eerst een glas limonade!

Max: Ik kan de limonadeglazen en koffiekopjes nergens meer vinden.

Sophie: Die staan in de gang. Heb je de gebakvorkjes in de la gelegd?

Max: Eh, die kan ik ook niet meer vinden ... maar hier heb je een stekje voor onze nieuwe stek!

UNDERSTANDING THE DIALOGUE

→ **Een nieuwe stek** *A new place.* The term **de stek** denotes a *place, niche, living space,* but also, as we see in the last line, *plant cutting,* which is usually in the diminutive: **het stekje.**

→ **Dan kan Chris de keukenspulletjes nog gauw in dozen stoppen.** *Then Chris can quickly put the kitchen things in boxes* ('can Chris the kitchen's-little-things still quickly in boxes put'). The verb **stoppen** can mean *to stop* or *to insert.*

→ **De koelkast kan (…) tegen de muur gezet.** *The refrigerator can (…) be put against the wall.* Note that **gezet** is the past participle of **zetten** *to set.* Here it functions as the adjective *set.*

→ **We zijn bijna klaar!** *We are almost done!* The term **klaar** means *clear* as well as *ready.*

→ **Wie wil er koffie met gebak?** *Who wants coffee and cake?* Note that **er** *of it, of them* is required when the subject is indefinite.

→ **Heb je de gebakvorkjes in de la gelegd?** *Did you put the little cake forks in the drawer?* This is the present perfect ('have you … laid?'): **gelegd** is the past participle of the verb **leggen** *to lay.*

SOME VOCABULARY FOR MOVING HOUSE

If you're moving to a new place, these terms might come in handy: **de verhuiswagen** *moving van,* **boven** *above, upstairs,* **beneden** *below, downstairs,* **omhoog** *up, upwards,* **omlaag** *down, downwards,* **leeg** *empty,* **vol** *full,* **de trap** *stairs, ladder,* **het trapje** *stepladder,* **het dak** *roof,* **de zolder** *attic, loft,* **de kelder** *basement, cellar.*

ITEMS OF FURNITURE, HOUSEHOLD APPLIANCES, DISHES, ETC.

Some terms for common household items include: **de kast** *cupboard, closet, wardrobe, cabinet,* **de stoel** *chair,* **de radio** *radio,* **de klok** *clock,* **de diepvriezer** *freezer,* **de oven** *oven,* **de wasmachine** *washing machine,* **het bord** *plate,* **de schotel** *dish, bowl, saucer,* **het mes** *knife,* **de vork** *fork,* **de lepel** *spoon.*

CULTURAL NOTE

The homes found along canals are called **grachtenpand** (**de gracht** *canal* + **het pand** *building, premises*). They are tall, narrow and deep, as are **de pakhuizen** *warehouses,* which also lie along canals. You will often see a hoist or lifting device on the upper part of the façade of these buildings, as the stairs are narrow (**smal**) and steep (**steil**), and it is not possible to get large pieces of furniture or merchandise into the upper floors using the stairwell. While these external hoists are far less common on modern buildings, you can still see them on historic **grachtenpanden**. As you stroll along the canals (or take a canal cruise) in cities such as Amsterdam, raise your eyes so you can take in the full view of these buildings, some of which tilt!

◆ GRAMMAR
CONTAINERS AND CONTENTS

The difference between **een glas limonade** *a glass of lemonade* and **een limonadeglas** *a lemonade glass* is that one refers to the contents and the other to the container. The term for a container is usually a compound word in Dutch, with the word stress on the first word or syllable: **koffiekop** *coffee cup*, **soepkom** *soup bowl*, **luciferdoos** *matchbox* (**de lucifer** *match* + **de doos** *box*).

FORMING THE PLURAL OF NOUNS ENDING IN -*IE* AND -*EE*

• To form the plural of nouns ending in **-ie**:
→   add **-ën** to words in which the word stress falls on the last (or only) syllable:
   de kopie *copy* → **de kopieën** *copies*
   de knie *knee* → **de knieën** *knees*
→   if the word stress does not fall on the last syllable, put a ¨ over the final **-e** of the singular word and then add an **-n**:
   de bacterie *bacterium* → **de bacteriën** *bacteria*
   de porie *pore* → **de poriën** *pores*
→   some words that end in **-ie** form the plural by adding an **-s**, wherever the word stress falls. You have to learn these as you come across them. For example:
   de balie *counter* → **de balies** *counters*
   de familie *family* → **de families** *families*

• To form the plural of nouns that end in **-ee**:
→   add **-ën**:
   het idee *idea* → **de ideeën** *ideas*
   de zee *sea* → **de zeeën** *seas*

FORMING THE NEGATIVE WITH *MEER* MORE

In lesson 16, we saw how to form the negative of an indefinite noun with **geen ... meer** *no ... more*. With a definite noun, it is formed with **niet ... meer**. But remember that in English, it is far more common to make the verb negative rather than the noun (e.g. *I can't* or *I didn't* or *I haven't*, etc.). Aside from **geen** and **niet**, the term **meer** *more* can be used with various negative words in Dutch: **nooit** *never* → **nooit meer** *never again* ('never more') or **nergens** *nowhere* → **nergens meer** *anywhere either* or *anywhere anymore* ('nowhere more').

▲ CONJUGATION
MORE ON VERBS OF POSITION

The verbs of position **staan** *to stand*, **liggen** *to lie*, **hangen** *to hang* and **zitten** *to sit* (which can all translate as *to be* when indicating the location of something) have corresponding verbs that are used when an object is in the process of being moved (i.e. *to put*). These are **(neer)zetten** *to set/put (down)*, **(neer)leggen** *to lay/put (down)*, **(op)hangen** *to hang/put (up)* and **doen/stoppen (in)** *to put (in)*.

De tafel staat tegen de muur. *The table is (standing) against the wall.* →
Ik zet de tafel tegen de muur. *I set/put the table against the wall.*
Het mes ligt in de la. *The knife is (lying) in the drawer.* →
Ik leg het mes in de la. *I lay/put the knife in the drawer.*
De lamp hangt aan de muur. *The lamp is (hanging) on the wall.* →
Ik hang de lamp aan de muur. *I hang/put the lamp on the wall.*
De rok zit in de wasmachine. *The skirt is (sitting) in the washing machine.* →
Ik doe/stop de rok in de wasmachine. *I put the skirt in the washing machine.*

The separable prefixes **neer-** and **op-** must be included if the place where the object is being put is not specified in the sentence: **Ik zet het glas neer.** *I set/put the glass down.* **Ik hang de lamp op.** *I hang/put the lamp up.*

⬡ EXERCISES

1. COMPLETE THESE SENTENCES WITH THE CORRECT VERB FOR 'PUT'.

a. Ze .... het bureau in de woonkamer. (2 possibilities)

b. Hebben jullie de fietsen voor het huis ....?

c. Hij .... het dossier op de grond.

d. Kun je de lamp aan de muur ....?

e. Ze .... het geld in haar portemonnee (*wallet*). (2 possibilities)

● VOCABULARY

de verhuizing *moving house*
de verhuiswagen *moving van*
de stek *place, niche*
het stekje *cutting, sprig*
zwaar *heavy*
het meubel *piece of furniture*
inladen *to load*
vast *firmly, surely*
rijden *to drive, to ride*
briljant *brilliant*
de keukenspulletjes *kitchen things*
nog *still, yet*
gauw *soon, shortly, before long*
de doos *box*
meenemen *to bring, to take along*
de buur *neighbour*
de buurman / de buurvrouw
  neighbour (m./f.)
leeg *empty*
vol *full*
geweldig *great, amazing, fantastic*
vlug *rapid, quick, fast*
de koelkast *refrigerator*
de kast *cupboard, cabinet*
de diepvriezer *freezer*
de hoek *corner, angle*
tegen *against*
het raam *window*
klaar *clear, ready*
klaar zijn *to be done*
de limonade *lemonade*
het pakhuis *warehouse*
smal *narrow*
steil *steep*
de luciferdoos *matchbox*
de lucifer *match*
de kopie *copy*
nergens *nowhere, not anywhere*
de gang *hall, corridor*

de la *drawer*
(neer)zetten *to set/put (down)*
(neer)leggen *to lay/put (down)*
(op)hangen *to hang/put (up)*
stoppen/doen (in) *to put (in)*
boven *above, upstairs*
beneden *below, downstairs*
omhoog *up, upwards*
omlaag *down, downwards*
de trap *stairs, ladder*
het trapje *stepladder*
het dak *roof*
de zolder *attic, loft*
de kelder *basement, cellar*
de stoel *chair*
de radio *radio*
de klok *clock*
de oven *oven*
de wasmachine *washing machine*
de afwasmachine *dishwasher*
de afwas *doing the dishes,*
  washing-up
het bord *plate*
de soepkom *soup bowl*
de kom *bowl*
de schotel *dish, bowl, saucer*
de gebakvork *cake fork*
het gebak *cake, pastry*
de vork *fork*
het mes *knife*
de lepel *spoon*
het grachtenpand *canal house*
de knie *knee*
de bacterie *bacterium*
de porie *pore*
de balie *counter*
de portemonnee *wallet*

2. LINK THE CONTAINER TO ITS CONTENTS, THEN TRANSLATE THEM.

a. een theekop   •
b. de soepkom   •
c. het luciferdoosje   •
d. twee wijnglazen   •

• 1. twee glazen wijn
• 2. een kop thee
• 3. de kom soep
• 4. het doosje lucifers

→ ....
→ ....
→ ....
→ ....

3. WRITE THE PLURAL FORMS OF THESE NOUNS AND THEN LISTEN TO THE RECORDING. REPEAT EACH WORD OUT LOUD IN THE SINGULAR AND THE PLURAL.

30

a. het idee → ....
b. de familie → ....
c. de bacterie → ....
d. de zee → ....
e. de kopie → ....

f. de epidemie → ....
g. de televisie → ....
h. de balie → ....
i. de advertentie → ....

4. LISTEN TO THE RECORDING AND WRITE EACH SENTENCE.

30

a. ....!

b. ....?

c. ....?

d. ....

e. ....

f. ....! ....! ....

254

29.
ON HOLIDAY

OP VAKANTIE

AIMS	TOPICS
• **TALKING ABOUT YOUR HOLIDAYS** • **DESCRIBING THE WEATHER AND THE SEASONS** • **DETAILING A TRIP**	• **SOME VOCABULARY RELATED TO WEATHER AND THE SEASONS** • **THE SIMPLE PAST OF REGULAR VERBS** • **THE PERFECT TENSES OF VERBS OF MOVEMENT: THE AUXILIARY VERB *ZIJN* TO BE OR *HEBBEN* TO HAVE**

ON HOLIDAY

Berend: I had *(have)* a strange dream!

It was summer and the weather was bad *(and bad weather)* and I decided to go on holiday.

I took the train to the airport. Because of strong *(the hard)* wind, branches had fallen on the rails *(had there branches ... fallen)* and we couldn't continue *(could we not further travel)*.

I wanted to transfer, but then I was suddenly sitting on *(then sat I suddenly in)* a bus.

The bus driver took *(made)* a detour: we went *(have ... ridden)* to Schiphol via Apeldoorn!

I had lost my passport, but a friendly flight attendant showed me to a seat anyway *(indicated to-me still a seat)*.

Once we landed *(Once landed)*, I took a taxi to a five-star hotel. There, a waiter set out a drink and a herring for me *(put a waiter an aperitif and a herring for me ready)*.

Then all of a sudden I was walking *(walked I suddenly)* in a supermarket in search of a beer and ...

Paulien: Then your alarm went off and you were terribly thirsty *(had terrible thirst)*!

Berend: Ik heb een vreemde droom gehad!

Het was zomer en slecht weer en ik besloot om op vakantie te gaan.

Ik nam de trein naar het vliegveld. Vanwege de harde wind waren er takken op de rails gevallen en konden we niet verder rijden.

Ik wilde overstappen maar toen zat ik opeens in een bus.

De buschauffeur maakte een omweg: we zijn via Apeldoorn naar Schiphol gereden!

Ik was m'n paspoort kwijt, maar een vriendelijke stewardess wees me toch een zitplaats aan.

Eenmaal geland, nam ik een taxi naar een vijfsterrenhotel. Daar zette een ober een borreltje en een haring voor me klaar.

Toen liep ik ineens in een supermarkt op zoek naar bier en …

Paulien: Toen liep je wekker af en je had vreselijke dorst!

■ UNDERSTANDING THE DIALOGUE

→ **ik besloot om op vakantie te gaan** / *decided to go on holiday*: **besloot** *decided* is the singular simple past of **besluiten (om)** *to decide (to)* (note that **te** is required before the following verb). There is more information about irregular verbs in the appendix (p. 282). Other useful holiday expressions include **op/met vakantie gaan** *to go on holiday* and **Prettige vakantie!** *Enjoy your holiday!*

→ **ik nam de trein** / *took the train*: **nam** *took* is the singular simple past of **nemen** *to take.*

→ **(...) konden we niet verder rijden** *we couldn't continue* ('could we not further travel'). The form **konden** *could* is the plural simple past of **kunnen** *to be able to, can*. Note that **rijden** in Dutch can mean *to ride*, but also refers to travelling in any form of transport with wheels: *to drive, to roll, to travel*, etc.

→ **(...) zat ik** / *was sitting*: **zat** *sat, was sitting* is the singular simple past of **zitten** *to sit.*

→ **we zijn (...) naar Schiphol gereden** *we went (...) to Schiphol* ('we have ... ridden'): **gereden** *ridden, travelled* is the past participle of **rijden** *to ride, to travel*. Remember that the present perfect of verbs of movement is formed with **zijn**.

→ **(...) wees me (...) aan** *indicated to me*: this is the singular simple past of the separable-prefix verb **aanwijzen** *to indicate, to designate, to point to.*

→ **(...) liep ik** / *walked, I was walking*: **liep** *walked, was walking* is the singular simple past of **lopen** *to walk.*

→ **(...) liep je wekker af** *your alarm went off* ('went your alarm off'). The separable-prefix verb **aflopen** means *to expire, to end*, but can also mean *to ring, to go off.*

VOCABULARY RELATED TO THE WEATHER AND THE SEASONS

On holiday or off, the weather is always a common topic of conversation. Here is some useful vocabulary you might need: **de lucht** *air, sky*, **de zon** *sun*, **de regen** *rain*, **de wolk** *cloud*, **de bui** *shower, storm, squall*, **de paraplu** *umbrella*, **droog** *dry*, **nat** *wet*, **waaien** *to blow, to gust* (wind), **schijnen** *to shine*, **voorspellen** *to predict, to forecast*, **het is licht/donker** *it is light/dark*, **het seizoen** *season*, **de lente** *spring*, **de zomer** *summer*, **de herfst** *autumn*, **de winter** *winter*.

CULTURAL NOTE

The Dutch appreciate an evening drink at **de borreltijd** ('drink-time'). The term **de borrel** *alcoholic drink* usually refers to a shot, of which **de jenever**, a type of Dutch gin, is one of the most common. It's a traditional spirit flavoured with juniper berries.

Eating herring is another Dutch tradition. At the end of the 16th century, Dutch fishermen began to **haring kaken**, clean and salt herring and put the salted fish in barrels to conserve them. At first this was done when the fish were brought to shore, and later larger fishing boats made it possible to process the fish on board. The Dutch continue to eat a lot of herring, especially between May and July when herring have the highest fat content and are known as **Hollandse Nieuwe** *new herring*.

▲ CONJUGATION
THE SIMPLE PAST OF REGULAR VERBS

The simple past of regular verbs has only two forms: a singular conjugation (*I, you, he, she, it*) and a plural conjugation (*we, they*). Like the past participle, the conjugation ending is determined by the last letter of the verb stem.

If the verb stem ends in **-t, -k, -f, -s, -ch** or **-p**,* the ending **-te** is added in the singular, and **-ten** in the plural. If the verb stem already ends in **-t**, the **-t** is doubled.
* Remember the mnemonic **'t kofschip**, or '**s**o**f**t **k**et**ch**u**p**'.
maken *to make*: **mak**** + **-te/-ten** →
maakte *I, you, he, she made, was making* **/ maakten** *we, they made, were making*
praten *to talk*: → **prat**** + **-te/-ten** →
praatte *I, you, he, she talked, was talking* **/ praatten** *we, they talked, were talking*
** Don't forget to double the vowel if it is long.

If the verb stem ends in any other letter, the ending **-de** is added in the singular, and **-den** in the plural. If the verb stem already ends in **-d**, the **-d** is doubled.
dineren *to dine*: **diner** + **-de/-den** →
dineerde *I, you, he, she dined, was dining* **/ dineerden** *we, they dined, were dining*
raden *to guess*: → **rad** + **-de/-den** →
raadde *I, you, he, she guessed, was guessing* **/ raadden** *we, they guessed, were guessing*

The simple past of verb stems ending in **-v** or **-z** is formed by adding **-de/-den**. Don't forget that the **v** turns into an **f** at the end of a word, and a **z** into an **s**.
geloven *to believe*: **gelov** + **-de/-den** →
geloofde *I, you, he, she believed* **/ geloofden** *we, they believed*
reizen *to travel*: → **reiz** + **-de/-den** →
reisde *I, you, he, she, it travelled, was travelling* **/ reisden** *we, they travelled, were travelling*

When conjugating separable-prefix verbs in the simple past, the prefix is detached and moved to the end of the clause:

terugbellen *to call back* →

Ik belde mijn broer meteen terug. *I called my brother back right away.* ('I called my brother immediately back.')

klaarzetten *to prepare* →

Hij zette een glas wijn voor me klaar. *He got me a glass of wine.* ('He set a glass wine for me ready.')

THE PERFECT TENSES OF VERBS OF MOVEMENT: THE AUXILIARY *ZIJN* TO BE OR *HEBBEN* TO HAVE

In most cases, **zijn** *to be* is used as the auxiliary to form the perfect tenses of verbs of movement. This is the case if the verb indicates a change of place or a destination (**zijn** is also used with verbs that indicate a change of state):

We zijn **naar Spanje gefietst.** *We cycled to Spain* ('have to Spain cycled').

However, in cases in which the means of movement rather than a change in place is emphasized, the perfect tenses are formed with **hebben** *to have*:

We hebben **in Spanje gefietst.** *We cycled in Spain* ('have in Spain cycled').

 **EXERCISES**

1. LINK THE TERMS THAT GO TOGETHER.

a. de regen •   • 1. schijnen

b. de jenever •   • 2. de bui

c. de zon •   • 3. voorspellen

d. het weer •   • 4. de borrel

2. CONJUGATE THESE VERBS IN THE SINGULAR AND PLURAL SIMPLE PAST.

a. maken →.....................................

b. landen →....................................

c. zetten →....................................

d. leggen → ....

e. fietsen →...................................

f. verwennen → ....

g. passen →...................................

h. bespelen →.................................

⬤ VOCABULARY

op/met vakantie *on vacation*
Prettige vakantie!
 Enjoy your holiday!
vreemd *strange*
de droom *dream*
slecht *bad*
het weer *weather*
besluiten (om) (te) *to decide (to) +*
 infinitive
het vliegveld *airport*
vanwege *because of, due to*
hard *hard, harsh, fierce*
de tak *branch*
de rail *rail*
vallen *to fall*
overstappen *to transfer, to change*
opeens / ineens *suddenly, at once*
de buschauffeur / de
 buschauffeuse *bus driver (m./f.)*
de chauffeur / de chauffeuse
 driver (m./f.)
de omweg *detour, diversion*
via *via*
het paspoort *passport*
kwijt (zijn) *(to have) lost*
vriendelijk *friendly*
de steward / de stewardess
 flight attendant (m./f.)
aanwijzen *to indicate, to designate*
de zitplaats *seat*
eenmaal *once*
landen *to land*
de taxi *taxi*

de ster *star*
klaarzetten *to set out, to lay out, to*
 prepare something for someone
de ober *server, waiter* (m.)
de serveerster *server, waitress* (f.)
toen *then*
de supermarkt *supermarket*
aflopen *to expire, to ring, to go off*
vreselijk *terrible, terribly*
de lucht *air, sky*
de zon *sun*
de regen *rain*
de wolk *cloud*
de wind *wind*
de bui *storm, shower, squall*
de paraplu *umbrella*
droog *dry*
nat *wet*
waaien *to blow, to gust* (wind)
schijnen *to shine*
voorspellen *to forecast*
Het is licht/donker. *It's light/dark.*
het licht *light*
het donker *dark*
het seizoen *season*
de lente *spring*
de zomer *summer*
de herfst *autumn*
de winter *winter*
de borrel *alcoholic drink, shot*
de borreltijd *'drink time'*
de jenever *Dutch gin*
de haring *herring*
de Hollandse Nieuwe
 new herring

3. PUT THESE SENTENCES INTO THE PRESENT PERFECT.

a. Ze belt haar zus meteen terug.

→...

b. Zet je een glas limonade voor hem klaar?

→...

c. Ze rijden naar het strand.

→...

d. Hij fietst tien kilometer (*kilometres*) op het eiland.

→...

31

4. LISTEN TO THE RECORDING AND SELECT *WAAR* IF THE SENTENCE MATCHES AND *NIET WAAR* IF IT DOESN'T. THEN READ EACH SENTENCE OUT LOUD AND LISTEN TO THE AUDIO AGAIN TO NOTE THE DIFFERENCES.

	WAAR	NIET WAAR
a. Toen liepen we opeens op de markt.		
b. Ze moest drie keer overstappen.		
c. De stewardess wees me geen zitplaats aan.		
d. Vanwege de harde regen waren er takken op de rails gevallen.		
e. De taxichauffeur maakte een omweg.		
f. De ober zette een borreltje en een haring voor hem neer.		
g. Waar is m'n paraplu?		

30.
AN UNKNOWN DESTINATION

EEN ONBEKENDE BESTEMMING

AIMS	TOPICS

- ASKING FOR AND GIVING INFORMATION

- DISCUSSING YOUR PLANS

- DESCRIBING YOUR STUDIES

- TALKING ABOUT FUTURE OR CONDITIONAL ACTIONS

- VOCABULARY RELATED TO STUDIES

- VOCABULARY RELATED TO TRAVELLING

- THE PREPOSITIONS *IN* IN AND *NAAR* TO

- THE PAST PERFECT (HAD ... TRAVELLED)

- THE FUTURE VERB *ZULLEN* WILL AND THE CONDITIONAL *ZOUDEN* WOULD

AN UNKNOWN DESTINATION

Agnes: Do you have any *(yet)* news regarding *(in connection with)* your daughter's studies?

Frank: Yes, she has been accepted at an institute of technology that scores quite highly in the international rankings *(which sizeably high in the international ranking scores)*. She moved into student housing a week ago *(has a week ago her entry taken in a student-house)*. I have the impression that she is very happy with it *(she there very pleased with is)*. And what are your son's plans?

Agnes: As soon as he had passed his exams *(Once he for his exams succeeded had)*, he *(has)* booked an around-the-world ticket.

Frank: Doesn't that scare you *(Find you that not scary)*?

Agnes: In the past *(Formerly)*, I would have found that dangerous, but not anymore. But I have to pack my bags, because my husband has booked a trip for us together to an unknown destination!

Frank: I would like that as well!

Agnes: Heb je al nieuws in verband met de studie van je dochter?

Frank: Ja, ze is aangenomen op een technische universiteit, die flink hoog op de internationale rangorde scoort. Ze heeft een week geleden haar intrek genomen in een studentenhuis. Ik heb de indruk dat ze er zeer tevreden mee is. En wat zijn de plannen van jouw zoon?

Agnes: Zodra hij voor z'n examens geslaagd was, heeft hij een wereldticket geboekt.

Frank: Vind je dat niet eng?

Agnes: Vroeger zou ik dat gevaarlijk hebben gevonden, maar nu niet meer. Maar ik moet m'n koffers pakken, want m'n man heeft een reis voor ons samen gereserveerd, naar een onbekende bestemming!

Frank: Dat zou ik ook wel willen!

⬛ UNDERSTANDING THE DIALOGUE

→ **ze is aangenomen op ...** *she has been accepted at ...* This is the present perfect, with **zijn** as the auxiliary (because the action is a change of state) and the past participle of the separable-prefix verb **aannemen** *to hire, to accept, to admit.*

→ **zijn/haar intrek nemen** *to move into* ('him/her entry to-take'): note this expression for moving.

→ Also note the useful expression **een week geleden** *a week ago.*

→ **(...) dat ze er zeer tevreden mee is** *(...) that she is really happy with it* ('that she there very contented with is'). The adverb **zeer** *very* is rather formal.

→ **Zodra hij voor z'n examens geslaagd was ...** *As soon as he had passed his exams ....* This is the past perfect of **slagen** *to succeed*, with **zijn** as the auxiliary (in the simple past) because the action is a change of state.

→ **m'n koffers pakken** *to pack my bags.* The primary meaning of **pakken** is *to take, to grab.* You could also say **(een koffer) inpakken** *to pack a suitcase.*

SOME VOCABULARY RELATED TO EDUCATION

het onderwijsprogramma *educational programme* (**het onderwijs** *education*), **de school** *school*, **het klaslokaal** *classroom* (**het lokaal** *meeting room*), **rekenen** *arithmetic, calculation*, **het vak** *academic subject*, **wiskunde** *mathematics* (**-kunde** *study*), **natuurkunde** *physics*, **geschiedenis** *history*, **aardrijkskunde** *geography* (**de aarde** *earth*), **culturele en kunstzinnige vorming** *cultural and artistic education* (**de kunst** *art*), **lichamelijke opvoeding** *physical education* (**het lichaam** *body*, **de opvoeding** *upbringing*), **Engels** *English*, **Duits** *German*, **maatschappijleer** *civics* (**de maatschappij** *society*, **-leer** *study*), **eindexamen doen** *to do one's final exams, to graduate*, **de faculteit** *faculty*, **de rechtenstudie** *law degree* (**het recht** *justice*).

SOME VOCABULARY RELATED TO TRAVELLING

het station *station*, **de vlucht** *flight*, **de/het vliegticket** *plane ticket* (**vliegen** *to fly*), **de boarding pass** *boarding pass*, **de vleugel** *wing*, **de staart** *queue*, **de rugzak** *backpack, rucksack*, **de reistas** *travel bag* (**de reis** *trip*, **de tas** *bag*), **de handbagage** *carry-on bag*, **het mededelingenbord** *notice board* (**de mededeling** *announcement*).

EDUCATION IN THE NETHERLANDS

Dutch children from ages 4 to 12 go to **het basisonderwijs** *primary school*. From ages 12 to 16/18, they are in **het voortgezet onderwijs** *secondary education*.

After this, depending on their academic pathway, they can opt to move directly into a professional career or to continue their studies. There are two types of higher education: **het hoger beroepsonderwijs** *higher vocational education* (**het beroep** *profession, occupation*) and **het wetenschappelijk onderwijs** *academic education* (**de wetenschap** *knowledge, science,* **de wetenschapper** *academic, scholar, scientist*).

◆ GRAMMAR
THE PREPOSITIONS *IN* IN AND *NAAR* TO

• The preposition **in** *in* is used before a month, a year or a place. As in English, it is used when referring to the place itself, without conveying an idea of moving from one place to another:

Het is koud in november. *It is cold in November.*
Hij is in 2018 geboren. *He was born in 2018.*
Ze loopt in de stad. *She walks in the city.*
in bad *in the bath*; **in bed** *in bed*; **in een winkel werken** *to work in a shop.*

• The preposition **naar** *to* is used to convey a direction, a destination or movement from one place to another, and is usually found with the verb **gaan** *to go* or another verb of movement:

naar het strand gaan *to go to the beach*; **naar bed gaan** *to go to bed*; **naar de stad fietsen** *to cycle to the city.*

Note the difference between these two sentences:
Hij gaat iets drinken in een café. *He goes for a drink in a café.*
Hij gaat naar het café. *He goes to the café.*

▲ CONJUGATION
THE PAST PERFECT

The past perfect (e.g. *had ... visited*) is used to refer to an action that happened before and directly influenced another event in the past. It is formed with **hebben** *to have* or **zijn** *to be* conjugated in the simple past and a past participle, which is generally placed at the end of the clause. The auxiliary can be placed before or after it:
Zodra hij voor z'n examens was geslaagd/geslaagd was**, heeft hij een wereldticket geboekt.**
As soon as he had passed his exams, he booked an around-the-world ticket.

Following **nadat** *after*, the past perfect is required:

Nadat ze hadden gegeten/gegeten hadden, zijn ze naar bed gegaan.

After they had eaten, they went to bed.

THE FUTURE VERB *ZULLEN* AND THE CONDITIONAL *ZOUDEN*

The present tense of **zullen** *will, shall* is **zal** in the singular and **zullen** in the plural. There is also an alternative form in the second-person singular: **je/u zult**. We've seen that most of the time, a future action is expressed with the present tense and a word or phrase that indicates a future time. The use of **zullen** is a bit more formal:

Ik zal morgen een vlucht voor mijn baas boeken.

Tomorrow I will book a flight for my boss.

This verb can also be used to:

→ make a suggestion (as a question, with the pronouns **ik** or **we/wij**):

Zullen we morgen een vlucht boeken? *Shall we book a flight tomorrow?*

→ express a probability (used with the adverb **wel**):

Hij zal wel moe zijn. *He must be tired.* ('He will well tired be.')

→ express a strong wish or necessity:

Je zult voor dat examen moeten slagen! *You will have to pass that exam!*

The simple past tense of **zullen** is **zou** in the singular and **zouden** in the plural. These verb forms are used to express the conditional *would*:

Vroeger zou ik dat gevaarlijk hebben gevonden/gevonden hebben.

In the past I would have found that dangerous.

Also note **zou(den) ... willen**: *would like*, which is often used with **graag** *gladly* or **wel** *well* (in the sense of *really*).

🛑 EXERCISES

1. COMPLETE THE SENTENCES WITH THE CORRECT PREPOSITION, *NAAR* OR *IN*.

a. Ze gaat met de tram .... de binnenstad.

b. Ze gaan iets eten .... de binnenstad.

c. We zijn moe en we gaan .... bed.

d. Waar is hij? Hij is moe en hij ligt .... bed.

e. Ben je ook .... maart geboren?

● VOCABULARY

onbekend *unknown*
de bestemming *destination*
het nieuws *news*
in verband met *in connection with, regarding*
aannemen *to accept, to admit*
technisch *technical, technological*
de universiteit *university*
flink *sizeable*
hoog *high*
internationaal *international*
de rangorde *rank, ranking*
scoren *to score*
geleden *ago*
de intrek nemen *to move in*
het studentenhuis *student housing*
de indruk *impression*
zeer *very*
tevreden *satisfied, pleased, content*
het plan *plan*
het examen *exam*
slagen *to succeed*
de/het wereldticket *around-the-world ticket*
de wereld *world*
de/het ticket *ticket*
boeken / reserveren *to book, to reserve*
eng *scary, frightening*
zodra *as soon as*
vroeger *previously, formerly*
gevaarlijk *dangerous*
de koffer *suitcase, baggage*
(een koffer) (in)pakken *to pack a bag*
de reis *trip*
verre *far*
samen *together*
de school *school*
het klaslokaal *classroom*
het lokaal *meeting room*
rekenen *arithmetic, calculation*

het vak *academic subject*
de wiskunde *mathematics*
de natuurkunde *physics*
de geschiedenis *history*
de aardrijkskunde *geography*
de culturele en kunstzinnige vorming *cultural and artistic education*
de kunst *art*
de lichamelijke opvoeding *physical education*
het lichaam *body*
de opvoeding *upbringing*
het Duits *German* (language)
de maatschappijleer *civics*
de maatschappij *society*
eindexamen doen *to do one's final exams*
het eindexamen *final exam*
de faculteit *faculty*
de rechtenstudie *law studies*
het station *station*
de vlucht *flight*
de/het vliegticket *plane ticket*
de vleugel *wing*
de staart *queue*
de rugzak *backpack, rucksack*
de reistas *travel bag*
de tas *bag*
de handbagage *carry-on bag*
het mededelingenbord *notice board*
het bord *board*
het onderwijs *education*
het onderwijsprogramma *educational programme*
het basisonderwijs *primary education*
het voortgezet onderwijs *secondary education*
het hoger beroepsonderwijs *higher vocational education*
het wetenschappelijk onderwijs *academic education*

2. USE THE ELEMENTS TO WRITE SENTENCES IN THE PAST PERFECT.

a. Ze een foute code gebruiken / ze blokkeren haar rekening

Nadat ....

b. Hij landen / een taxi nemen

Nadat ....

c. Ik voor mijn examen slagen / verre *(far)* reis maken

Zodra ....

d. We tas inpakken / een vakantie boeken

Toen ....

3. TRANSLATE THESE SENTENCES INTO ENGLISH.

a. Ze is een week geleden op een technische school aangenomen.

→...

b. Ik zal voor dat examen moeten slagen!

→...

c. Nadat ze de zware meubels hadden ingeladen, zijn ze naar hun nieuwe woning gereden.

→...

d. Zodra hij zijn bril had opgezet, heeft hij het pakje opengemaakt.

→...

4. LISTEN TO THESE SENTENCES AND COMPLETE THEM. WHAT DO THEY MEAN?

32

a. Je .... moe zijn!

→...

b. Vroeger .... ik dat gevaarlijk.................................... .

→...

c. We .... dat .... doen.

→...

d. Ik .... morgen een .... Frankrijk ....

→...

e. .... een taxi ....?

→...

270

EXERCISE ANSWERS

NOTE

On the following pages, you'll find the answers to the exercises in the lessons. The exercises accompanied by audio are indicated by the (◁) icon, along with the number of the corresponding track. The exercise recordings are found on the same track as the lesson dialogue, following just after it (or after the list of numbers in lessons 6, 7 and 12); they have the same track number.

1. FIRST ENCOUNTER

1. a. 2 **b.** 4 **c.** 1 **d.** 3

2. a. in **b.** op **c.** Tot **d.** op

3. a. Jullie <u>wonen</u> in Amsterdam.
b. <u>Heten</u> jullie Mark en Bernie?
c. <u>Komt</u> u voor de kaasproeverij?
d. En waar <u>woont</u> u?

03 🔊 **4. a.** Waar <u>wonen</u> jullie?
b. <u>Komt</u> u voor de proeverij?
c. De kaasmaker <u>heet</u> meneer Peters.
d. <u>Staan</u> jullie op de lijst?
e. <u>Woont</u> u in Amsterdam?

2. TALKING ABOUT YOURSELF

1. a. de **b.** het **c.** de **d.** het

2. a. <u>Ik</u> kom uit Utrecht. **b.** <u>Ze</u> hebben een hond en een kat. **c.** <u>Ze</u> heeft een broer.
d. Heeft <u>u</u> een huisdier? **e.** <u>We</u> zijn hier.
f. <u>Je</u> hebt een zus. **g.** Waar wonen <u>jullie</u>?

3. a. hebben **b.** bent **c.** is **d.** hebt

04 🔊 **4. a.** Mijn <u>voornaam</u> is David. **b.** Ik <u>heet</u> Maud. **c.** We komen <u>uit</u> Giethoorn. **d.** Is uw <u>achternaam</u> Smid? **e.** <u>Heeft</u> Bernie een huisdier?

3. DESCRIBING SOMEONE

1. a. Ik <u>werk</u> voor de televisie. **b.** <u>Spreekt</u> u Spaans en Frans? **c.** De tulp is <u>rood.</u>
d. Hij <u>woont</u> in dat <u>grote</u> huis. **e.** Ze <u>werken</u> in Zaandam.

2. a. Mag ik je even voorstellen? Dit is de buurvrouw en dat is de oppas. Aangenaam. **b.** Mag ik je even voorstellen? Dit is Maud en dat is Thijs. Aangenaam. **c.** Mag ik je even voorstellen? Dit is de nieuwe leerling en dat is de nieuwe docente. Aangenaam.

3. a. Argentijnse **b.** rood **c.** groot **d.** nieuwe

05 🔊 **4. a.** Ze komt uit <u>Argentinië</u>. **b.** Hij spreekt <u>Nederlands</u> en <u>Spaans</u>. **c.** Mijn <u>Franse</u> oppas is niet lief. **d.** Hij is <u>Nederlander</u> en zij is <u>Française</u>.

4. CHEERS!

1. a. She is Italian and he is Dutch. **b.** They come from Portugal. **c.** He speaks Dutch, French and Spanish. **d.** We say 'France', but the Netherlands. **e.** A Frenchman speaks French.

2. a. 2. Zullen we <u>wat gaan drinken?</u>
b. 3. Ze wonen <u>hier al tien jaar.</u>
c. 1. Spreekt zij <u>Italiaans en Portugees?</u>
d. 4. Ik neem <u>een glas witte wijn.</u>

3. a. zeggen **b.** kennen **c.** witte **d.** grappig

06 🔊 **4. a.** <u>Nou</u>, eigenlijk heet ik Bernard. / Well, actually my name is Bernard. **b.** Zeg <u>maar</u> gewoon Ben! / You can just call me Ben! **c.** Dat is een Nederlandse naam <u>hoor</u>! / That is a Dutch name, you know!

5. AT THE MARKET

1. a. Hoe duur zijn de bananen?
b. Hoeveel kost de haring?
c. Wat kosten de bessen?

2. a. De bananen kosten twee euro per kilo. **b.** De haring is duur: een euro per stuk. **c.** Een ons bessen kost zeven euro.

3. a. de bessen **b.** de kleuren **c.** de bananen **d.** de visboeren **e.** de appels/ appelen

07 🔊 **4. a.** Zegt u het maar! / What would you like? (formal) **b.** Wat duur! / That's expensive! **c.** Dank u wel. / Thank you very much. (formal) **d.** Ja, graag! / Yes, please!

6. FAMILY

1. a. vier **b.** veertien **c.** acht **d.** achttien **e.** drie **f.** dertien

2. a. They have a daughter who's 16 and a son who's 11. **b.** On this photo are my grandad and granny. **c.** What a cute child! **d.** Do you already have grandchildren? Yes, I am already a grandmother.

3. a. groot **b.** grote **c.** leuk **d.** leuke

08 🔊 **4. a.** niet waar **b.** niet waar **c.** waar **d.** niet waar **e.** waar

7. ON THE PHONE

1. a. achtentachtig   **b.** negenenveertig   **c.** zesendertig   **d.** achtentwintig   **e.** negenennegentig   **f.** honderdeen

2. a. <u>Waar</u> werkt de buurvrouw? **b.** <u>Waarom</u> wonen jullie in een huis op de dijk? **c.** <u>Wanneer</u> begint de kaasproeverij? **d.** <u>Wat</u> is je naam? **e.** <u>Wat</u> doe je straks?

3. a. Good morning, this is Mr Hans. Is your father home?
b. Excuse me. I have the wrong number.
c. You can reach her on her mobile.
d. Hello, who am I speaking to?
e. This is the answering machine of Ivo. Leave a message after the tone.

09 🔊 **4. a.** Hebben zij niet een <u>dochter</u> van <u>achttien</u> en een <u>zoon</u> van <u>zestien</u>? Ja, dat klopt. **b.** <u>Wat</u> doet ze <u>straks</u>? <u>Dat weet ik niet</u>. **c.** Wat <u>wil</u> je drinken? Ik <u>neem</u> een glas <u>rode wijn</u>. En jij? **d.** Zullen we <u>naar het café</u> gaan? Ja, <u>goed</u> idee! **e.** Sorry, hij is <u>momenteel niet thuis</u>.

8. A NEW ID CARD

1 a. 3   **b.** 4   **c.** 1   **d.** 2

2. a. U staat <u>op</u> de lijst. / U staat niet op de lijst.   **b.** Ik zie je naam <u>in</u> het bestand. / Ik zie je naam niet in het bestand.   **c.** We kunnen <u>op</u> donderdag. / We kunnen niet op donderdag.   **d.** Ze reizen <u>op</u> 3 maart <u>naar</u> het buitenland. / Ze reizen niet op 3 maart naar het buitenland. / Ze reizen op 3 maart niet naar het buitenland.

3. a. Ik <u>geef</u> u een nieuwe identiteitskaart. **b.** Hij <u>leest</u> de krant. **c.** Ze <u>reist</u> niet vaak. **d.** <u>Geeft</u> u mij dan maar drie tulpen.

10 🔊 **4. a.** <u>Hoe oud</u> zijn je kinderen? **b.** Jullie moeten eerst <u>een afspraak maken</u>. **c.** We <u>komen</u> onze kaarten <u>ophalen</u>. **d.** Doe <u>dan maar</u> twee ons bessen! **e.** Hij <u>heeft</u> een nieuwe rekenmachine <u>nodig</u>.

9. DAILY ACTIVITIES

1. a. Het is negen uur vijfenveertig. Het is kwart voor tien 's ochtends/'s morgens.

b. Het is zeventien uur vijf. Het is vijf over vijf 's middags. **c.** Het is drie uur vijftien. Het is kwart over drie 's nachts. **d.** Het is twintig uur vijfendertig. Het is vijf over half negen 's avonds.

2. a. Het is tien <u>voor/over</u> half negen. / It's 8:20. / It's 8:40. **b.** Zij heeft zin <u>in</u> een glas witte wijn en hij <u>in</u> een patatje <u>met</u> mayonaise. / She fancies a glass of white wine, and he wants fries with mayonnaise. **c.** We hebben zin <u>om naar</u> het buitenland te gaan. / We feel like going abroad. **d.** De pont komt <u>over</u> een kwartier. / The ferry arrives in a quarter of an hour. **e.** Ga je een kroketje <u>uit</u> de muur trekken? / Are you going to get a croquette (from the wall)? **f.** Hoe laat ben je terug? <u>Om</u> negen uur. / What time will you be back? At 9:00. **g.** Ze blijven <u>in</u> bed <u>tot</u> tien uur. / They stay in bed until 10:00.

3. a. Ik <u>doe</u> mijn joggingpak aan en ik <u>ga</u> mee. **b.** <u>Staat</u> Jasper niet op de lijst? **c.** <u>Gaat</u> u op de fiets of met de tram? **d.** <u>Blijf</u> je in bed tot twaalf uur of <u>sta</u> je nu op?

11 🔊 **4. a.** Het is <u>tien over drie</u> 's middags. **b.** Heb je <u>honger</u>? **c.** Ze nemen <u>de pont</u> over <u>het IJ</u>. **d.** Hij <u>trekt</u> een <u>kroketje</u> uit de <u>muur</u>. **e.** Doe je <u>joggingpak</u> maar aan.

10. AN EMAIL FROM EVA

1. a. <u>Stop</u> je met je studie? **b.** De vakantie <u>begint</u> vanavond. **c.** <u>Zegt</u> u het maar! **d.** Hoe <u>spel</u> je dat? **e.** Ik <u>wil</u> je straks even aan hem <u>voorstellen</u>.

2. a. 2   **b.** 1   **c.** 4   **d.** 3.

12 🔊 **3. a.** Doe haar de groeten! **b.** Ze start haar eigen bedrijf. **c.** Hoe gaat het met u? **d.** Ze hopen dat het beter met je vader gaat.

12 🔊 **4. a.** Hoe <u>gaat</u> het met <u>haar</u>? **b.** Hij heeft het <u>druk</u> maar <u>alles</u> is <u>prima</u> met <u>hem</u>. **c.** We zien <u>hen niet</u> zo <u>vaak</u> meer. **d.** Jullie zijn <u>altijd</u> <u>welkom</u> bij <u>ons</u>.

11. LOOKING FOR AN APARTMENT

1. Yes: **a, d, e, h**
No: **b, c, f, g**

2. a. schattiger / cuter **b.** verder / further, farther **c.** verser / fresher **d.** later / later **e.** leuker / nicer, funnier **f.** ruimer / roomier, more spacious **g.** duurder / more expensive **h.** liever / sweeter, dearer

3. a. de badkamers **b.** de grootouders **c.** de berichten **d.** de groeten **e.** de jongens **f.** de nummers **g.** de dochters **h.** de tunnels **i.** de postcodes **j.** de meisjes **k.** de keukens **l.** de visboeren

13 🔊 **4. a.** Wat vind je van dat uitzicht? **b.** Ben je op zoek naar een flat? **c.** Deze woning heeft een balkon op het zuiden. **d.** De extra berging is op de begane grond. **e.** Wat is de huurprijs van dit appartement?

12. ASKING THE WAY

1. a. 2 **b.** 3 **c.** 1

2. a. Daar gaat over drie minuten een tram heen. **b.** U loopt hier rechtdoor tot de stoplichten. **c.** Dan is het de tweede straat rechts.

14 🔊 **3. a.** eerste **b.** derde **c.** zevenentwintigste **d.** achtste **e.** veertiende

14 🔊 **4. a.** Ze komen uit het noordwesten van het land. / They come from the northwest of the country. **b.** Goedemiddag, ben je hier bekend? / Good afternoon, are you from around here? **c.** Hij heeft een zuidelijk accent. / He has a southern accent. **d.** Waar ga je naartoe? Daarnaartoe! / Where are you going? – Over there!

13. SHALL WE … ?

1. a. Hij heeft geen zin in een kop koffie. **b.** Ze hebben geen dorst en geen honger. **c.** Deze flat is niet duurder dan die andere. **d.** Ze stopt niet met de studie want ze gaat geen bedrijf starten. **e.** Mijn buurvrouw heeft geen fiets. **f.** Heb je geen kinderen of geen huisdieren?

2. a. Zullen we Emma uitnodigen? Ja, dat

is een goed idee. **b.** Ik heb zin om naar de film/bioscoop te gaan. Nee, laten we hier blijven! **c.** Wat vinden jullie van het idee om naar de markt te gaan? Oké/Dat is goed, laten we dat doen! **d.** Wil je een biertje? Ja, graag! Ik heb dorst.

3. a. We kunnen vanavond thuisblijven <u>of</u> naar het café gaan. **b.** Waar kom je vandaan, <u>want</u> je hebt een licht accent? **c.** Zij werkt in Zaandam <u>maar/en</u> hij werkt in Maastricht. **d.** Ze hebben geen honger, <u>dus</u> ze willen niet blijven eten. **e.** Ik noteer de datum <u>en</u> geef u vast het formulier.

15 🔊 **4. a.** <u>Hé, dag</u> Mariska. Hoe gaat het met je? **b.** Hebben jullie <u>vanochtend</u> geen zin om te werken? **c.** <u>Goedenavond!</u> Wilt u een glas wijn of een biertje? **d.** <u>Ha</u> Marc! <u>Hoi</u> Ben, ik kan niet blijven hoor! <u>Doei.</u> **e.** <u>Hè</u> jammer! Ik kan <u>vanavond</u> niet met je meegaan. Oké, nou <u>dag!</u>

14. THE HOROSCOPE

1. Optional: **a, d, e**   Required: **b, c**

2. a. Zij kent geen compromis. Het is voor haar altijd <u>alles</u> of <u>niets</u>. **b.** Willen jullie ons <u>iets/wat/niets</u> vragen? **c.** <u>Niemand</u> is zo voorzichtig als hij. **d.** Niet <u>iedereen</u> vindt dat een mooie film.

3. a. <u>Geeft</u> u mij maar een kilo peren! **b.** <u>Laat</u> maar snel iets van je horen! **c.** <u>Wees</u> niet zo dom! **d.** <u>Maakt</u> u niet kwaad! **e.** <u>Leer</u> eens je mening te uiten!

16 🔊 **4. a.** Heeft zij <u>nooit</u> honger of <u>dorst</u>? **b.** Ze heeft <u>soms</u> zin om <u>wat</u> te eten <u>of</u> te drinken. **c.** <u>Wat</u> maak je 't jezelf <u>vaak</u> moeilijk! **d.** Je bent <u>zo'n</u> harde werker! Maar <u>neem 'ns</u> vakantie! **e.** Hij wil <u>steeds</u> de baas zijn, maar niet <u>iedereen</u> vindt dat leuk. **f.** Stop 's met <u>altijd</u> tot morgen te <u>wachten</u>!

15. A NAVIGATION APP

1. a. <u>Zijn</u> zoon heeft geen smartphone. **b.** <u>Haar</u> dochters staan elke dag in de file. **c.** <u>Onze</u> kinderen nemen iedere ochtend de bus. **d.** <u>Ons</u> huis heeft een grote woonkamer en een open keuken.

2. a. Hoe is 't met 'm? **b.** Ik zie je naam niet in m'n bestand staan. **c.** We houden veel van d'r/'r. **d.** Ze willen 'r één met internetverbinding.

3. a. He wants to go to work by public transport. **b.** Can you install some apps on my smartphone? **c.** There is an easy and cheap system. **d.** They need one in order to be able to travel abroad.

17  **4. a.** niet waar **b.** niet waar **c.** waar **d.** niet waar **e.** waar

16. DOING THE SHOPPING

1. a. 2 **b.** 3 **c.** 4 **d.** 1

2. a. Hij heeft haar nummer nodig om haar uit te nodigen. / separated **b.** Het is niet gemakkelijk om iets leuks voor haar uit te kiezen. / separated **c.** Waarom ga je niet met ons mee? / separated **d.** Je kunt na de piep een boodschap inspreken. / attached **e.** Ze stelt hem aan de buurvrouw voor. / separated **f.** Hoe laat wil je opstaan? / attached **g.** Daar komt de trein aan. / separated

3. a. wil **b.** heeft, heeft **c.** wil(t) **d.** raad

18 **4. a.** Hoeveel brood hebben we per persoon nodig? **b.** De klant is koning! **c.** Gaat u maar van ongeveer 200 gram uit. **d.** Hij wil een roggebrood, een runderrollade en een stuk leverworst. **e.** We hebben vijf kazen nodig om een kaasplankje samen te stellen.

17. GOING TO THE RESTAURANT

1. a. hoofdgerecht **b.** kaas **c.** bestellen **d.** koffie **e.** pannenkoek

2. a. de foto's **b.** de risico's **c.** de flats **d.** de oma's

3. a. Ik wil/heb graag (een) koffie. **b.** Drink je liever wijn of bier? **c.** Ze/zij gaan het liefst naar het strand. **d.** Hij is dol/gek op brood met jonge kaas. **e.** Eet smakelijk! / Smakelijk eten!

19 **4. a.** Ik houd niet van friet met satésaus. **b.** We vinden die toetjes niet lekker.

c. Waarom zijn Nederlanders niet gek op gerechten uit Indonesië? **d.** Ze eten niet graag pannenkoeken.

18. AT THE DOCTOR'S

1. a. Er staat geen fiets in de berging. **b.** Er komt een auto aan. **c.** Er wonen veel makelaars in dat flatgebouw. **d.** Er lopen een paar mannen op het strand.

2. a. Ze/Zij zijn erg moe en ze/zij hoesten. **b.** Ze/Zij heeft buikpijn en rugpijn, maar ze/zij heeft geen keelpijn.; Ze/Zij heeft pijn in haar buik en in haar rug, maar ze/zij heeft geen pijn in haar keel. **c.** Uw/Jullie symptomen lijken er in ieder geval op. **d.** Mijn voeten en tenen doen pijn.

3. a. We bellen straks wel even terug. **b.** Ze hebben geen zin om op te hangen. **c.** Hij verbindt haar met de dokter door. **d.** Kom je vanavond even langs?

4.

het oog *eye*
de neus *nose*
de mond *mouth*
de hand *hand*
de buik *stomach*
de voet *foot*
de vinger *finger*
het hoofd *head*
het oor *ear*
de keel *throat*
de rug *back*
de schouder *shoulder*
de arm *arm*
het been *leg*
de teen *toe*

20 **5. a.** Waar hebben jullie last van? **b.** Mijn arm, handen en vingers doen pijn. **c.** Ben je verkouden en heb je hoofdpijn? **d.** Ze is in gesprek. Blijf je aan de lijn of wil je liever terugbellen? **e.** De assistente hangt net op. Ik verbind je door. **f.** Wat erg! Beterschap!

19. THE ROUTINE

1. a. Hij vindt de zondag <u>zo'n</u> fijne dag! **b.** Ze hebben <u>zulke</u> lieve kinderen! **c.** <u>Zulke</u> lekkere broodjes vind je alleen in Nederland. **d.** Zij heeft <u>zo'n</u> grappige achternaam! **e.** Waarom drink je <u>zulk</u> koud water?

2. a. Ze heeft er zin in. / Daar heeft ze zin in. **b.** Kan ik er over een maand in? / Kan ik daar over een maand in? **c.** Wat is er leuk aan? / Wat is daar leuk aan?

3. a. dezelfde **b.** hetzelfde **c.** dezelfde **d.** dezelfde **e.** hetzelfde

21 🔊 **4. a.** Ze begint met brieven typen op haar laptop. / She begins by typing letters on her laptop. **b.** We gaan er tussen de middag even tussenuit. / We are going to take a break at lunchtime. **c.** Hij heeft zulke negatieve ideeën! / He has such negative thoughts! **d.** Ik houd niet van fotokopieën maken. / I don't like making photocopies.

20. THE JOB INTERVIEW

1. a. <u>Kun/Kan</u> je goed overweg met computers? **b.** Ze <u>kan/kunnen</u> niet wachten en <u>wil/willen</u> meteen beginnen. **c.** <u>Mag</u> ik de kaart? **d.** We <u>willen</u> graag hier blijven.

2. a. Ze neemt een glas wijn <u>want</u> ze heeft dorst. **b.** Hij eet een broodje <u>omdat</u> hij honger heeft.

3. a. Hij heeft helemaal geen werkervaring. **b.** Ik ben momenteel niet beschikbaar. **c.** Ze gaat op een interessante vacature solliciteren.

4. a. Je bent sociaal heel vaardig <u>als</u> ik het goed begrijp. **b.** Waarom studeer je communicatiewetenschappen? <u>Omdat</u> ik dat een leuke studie vind! **c.** <u>Voordat</u> hij met zijn werk begint, drinkt hij eerst een kop koffie. **d.** <u>Hoewel</u> ze geen werkervaring heeft, neemt hij haar toch aan. **e.** Ze zijn blij <u>dat</u> ze niet meer iedere ochtend in de file staan.

22 🔊 **5. a.** Ik <u>beschik</u> over <u>veel competenties voor deze</u> baan. **b.** Jullie <u>kunnen erg</u> goed <u>typen</u>! **c.** Hij is <u>een geschikte kandidaat</u>, want hij is <u>nu meteen beschikbaar</u>. **d.** Wat een fijn <u>sollicitatiegesprek</u> is <u>dit</u>! **e.** Ik studeer <u>communicatiewetenschappen</u>. **f.** Het is <u>een leuke organisatie</u>.

21. AT THE OFFICE

1. a. Het bureau <u>staat</u> in de woonkamer. **b.** De fietsen <u>staan</u> voor het huis. **c.** Het dossier <u>ligt</u> op de grond. **d.** De lamp <u>hangt</u> aan de muur. **e.** De delete-toets <u>zit</u> op het toetsenbord.

2. a. Ik neem er geen. **b.** Er staan er drie in de berging. **c.** We hebben er vijf nodig. **d.** Er liggen er twee op tafel. **e.** Hij kent er vier.

23 🔊 **3. a.** de redactrice / editor (f.) **b.** de kandidate / candidate (f.) **c.** de bazin / boss (f.) **d.** de medewerkster / employee (f.) **e.** de vriendin / friend (f.), girlfriend **f.** de docente / teacher (f.) **g.** de leerlinge / learner (f.) **h.** de vertaalster / translator (f.) **i.** de koningin / queen **j.** de studente / student (f.)

23 🔊 **4. a.** We <u>krijgen steeds</u> een <u>foutmelding</u>. **b.** Het is te laat! Je <u>hoeft niet meer</u> te komen. **c.** Je moet eerst <u>dubbel klikken</u> en dan <u>knippen</u> en <u>plakken</u>. **d.** Hij bestelt <u>alle kantoorbenodigdheden</u> in <u>maart</u> en <u>juli</u>. **e.** <u>Weet</u> je niet wat <u>een apenstaartje</u> is? **f.** Hoe spel je <u>paperclip</u>, <u>delete-toets</u> en <u>mail</u>?

22. HOLIDAYS

1. a. 3 peperduur **b.** 4 ijskoud **c.** 1 doodstil **d.** 2 dolblij

2. a. biertje **b.** uitje **c.** visje **d.** mobieltje **e.** bosje **f.** kroketje **g.** kwartiertje **h.** patatje **i.** kaasplankje **j.** stukje **k.** rolletje **l.** gedichtje

3. a. Bedank haar maar snel! **b.** Er staan heel erg veel pakjes voor de deur. **c.** Gefeliciteerd (met je/uw verjaardag)! **d.** Het is zeven graden onder nul en ik heb het ijskoud.

24 🔊 **4. a.** niet waar **b.** niet waar **c.** waar **d.** niet waar **e.** waar

23. HOBBIES

1. **a.** belangrijker, belangrijkst **b.** gelukkiger, gelukkigst **c.** beter, best **d.** korter, kortst **e.** lekkerder, lekkerst **f.** meer, meest **g.** slimmer, slimst **h.** warmer, warmst **i.** minder, minst **j.** liever/liefst **k.** duurder, duurst **l.** mooier, mooist

2. **a.** Haar dochter is jonger <u>dan</u> zijn zoon. **b.** Deze kaas is net zo lekker <u>als</u> die andere. **c.** Zij sporten meer <u>dan</u> wij. **d.** Hij gaat liever naar de bioscoop <u>dan</u> naar het restaurant. **e.** Deze vis is niet zo vers <u>als</u> die daar.

3. a. She walks around singing. **b.** Let's go to the beach on foot (walking)! **c.** When do you get a stomachache? – While laughing. **d.** If you listen to me carefully, you will understand.

4. (The word stress is shown in colour.) **a.** 2 het televisieprogramma **b.** 4 het telefoonnummer **c.** 1 het volkorenbrood **d.** 3 de sollicitatiebrief

24. GOING SHOPPING

1. a. Hij gelooft in <u>zich</u>zelf. **b.** Ze wassen <u>zich/elkaar</u> niet vaak. **c.** Vermaakt u <u>zich</u> hier wel? **d.** Ik erger <u>me/mij</u> aan die verkoopster. **e.** Je vergist <u>je</u>.

2. a. to be ashamed **b.** to be mistaken **c.** to enjoy oneself/to have fun **d.** to marry/to get married **e.** to be called **f.** to be aware/to know **g.** to like/to love **h.** to be annoyed

3. a. Waar is mijn overhemd/bloes? **b.** Die laarsjes met hoge hakken staan u goed. **c.** Mag ik deze rok (even) passen/proberen? **d.** Heeft u deze schoenen in maat 42? **e.** Hij zoekt een kledingwinkel.

4. a. Is de binnenstad van Den Bosch autovrij? **b.** Zit er een gaatje in die jas? **c.** Vindt u dat eenvoudige model bijzonder mooi? **d.** Bedoel je die bank in de buurt van de kapper?

25. A WEEKEND AWAY

1. a. <u>de</u> rondvaart <u>die</u> **b.** <u>het</u> zwembad <u>dat</u> **c.** <u>de</u> boten <u>die</u> **d.** <u>de</u> broden <u>die</u>

2. a. de zee: <u>Die</u> is nogal koud. **b.** de kaas: <u>Die</u> is heerlijk! **c.** haar gezicht: <u>Dat</u> herinner ik me niet meer. **d.** onze zoon: <u>Die</u> woont in Haarlem.

3. a. Wat <u>betekent</u> dat woord? **b.** Ze <u>begrijpt/begrijpen</u> niet waarom dat belangrijk is. **c.** Hij <u>bedankt</u> haar voor het cadeau. **d.** <u>Bedoel</u> je die winkel in de buurt van de bank?

4. a. Het schijnt dat je daar verrukkelijk kunt brunchen! **b.** Had je mooi weer? **c.** Het heeft niet geregend. **d.** We gaan volgend weekend waarschijnlijk naar Texel. **e.** Ze zijn naar Zierikzee geweest. **f.** Waar staan de pindakaas en de hagelslag?

26. AT THE TOURIST OFFICE

1. a. Hij gaat <u>met/op</u> de brommer naar het strand. **b.** Ik ga het liefst <u>met</u> het vliegtuig. **c.** <u>Met/Op</u> de fiets kunnen ze stoppen waar ze willen. **d.** Ga je <u>met</u> de boot naar Engeland of <u>met</u> de trein?

2. a. afstappen **b.** uitstappen **c.** instappen **d.** opstappen

3. a. This time, she would like to go somewhere different/else. **b.** What type of holiday accommodation does he prefer? **c.** They would like information about a cycling holiday in the month of March. **d.** A nice spot in a campsite? Yes, that sounds good to her.

4. a. Kamperen? Nee, dat bevalt me niet. / Camping? No, I don't like that. **b.** Wat dacht je van een rondreis op de fiets rond het IJsselmeer? / How about a cycling tour around Lake IJssel? **c.** Ze fietst door schitterende natuurgebieden. / She cycles through gorgeous natural areas. **d.** Ze komen langs bekende historische dorpjes met gezellige middeleeuwse straatjes. / They pass by well-known historic villages with bustling medieval streets. **e.** Heb je voorkeur voor een vakantiehuisje of voor een stacaravan? / Do you prefer a holiday home or a mobile home?

27. THE ONLINE BANK

1. a. uncountable: one litre of beer / a few or a couple of beers **b.** countable: three cents / How many cents? **c.** countable: 37 degree fever / a few degrees **d.** countable: six times / the sixth time **e.** countable: a few or a couple of hours / five hours **f.** uncountable: a glass of wine / two wines

2. a. Ze heeft een foute code <u>gebruikt</u> en daarom is haar spaarrekening <u>geblokkeerd</u>. **b.** Hij heeft gisteren eerst een account <u>aangemaakt</u> en daarna een code <u>ingevoerd</u>. **c.** Ze hebben haar <u>gefeliciteerd</u> met haar verjaardag. **d.** Ik heb op een leuke vacature <u>gesolliciteerd</u>. **e.** Heb je veel geld <u>verdiend</u>? **f.** Ze zijn al zes keer <u>verhuisd</u>!

3. a. Na de derde keer wordt alles geblokkeerd. **b.** Waarom neem je zoveel geld op? **c.** Daar ben ik het niet mee eens! **d.** Ik kon geen goed wachtwoord bedenken. **e.** In de maand mei heb ik niets uitgegeven.

29 🔊 **4. a.** Wat is er aan de hand? **b.** Ik wil graag contant betalen. **c.** Hij heeft gisteren een account aangemaakt. **d.** Hoe is dat gebeurd? **e.** Wanneer en waar ben je geboren? **f.** Het lijkt me logisch dat ze al die dingen willen weten.

28. MOVING HOUSE

1. a. Ze <u>zet/zetten</u> het bureau in de woonkamer. **b.** Hebben jullie de fietsen voor het huis <u>gezet</u>? **c.** Hij <u>legt</u> het dossier op de grond. **d.** Kun je de lamp aan de muur <u>hangen</u>? **e.** Ze <u>doet/stopt</u> het geld in haar portemonnee.

2. a. a teacup / **2** a cup of tea **b.** the soup bowl / **3** the bowl of soup **c.** the matchbox / **4** the box of matches **d.** two wine glasses / **1** two glasses of wine

30 🔊 **3. a.** de ideeën **b.** de families **c.** de bacteriën **d.** de zeeën **e.** de kopieën **f.** de epidemieën **g.** de televisies **h.** de balies **i.** de advertenties

30 🔊 **4. a.** Wat heb jij toch altijd briljante ideeën! **b.** Wie wil er koffie met gebak? **c.** Heb je m'n short in de wasmachine gestopt?

280

d. Haar knieën doen niet meer pijn. **e.** Hij kan de gebakvorkjes nergens meer vinden. **f.** Geweldig! Het gaat lekker vlug! Alles staat al in de gang.

29. ON HOLIDAY

1. a. 2 or 3 **b.** 4 **c.** 1 **d.** 3

2. a. maakte/maakten **b.** landde/landden **c.** zette/zetten **d.** legde/legden **e.** fietste/fietsten **f.** verwende/verwenden **g.** paste/pasten **h.** bespeelde/bespeelden

3. a. Ze heeft haar zus meteen teruggebeld. **b.** Heb je een glas limonade voor hem klaargezet? **c.** Ze zijn naar het strand gereden. **d.** Hij heeft tien kilometer op het eiland gefietst.

31 🔊 **4. a.** niet waar **b.** waar **c.** niet waar **d.** waar **e.** niet waar **f.** niet waar **g.** waar

30. AN UNKNOWN DESTINATION

1. a. Ze gaat met de tram <u>naar</u> de binnenstad. **b.** Ze gaan iets eten <u>in</u> de binnenstad. **c.** We zijn moe en we gaan <u>naar</u> bed. **d.** Waar is hij? Hij is moe en hij ligt <u>in</u> bed. **e.** Ben je ook <u>in</u> maart geboren?

2. a. Nadat ze een foute code had gebruikt/gebruikt had, hebben ze haar rekening geblokkeerd. **b.** Nadat hij was geland/geland was, heeft hij een taxi genomen. **c.** Zodra ik voor mijn examen was geslaagd/geslaagd was, heb ik een verre reis gemaakt. **d.** Toen we onze tas hadden ingepakt/ingepakt hadden, hebben we een vakantie geboekt.

3. a. She was accepted at a technical school a week ago. **b.** I will have to pass that exam! **c.** After they had loaded the heavy furniture, they drove to their new residence. **d.** As soon as he put on his glasses, he opened the package/gift.

32 🔊 **4. a.** Je <u>zult wel</u> moe zijn! / You must be tired! **b.** Vroeger <u>zou</u> ik dat gevaarlijk <u>hebben gevonden</u>. / In the past I would have found that dangerous. **c.** We <u>zouden</u> dat <u>graag willen</u> doen. / We would like to do that. **d.** Ik <u>zal</u> morgen een <u>vlucht naar</u> Frankrijk <u>boeken</u>. / I will book a flight to France tomorrow. **e.** <u>Zullen we</u> een taxi <u>naar het vliegveld nemen</u>? / Shall we take a taxi to the airport?

GRAMMATICAL
APPENDIX

▲ CONJUGATION
STRONG VERBS AND IRREGULAR VERBS

Dutch verbs in which the vowel in the verb stem changes in the simple past are called strong verbs. The good news is that like regular verbs, there is only one simple past conjugation for the singular (*I, you, he, she, it*) and one for the plural (*we, they*). The table below gives the irregular simple past conjugations of the strong verbs in this course (if only one form is given, the other is regular).

The past participle of strong verbs is formed by adding the prefix **ge-** and the ending **-en** to the verb stem. The past participles indicated with an asterisk (*) below take the auxiliary **zijn** *to be* in the perfect tenses. For separable-prefix verbs, use the simple past or past participle of the base verb (for example, **komen** *to come* → **kwam** *I/you/(s)he/it came* / **kwamen** *we, they came*, **gekomen** *come*) to conjugate the derived verbs (**aankomen** *to arrive*, **binnenkomen** *to come in, to enter*, etc.).

INFINITIVE		SIMPLE PAST	PAST PARTICIPLE
(op)hangen	to hang up	hing op	opgehangen
aangeven	to indicate, to point out, to pass	gaf aan / gaven aan	aangegeven
aannemen	to take on, to hire, to accept	nam aan / namen aan	aangenomen
aantrekken	to put on (clothes)	trok aan	aangetrokken
aanwijzen	to indicate	wees aan	aangewezen
aflopen	to run out, to expire	liep af	afgelopen*
beginnen	to begin	begon	begonnen*
begrijpen	to understand	begreep	begrepen
besluiten	to decide	besloot	besloten
binnenkrijgen	to receive	kreeg binnen	binnengekregen
blijven	to stay	bleef	gebleven*
doorbreken	to break, to break through	doorbrak / doorbraken	doorbroken
doorverbinden	to transfer, to connect, to put through (a call)	verbond door	doorverbonden
dragen	to wear, to bear	droeg	gedragen
drinken	to drink	dronk	gedronken

282

eten	to eat	at / aten	gegeten
helpen	to help	hielp	geholpen
inladen	to load	laadde in	ingeladen
inspreken	to speak	sprak in / spraken in	ingesproken
kijken	to look	keek	gekeken
laten	to let, to allow	liet	gelaten
lezen	to read	las / lazen	gelezen
liggen	to lie, to be lying	lag / lagen	gelegen
lijken	to be like, to seem	leek	geleken
ontbijten	to have breakfast	ontbeet	ontbeten
ontvangen	to receive	ontving	ontvangen
rijden	to ride, to drive, to travel (on wheels)	reed	gereden
schijnen	to shine	scheen	geschenen
sluiten	to close	sloot	gesloten
trekken	to pull	trok	getrokken
uitkiezen	to choose, to pick out, to select	koos uit	uitgekozen
vallen	to fall	viel	gevallen*
vergeten	to forget	vergat / vergaten	vergeten
verzenden	to send, to ship	verzond	verzonden
vinden	to find	vond	gevonden
worden	to become	werd	geworden*
zingen	to sing	zong	gezongen
zitten	to sit, to be sitting	zat / zaten	gezeten

In the simple past of irregular verbs, the vowel(s) or consonant(s) of the verb stem can change, and the past participle can end in -en, -t or -d. When the singular simple past ends in a vowel, a -d is added before the plural -en ending: zei *I, you, he, she said* → zeiden *we, they said*; wou *I, you, he, she wanted* → wouden *we, they wanted*.

INFINITIVE		SIMPLE PAST	PAST PARTICIPLE
aandoen	to put on, to turn on	deed aan	aangedaan
aankomen	to arrive	kwam aan / kwamen aan	aangekomen*

afgaan	to go off	ging af	afgegaan*
bedenken	to think of/about	bedacht	bedacht
bestaan	to exist	bestond	bestaan
bezoeken	to visit	bezocht	bezocht
brengen	to bring	bracht	gebracht
doorgaan	to go on, continue	ging door	doorgegaan*
heten	to be called	heette	geheten
hoeven	to need	hoefde	gehoeven
houden van	to love, to care for	hield van	gehouden van
inzien	to see, to realize	zag in / zagen in	ingezien
kunnen	to be able to (can)	kon / konden	gekund
moeten	to have to (must)	moest	gemoeten
mogen	to have permission to (may)	mocht	gemogen
opslaan	to save, to store	sloeg op	opgeslagen
vragen	to ask	vroeg	gevraagd
weten	to know	wist	geweten
willen	to want	wilde (reg.), wou / wouden	gewild
zeggen	to say	zei / zeiden	gezegd
zien	to see	zag / zagen	gezien
zijn	to be	was /waren	geweest*
zoeken	to look for, to seek	zocht	gezocht
zullen	will (future aux.)	zou / zouden	*

PAST PARTICIPLES WITHOUT THE *GE-* PREFIX

Verbs that start with the prefixes **be-, ge-, (h)er-, ont-** or **ver-**, do not add the prefix **ge-** to form the past participle. Neither do separable-prefix verbs. Remember that the word stress on these two types of verbs is on the verb, not the prefix:

door<u>bre</u>ken *to break* → **doorbroken** *broken*
voor<u>spel</u>len *to announce, to forecast* → **voorspeld** *announced, forecasted*
be<u>spa</u>ren *to save, to economize* → **bespaard** *saved, economized*
ge<u>beu</u>ren *to happen, to occur* → **gebeurd** *happened, occurred*
ont<u>van</u>gen *to receive* → **ontvangen** *received*
ver<u>hui</u>zen *to move house* → **verhuisd** *moved house*

Here are some frequently used verbs with the prefixes **her-** or **ver-**:

(zich) herinneren	*to remember*
herhalen	*to repeat*
verbieden	*to forbid, to prohibit*
vergelijken	*to compare*
verkopen	*to sell*
verliezen	*to lose*
(zich) verontschuldigen	*to excuse*
verstaan	*to understand*
vertalen	*to translate*
vertrekken	*to leave*

 # GRAMMAR
VERBS WITH FIXED PREPOSITIONS

Some verbs are used with a particular preposition to convey a specific meaning. These are known as phrasal or prepositional verbs. The preposition must be included when the verb is used – if it is left out, or another preposition is used, this changes its meaning. Note, for example, the difference between **houden** *to hold* and **houden van** *to love*. Below are some of the verbs with fixed prepositions we have seen:

beschikken over	*to have access to, to have available*
denken aan	*to think about*
doorgaan met	*to carry on, to proceed with*
doorverbinden met	*to transfer, to connect with, to put through* (a call)
gaan naar	*to go to*
houden van	*to love, to care for*
kijken naar	*to look at*
komen uit	*to come from*
lijken op	*to resemble, to seem like*
luisteren naar	*to listen to*
meegaan met	*to go along with, to accompany*
ophouden met	*to quit, to stop*
passen bij	*to go with, to suit, to match*
praten met	*to talk with/to*

praten tegen	to talk to
spreken met	to speak with/to
trekken uit	to pull out
vinden van	to think of, to find
vragen aan	to ask (someone)
wachten op	to wait for
zeggen tegen	to say to

SEPARABLE-PREFIX VERBS

Be careful not to confuse separable prefixes with prepositions. Usually a separable prefix is placed at the end of the main clause. While it is also possible to place it before a prepositional phrase, it is clearest to put it at the end of the clause:

meegaan met *to go with*: **Ga je niet** mee **met je vrienden / met je vrienden** mee? *Aren't you going with your friends?*

ophouden met *to stop*: **Hij houdt** op **met zijn studie / met zijn studie** op. *He is stopping his studies.*

doorverbinden met *to put through*: **Ze verbindt haar** door **met de dokter / met de dokter** door. *She puts her through to the doctor.*

THE POSITION OF THE PAST PARTICIPLE IN A SUBORDINATE CLAUSE

In a subordinate clause with a perfect tense, the word order of the auxiliary verb and the past participle is interchangeable: the auxiliary verb first followed by the past participle or the other way around. This can depend on several factors: regional differences, personal preference or for reasons of emphasis. Often, in spoken language the order is past participle followed by the auxiliary verb, and in written language it is auxiliary verb followed by past participle. However, you'll hear and read both, the choice is somewhat intuitive.

Zodra hij voor z'n examens was geslaagd / geslaagd was**, heeft hij een treinticket geboekt.**
As soon as he had passed his exams, he booked a train ticket.
Nadat ze hadden gegeten / gegeten hadden**, zijn ze naar bed gegaan.**
After they had eaten, they went to bed.

WORD ORDER

In a main clause, the conjugated verb is in the second position. If the object of the action of the verb is included, it is usually placed after a phrase that indicates location if the object is indefinite (*a/an*), or before if the object is definite (*the, this, that*):

We gaan in de stad een nieuw horloge kopen.
We're going into town to buy a new watch.
We gaan dat nieuwe horloge in de stad kopen.
We're going into town to buy that new watch.

A word or phrase indicating time comes before a phrase indicating location. If the means/manner of getting to a location is included, it comes between the two:

We gaan dat nieuwe horloge morgen in de stad kopen.
We're going into town to buy that new watch tomorrow.
We gaan morgen met de auto naar de stad. *We're going into town tomorrow by car.*

An indirect object without a preposition (here, **me** in the sense of *to me*: who or what receives the direct object) comes before the direct object (who or what receives the action of the verb: here, the salt):

Kan je me het zout aangeven? *Can you pass me the salt?*

However, an indirect object with a preposition comes after the direct object:

Hij heeft de koffers in de verhuiswagen gezet.
He put the suitcases in the moving van.
Ze wil nieuwe schoenen voor hem kopen.
She wants to buy new shoes for him.

If the direct and indirect objects are both pronouns, an unstressed pronoun comes before a stressed pronoun:

Zij heeft haar dat gegeven. *She gave her that.*
Ze heeft ze daar opgehangen. *She hung them up over there.*

However, if there is no difference in stress, the direct object pronoun comes before the indirect object pronoun:

Zij heeft het haar gegeven. *She has given it to her.*
Ze heeft het hem aangewezen. *She pointed it out to him.*

If the two pronouns are the same or similar (**hem hem, haar haar, haar hem, hem haar**), the direct object pronoun is replaced by **die** or **dat**:

Ze heeft de jas aan Wim gegeven. → **Ze heeft hem die gegeven.**
She gave the coat to Wim. → *She gave it to him.*

CONJUNCTIONS

→ Coordinating conjunctions:

dus	so, thus, therefore
en	and
maar	but
of	or
want	because

→ The most common subordinating conjunctions:

als	when, as, if (condition)
dat	that, which
doordat	because, due to the fact that
hoewel	although, even though
nadat	after
omdat	because, as
sinds	since
terwijl	while
toen	when, just as, then
voor(dat)	before, until
wanneer	when, whenever, if (condition)
zodat	so that
zodra	as soon as

Don't forget that a subordinating conjunction introduces a subordinate clause in which the conjugated verb moves to the last position.

RELATIVE CLAUSES

A relative clause gives more information about a previously mentioned noun. The clause is introduced by a relative pronoun such as *that, which, who*, etc. (although in English these are often omitted). In Dutch, **die** and **dat** are used when the verb is not accompanied by a preposition: **die** refers to common nouns and **dat** to neuter nouns:

De man die je daar ziet ... *The man (who) you see over there ...*
Het meisje dat daar staat ... *The girl (who is) standing over there ...*

After **iets** *something* or **alles** *everything*, the relative pronoun is **wat**:

Als er iets is wat **ik voor je kan doen ...** *If there is anything (that) I can do for you ...*

Dit is alles wat **ik voor hem heb.** *This is all (that) I have for him.*

When the verb is used with a preposition, the latter is attached to the term **waar** *where* (**waar** + preposition) if it refers to an inanimate object:

de taxi waarmee **je naar huis bent gegaan**
the taxi in which you went home / the taxi you went home in

de stoel waarop **je zit** *the chair on which you're sitting / the chair you're sitting on*

Or **waar** can be separated from the preposition, which is more casual:

De auto waarin **de bazin het liefst rijdt. /De auto** waar **de bazin het liefst in rijdt.** *The car in which the boss prefers to ride. / The car the boss prefers to ride in.*

When referring to people, use preposition + **wie** *who*:

De jongen met wie **je sprak.**
The boy with whom you spoke. / The boy you spoke to.

De vrouw aan wie **ik dit wil geven.**
The woman to whom I want to give this. / The woman I want to give this to.

However, in spoken language you'll often hear the form for objects used for people:

De jongen waarmee **je sprak.** *The boy with which you spoke.*

◆ FORMING QUESTIONS
QUESTION WORDS

Hoe?	*How?*
Hoe veel? Hoeveel?	*How many/much?*
Waar?	*Where?*
Waarheen? Waarnaartoe?	*Where to?* (conveying movement to)
Waarom?	*Why?*
Waarvandaan?	*Where from?*
Waarvoor?	*What for?*
Wanneer?	*When?*
Wat?	*What?*
Wat voor?	*What kind of?*
Welk(e)?	*Which?*
Wie?	*Who?*

Questions to quantify something start with **hoe** *how*, followed by an adjective:

Hoe groot?	How big/large?
Hoe laat?	What time?
Hoe lang?	How long?
Hoe oud?	How old?
Hoe ver?	How far?
Hoe zwaar?	How heavy?

INDIRECT QUESTIONS

An indirect question is a question embedded inside another sentence that starts with an introductory question or phrase. This tends to be considered more polite than a direct question. Another example of an indirect question is a question reported in speech or writing.

In Dutch, an indirect question can be formed with:

• a question word:
Weet jij waar **hij vandaan komt?** *Do you know where he comes from?*
Heb je haar gevraagd hoe **laat het is?** *Have you asked her what time it is?*

• the conjunction **dat** *that*:
Weet je zeker dat **je fiets hier stond?** *Are* ('Know') *you sure that your bike was here?*

• the conjunction **of** *if*:
Weet u of **Wim naar huis is gegaan?** *Do you know if Wim has gone home?*
Ik vraag me af of **Wim thuis is.** *I wonder* ('ask myself') *if Wim is at home.*

NOUNS WITH IRREGULAR PLURAL FORMS

Most Dutch nouns form the plural by adding either **-en** or **-s**, though there are some exceptions to this. Most nouns of Latin origin, for example, have two possible plural forms: one ending in **-a** and the other ending in **-ums**.

centrum	centre	centra	centrums
museum	museum	musea	museums
datum	date	data	datums
stadium	stadium	stadia	stadiums

Sometimes, an **-i-** is added before the plural ending, or the vowel in the noun stem changes. And some nouns take the plural ending **-eren**.

NOUN		PLURAL FORM	IRREGULARITY
koe	cow	**koeien**	**-i-** before ending
vlo	flea	**vlooien**	**-i-** before ending
bad	bath	**baden**	long vowel
dag	day	**dagen**	long vowel
dak	roof	**daken**	long vowel
gat	hole	**gaten**	long vowel
glas	glass	**glazen**	long vowel
weg	road, track	**wegen**	long vowel
slot	lock	**sloten**	long vowel
stad	city	**steden**	change of vowel in noun stem
schip	boat, ship	**schepen**	change of vowel in noun stem
ei	egg	**eieren**	ends in **-eren**
goed	good (merchandise)	**goederen**	ends in **-eren**
kalf	calf	**kalveren**	ends in **-eren**
kind	child	**kinderen**	ends in **-eren**
rund	bovine	**runderen**	ends in **-eren**

Note that the nouns **het fruit** *fruit* and **het nieuws** *news* have no plural form.

ADJECTIVES

When an adjective comes before a noun, typically an **-e** ending is added. However, adjectives showing what something is made from and ending in **-en** do not change.

NOUN		ADJECTIVE	
het goud	gold	**gouden**	golden
het hout	wood	**houten**	wooden
het ijzer	iron	**ijzeren**	(of) iron
het papier	paper	**papieren**	(of) paper
het staal	steel	**stalen**	(of) steel
de steen	stone	**stenen**	(of) stone

The adjectives of colour **roze** *pink* and **oranje** *orange* do not add **-e** either.

→ Some frequent adjectives and their opposites:

arm	poor	rijk	rich
dun/mager	thin, slim	dik	fat
heel	whole	stuk/kapot	part, piece / broken
hoog	high	laag	low
kort	short	lang	long
langzaam	slow	snel/vlug	fast, quick
schoon	clean	vies/vuil	dirty
smal	narrow	breed	wide
sterk	strong	zwak	weak
zacht	soft	hard	hard
zoet	sweet	zout	salty

In Dutch, the prefix **on-** is often added to give the negative or opposite of an adjective, such as *un-* or *in-* in English with the meaning *not*: **bekend** *known* → **on**bekend *unknown*; **belangrijk** *important* → **on**belangrijk *unimportant, insignificant*; **gelukkig** *happy* → **on**gelukkig *unhappy*; and even **diep** *deep* → **on**diep *shallow*.

THE COMPARATIVE AND SUPERLATIVE

The comparative form of adjectives (*more* or *-er*) is formed by adding the ending **-er**. The superlative (*most* or *-est*) is formed by adding **-st**:
zoet *sweet* → **zoet**er *sweeter* → **zoet**st *sweetest*

The comparative of adjectives ending in **-r** is formed by adding the ending **-der**:
mager *thin* → **mager**der *thinner* → **mager**st *thinnest*

The comparative and superlative can be used before or after a noun. If used before a noun, the adjective adds an **-e** ending, except if it is followed by an indefinite singular neuter noun: **een smaller huis** *a narrower house*, but **het smaller**e **huis** *the narrower house*; **het smalst**e **huis** *the narrowest house*. Also note these irregular comparative and superlative forms:

dichtbij *near*	dichterbij *nearer*	dichtstbij *nearest*
goed *good*	beter *better*	best *best*
graag *gladly*	liever *more gladly*	liefst *most gladly*
veel *many*	meer *more*	meest *most*
weinig *few, little*	minder *fewer, less*	minst *fewest, least*

292

Here are a few examples with the comparative and superlative of **weinig**:

Ze houdt het minst van die rode jurk. *She likes this red dress the least.*

Deze wijn past minder bij die kaas dan die andere.
This wine goes less well with the cheese than the other.

Dit is het minst leuke café van de stad. *It's the least nice café in the city.*

The combination **meest** + adjective is mostly used with adjectives ending in **-s** or **-st** or by a series of consonants that are difficult to pronounce: **de meest geschikte kandidate** *the most suitable candidate*; **het meest precieze cijfer** *the most accurate figure.*

To make a comparison of equality, **als** *as* is used: **dezelfde trein** als *the same train as*; **hetzelfde huis** als *the same house as*. The expression for comparing two things that are equal is **net zo ... als** *just as ... as*, or that are not equal: **niet zo ... als** *not as ... as*. To say that something is more or less than something else, use **dan** *than*: **minder groot** dan *smaller than*, **groter** dan *bigger than.*

● VOCABULARY
SOME KEY PREPOSITIONS

aan	to, on
achter	behind
bij	at, by, near
boven	above, over
door	through, by
in	in, at
langs	along
met	with
na	after
naar	to, towards
naast	next to, beside
om	around, to, at (+ time)
onder	under, below
op	on, at, up
over	about, over, of, on, past (+ time)
rond	around
te	at

tegen	against
tegenover	across, facing, opposite
tot	until, to
tussen	between, among
uit	of, from (place of origin)
van	of, from
vanaf	from, since
vanwege	because of, due to
via	via, by
volgens	according to
voor	in front of, for, before, to (+ time)
zonder	without

LOAN WORDS AND FALSE FRIENDS

Dutch has borrowed many English words, particularly in the areas of IT, marketing, sports, business, higher education and youth culture. In past centuries, a large number of words were also taken from French, such as **het cadeau** *gift, present* and **de paraplu** *umbrella*.

There are also some false friends to be aware of: that is, words that sound or look the same between two languages, but have a different meaning. Here are a few of the classic traps for English speakers in Dutch: **de boot** means *boat*, **de chef** can also mean *boss*, **de concurrent** *competitor, rival*, **het dier** *animal* (not *deer*), **de dozen** *boxes*, **de eekhoorn** *squirrel* (not *acorn*), **de file** *traffic jam*, **het magazijn** *warehouse*, **de mening** *opinion* (not *meaning*), **het monster** can also mean *sample*, **de pet** *cap*, **de trap** *stairs*, **douchen** *to shower*, **willen** *to want*, **actueel** *current, up to date*, **brutaal** *cheeky, brash*, **dapper** *brave*, **eventueel** *possible*, **glad** *slippery, smooth*, **hard** *firm, solid* (but not *difficult*), **raar** *strange, odd, weird*, **slim** *clever, intelligent*, **smal** *narrow*.

Graphic design and cover: Sarah Boris
Sound engineer: Léonard Mule @ Studio du Poisson Barbu

© 2023 Assimil
Legal deposit: July 2023
Publication number: 4282
ISBN: 978-2-7005-0943-4
www.assimil.com

Printed in Spain by Ganboa